MANHATTAN GMAT

Critical Reasoning

GMAT Strategy Guide

This unique guide illustrates how to deconstruct arguments using a four-step process designed to build speed and improve accuracy. Understanding the underlying structure of arguments and answer choices is the key to quick reading and accurate analysis.

guide **6**

Critical Reasoning GMAT Strategy Guide, Fifth Edition

10-digit International Standard Book Number: 1-935707-61-2
13-digit International Standard Book Number: 978-1-935707-61-5
eISBN: 978-1-937707-02-4

Layout Design: Dan McNaney and Cathy Huang
Cover Design: Evyn Williams and Dan McNaney
Cover Photography: Alli Ugosoli

SUSTAINABLE FORESTRY INITIATIVE

Certified Chain of Custody
Promoting Sustainable Forestry
www.sfiprogram.org
SFI-00756

INSTRUCTIONAL GUIDE SERIES

SUPPLEMENTAL GUIDE SERIES

MANHATTAN
GMAT

April 24th, 2012

Dear Student,

Thank you for picking up a copy of *Critical Reasoning*. I hope this book provides just the guidance you need to get the most out of your GMAT studies.

As with most accomplishments, there were many people involved in the creation of the book you are holding. First and foremost is Zeke Vanderhoek, the founder of Manhattan GMAT. Zeke was a lone tutor in New York when he started the company in 2000. Now, 12 years later, the company has instructors and offices nationwide and contributes to the studies and successes of thousands of students each year.

Our Manhattan GMAT Strategy Guides are based on the continuing experiences of our instructors and students. For this volume, we are particularly indebted to Dave Mahler, Ian Jorgeson, and Stacey Koprince. Dave deserves special recognition for his contributions over the past number of years. Dan McNaney and Cathy Huang provided their design expertise to make the books as user-friendly as possible, and Noah Teitelbaum and Liz Krisher made sure all the moving pieces came together at just the right time. And there's Chris Ryan. Beyond providing additions and edits for this book, Chris continues to be the driving force behind all of our curriculum efforts. His leadership is invaluable. Finally, thank you to all of the Manhattan GMAT students who have provided input and feedback over the years. This book wouldn't be half of what it is without your voice.

At Manhattan GMAT, we continually aspire to provide the best instructors and resources possible. We hope that you will find our commitment manifest in this book. If you have any questions or comments, please email me at dgonzalez@manhattanprep.com. I'll look forward to reading your comments, and I'll be sure to pass them along to our curriculum team.

Thanks again, and best of luck preparing for the GMAT!

Sincerely,

Dan Gonzalez
President
Manhattan GMAT

HOW TO ACCESS YOUR ONLINE RESOURCES

If you…

⊚ **are a registered Manhattan GMAT student**

and have received this book as part of your course materials, you have AUTOMATIC access to ALL of our online resources. This includes all practice exams, question banks, and online updates to this book. To access these resources, follow the instructions in the Welcome Guide provided to you at the start of your program. Do NOT follow the instructions below.

⊚ **purchased this book from the Manhattan GMAT online store or at one of our centers**

1. Go to: http://www.manhattangmat.com/practicecenter.cfm.

2. Log in using the username and password used when your account was set up.

⊚ **purchased this book at a retail location**

1. Create an account with Manhattan GMAT at the website: https://www.manhattangmat.com/createaccount.cfm.

2. Go to: http://www.manhattangmat.com/access.cfm.

3. Follow the instructions on the screen.

Your one year of online access begins on the day that you register your book at the above URL.

You only need to register your product ONCE at the above URL. To use your online resources any time AFTER you have completed the registration process, log in to the following URL: http://www.manhattangmat.com/practicecenter.cfm.

Please note that online access is nontransferable. This means that only NEW and UNREGISTERED copies of the book will grant you online access. Previously used books will NOT provide any online resources.

⊚ **purchased an eBook version of this book**

1. Create an account with Manhattan GMAT at the website: https://www.manhattangmat.com/createaccount.cfm.

2. Email a copy of your purchase receipt to books@manhattangmat.com to activate your resources. Please be sure to use the same email address to create an account that you used to purchase the eBook.

For any technical issues, email books@manhattangmat.com or call 800-576-4628.

Please refer to the following page for a description of the online resources that come with this book.

YOUR ONLINE RESOURCES

Your purchase includes ONLINE ACCESS to the following:

⊛ 6 Computer-Adaptive Online Practice Exams

The 6 full-length computer-adaptive practice exams included with the purchase of this book are delivered online using Manhattan GMAT's proprietary computer-adaptive test engine. The exams adapt to your ability level by drawing from a bank of more than 1,200 unique questions of varying difficulty levels written by Manhattan GMAT's expert instructors, all of whom have scored in the 99th percentile on the Official GMAT. At the end of each exam you will receive a score, an analysis of your results, and the opportunity to review detailed explanations for each question. You may choose to take the exams timed or untimed.

The content presented in this book is updated periodically to ensure that it reflects the GMAT's most current trends and is as accurate as possible. You may view any known errors or minor changes upon registering for online access.

Important Note: The 6 computer adaptive online exams included with the purchase of this book are the SAME exams that you receive upon purchasing ANY book in the Manhattan GMAT Complete Strategy Guide Set.

⊛ *Critical Reasoning* Online Question Bank

The Bonus Online Question Bank for *Critical Reasoning* consists of 25 extra practice questions (with detailed explanations) that test the variety of concepts and skills covered in this book. These questions provide you with extra practice beyond the problem sets contained in this book. You may use our online timer to practice your pacing by setting time limits for each question in the bank.

⊛ Online Updates to the Contents in this Book

The content presented in this book is updated periodically to ensure that it reflects the GMAT's most current trends. You may view all updates, including any known errors or changes, upon registering for online access.

TABLE *of* CONTENTS

guide **6**

Chapter 1 of Critical Reasoning

Argument Structure

In This Chapter...

Chapter 1:

Argument Structure

Here is an example of a typical GMAT argument.

S1: Background

S2: Counterpoint

The expansion of the runways at the Bay City Airport will allow for larger planes to travel to and from Bay City. These new planes will create a large amount of noise, a nuisance for residents who live near the airport. However, many of the residents in this neighborhood work in construction, and the contract to expand the runways has been awarded to a local construction company. Thus, the expansion of the runways will lead to an increased quality of life for the residents of this neighborhood.

S3: Premise

S4: Conclusion

There are two broad things we need to study in order to answer Critical Reasoning questions effectively and efficiently. We need to understand the specific information given for that question, and we also need to know how to conduct the necessary reasoning to answer a question of that type.

Let's begin first by understanding what we are *given*. What are the pieces of an argument, how do they fit together, and how do we categorize them properly? In later chapters, we'll talk about what we need to *do* with that information.

On the GMAT:

(1) All arguments contain at least one **premise**. A premise is information used by the author to support some claim or conclusion. That information may be a fact or an opinion. In the above example, sentence 3 is a premise because it helps to support the author's conclusion.

1

(2) Most (though not all) arguments contain a **conclusion**, the primary claim the author is trying to prove. In the above example, sentence 4 is a conclusion.

(3) Many arguments (though not all) contain **background** information, which provides context to allow us to understand the basic situation. In the above example, sentence 1 provides background.

(4) Some arguments contain a **counterpoint** or **counterpremise**—a piece of information that goes against the author's conclusion. In the above example, sentence 2 represents a counterpoint because it goes against the author's conclusion.

Collectively, these categories represent the **building blocks** of an argument. How do we know which sentences fall into which categories? Try to articulate your own thought process for the above argument, then take a look at this example "decision process" of a fictional student:

Argument	Reader's Thoughts
The expansion of the runways at the Bay City Airport will allow for larger planes to travel to and from Bay City.	*Hmm. This is a fact. It could be **premise** or it could just be **background**. I'm not sure yet.*
These new planes will create a large amount of noise, a nuisance for residents who live near the airport.	*Now we're moving into claim territory. Something negative will come from this project. Why are they telling me this? I can't figure that out until I know the conclusion.*
However, many of the residents in this neighborhood work in construction, and the contract to expand the runways has been awarded to a local construction company.	*The word "however" indicates a contrast between sentences two and three. What's the contrast? The noise is a negative consequence of the expansion, while winning a work contract is a positive consequence. Looks like I've got a **premise** and a **counterpoint** in these two sentences, but I don't know which one is which yet.*
Thus, the expansion of the runways will lead to an increased quality of life for the residents of this neighborhood.	*The word "thus" usually indicates a **conclusion**. And, yes, this does seem like a conclusion—this project will have a certain outcome (better quality of life in this neighborhood), and I can now see how the previous two sentences fit into this conclusion. Sentence 3 is a **premise** because it tells me one way in which the quality of life might be better for these people (they might make more money), and sentence 2 is a **counterpremise** because it tells me a negative consequence.*

Notice how many times the reader thought "I'm not sure yet" (or something along those lines). That will happen frequently while reading an argument. We're gathering information and trying to understand what each piece might be, but we won't really know how everything fits together until we know what the conclusion is—and that might not be until the end.

The Core

The premise (or premises) and conclusion represent the **core** of the argument. Remember that not all arguments will have a conclusion, but all will have at least one premise, so we will always have at least a partial core. The core represents what the author is trying to tell me or prove to me.

It's important for us to be able to identify what specific information in an argument falls into which category, because that helps us to take our next step: conducting the necessary reasoning in order to answer the question. It turns out that different question types require us to perform different kinds of reasoning; we'll discuss this in much more detail in subsequent chapters. Let's take one step now, though, just to whet our appetites: how do the premises support the conclusion? In other words, how does the "core" actually function in this particular argument?

In this problem, our core consists of these two pieces:

However, many of the residents in this neighborhood work in construction, and the contract to expand the runways has been awarded to a local construction company. Thus, the expansion of the runways will lead to an increased quality of life for the residents of this neighborhood.

The conclusion, on the right, claims that the runway expansion project will have a good outcome (better quality of life for certain people). The premise, on the left, provides one piece of information to support this claim: the people in question may make money as a result of this project.

The premise provides one piece of evidence toward a positive outcome, but the argument is not airtight. For example, do we know for sure that the residents of the neighborhood are the ones who work for the local construction company that won the contract? We don't. As we'll see, that kind of thinking will help us when we get to the question-answering stage. For now, remember this: when we have both a premise and a conclusion, it's critically important to understand *how* the premise supports the conclusion.

Building Blocks of an Argument

Let's fully define all of the **building blocks** we've discussed so far.

Premise

- Part of the **core** of the argument; present in every argument
- *Supports* the author's conclusion
- Can be a fact or an opinion; can be a description, historical information, statistical or numerical data, or a comparison of things
- Often signaled by words or phrases such as *because of*, *since*, *due to*, and *as a result of*

Conclusion

- Part of the **core** of an argument; present in most arguments
- Represents the author's main opinion or claim; can be in the form of a prediction, a judgment of quality or merit, or a statement of causality
- Is supported by at least one **premise**
- Often signaled by words such as *therefore*, *thus*, *so*, and *consequently* (though note that harder arguments might use such a word elsewhere in the argument in an attempt to confuse us)

Background

- Not part of the **core**; often present, but not always
- Provides context to help understand the **core**·
- Almost always fact-based; can be in almost any form: historical information, numerical or other data, descriptions of plans or ideas, definitions of words or concepts, and so on

Counterpoint

- Not part of the **core**; only present occasionally
- Opposes or goes against the author's **conclusion** in some way
- Introduces multiple opportunities for traps: believing that the **conclusion** is the opposite of what it is, mistakenly labeling a **counterpoint** the **premise** (and vice versa), and so on
- Often signaled by transition words such as *however*, *yet*, and *but*; typically, the transition word will be found somewhere between the counterpremise and the conclusion (though the two sentences may not be right next to each other)

MANHATTAN
GMAT

Argument Structure

The argument above used all four of our building blocks; its "structure" looks like this:

Background – Counterpoint – Premise – Conclusion

We call that the structure because it shows the building blocks used and the order in which each appeared. The simplest possible argument will contain only premises; its structure might look like this:

Premise – Premise

The GMAT can vary the type of building blocks used in a particular argument, and it can also vary the order of those building blocks. If we can label the building blocks given in any particular argument, that helps us to understand the purpose of each step in the chain of information, and we'll be one good step closer to answering the question correctly.

Let's try some sample arguments. You have two tasks. First, read the argument and try to identify the role of each sentence or major piece of information (note that one sentence could contain two different pieces of information). Use that information to write out the structure as we just did above. Second, try to articulate in your own words *how* the premises support the conclusion.

1. Budget Fitness will grow its membership base by 10% in the next six months. Budget Fitness has recently crafted a clever ad campaign that it plans to air on several local radio stations.

2. Last year, the Hudson Family Farm was not profitable. However, the farm will be profitable this year. The farm operators have planted cotton, rather than corn, in several fields. Because cotton prices are expected to rise dramatically this year, the farm can expect larger revenues from cotton sales than it previously earned from corn.

Answers can be found on page 21.

Intermediate Conclusions and the Therefore Test

We have one more building block to introduce in this chapter. Try the below problem.

The owner of a small publishing company plans to lease a new office space that has floor-to-ceiling windows and no internal walls, arguing that the new space will enhance worker productivity. The owner cites a recent study showing that workers exposed to natural light throughout the day tended to report, on average, a higher level of job satisfaction than did those who worked in office spaces that used fluorescent lighting. Thus, the owner concluded, exposure to natural light has a positive effect on workers' job satisfaction.

The owner of a small publishing company plans to lease a new office space that has floor-to-ceiling windows and no internal walls,	*This is likely to be background information because it introduces a "plan" to do something. The argument is probably about the plan, or a result of the plan.*
arguing that the new space will enhance worker productivity.	*This might be the conclusion because it describes the predicted future benefit of the company's plan.*
The owner cites a recent study showing that workers exposed to natural light throughout the day tended to report, on average, a higher level of job satisfaction than did those who worked in office spaces that used fluorescent lighting.	*And this seems to be a premise in support of that conclusion. The workers will be more productive because the new space will provide exposure to natural light through the floor-to-ceiling windows.*
Thus, the owner concluded, exposure to natural light has a positive effect on workers' job satisfaction.	*Hmm, this is strange. This appears to be the conclusion as well. It uses the word "thus," it represents an explanation for the study's results, and it even says that "the owner concluded" this!*

This is a tough one! In this case, we have *two* claims that look like the conclusion. Now what?

This brings us to another building block, the **intermediate conclusion** (also known as the secondary conclusion). What is an intermediate conclusion? Look at this simpler example:

> The burglar is clumsy and often makes a lot of noise while robbing homes. As a result, he is more likely to get caught. Thus, in the near future, he will probably end up in jail.

The first sentence is a basic premise: it tells us some factual information about the robber. The second sentence is a claim made based upon that premise: *because* he makes noise, he is more likely to get caught. This is a conclusion… but, wait, there's a third sentence! That third sentence also contains a claim, and this claim follows from the previous claim: *because* he is more likely to get caught, there is a good chance he will end up in jail.

Essentially, a premise supports a conclusion, and that conclusion then supports a further conclusion. The first conclusion is called the **intermediate conclusion** (also known as the secondary conclusion). The second conclusion can be called the final conclusion to distinguish it from the intermediate conclusion.

In the example above, the three pieces were given in this order: **Premise – Intermediate Conclusion – Final Conclusion**. Arguments won't always do this, however; they might mix up the order and have additional information thrown in. When an argument contains more than one conclusion and we're not sure how to classify each, we can use the **Therefore Test**.

We have two conclusions; let's call them *A* (he's more likely to get caught) and *B* (he will probably end up in jail). All we need to do is plug the two conclusions into two sentences and ask which one is true:

> Is it the case that *A* (he's more likely to get caught) is true, THEREFORE *B* (he will probably end up in jail) is true?

> Or is it the case that *B* (he will probably end up in jail) is true, THEREFORE *A* (he's more likely to get caught) is true?

What do you think? Right, the first scenario makes sense, but the second one doesn't. That tells us that *B* (he will probably end up in jail) is the final conclusion and *A* (he's more likely to get caught) is the intermediate conclusion.

Let's return to the job satisfaction argument. We have two possible conclusions:

> (*A*) …arguing that the new space will enhance worker productivity.

> (*B*) Thus, the owner concluded, exposure to natural light has a positive effect on workers' job satisfaction.

Which scenario makes more sense?

> The new space will enhance worker productivity, THEREFORE exposure to natural light has a positive effect on workers' job satisfaction.

> OR

> Exposure to natural light has a positive effect on workers' job satisfaction, THEREFORE the new space will enhance worker productivity.

The second scenario seems to make sense. That means that (*B*) is the intermediate conclusion and (*A*) is the final conclusion.

As is typical of arguments with an intermediate conclusion, the premise supports the intermediate conclusion, which then supports the final conclusion. The premise (the second sentence) says that a study found a correlation between natural lighting and job satisfaction. The third sentence in that argument then makes a claim based on the study's results: the owner (not the study) concludes that exposure to natural light actually causes better job satisfaction.

The owner claims that the new space will enhance productivity at her company because, first, a study showed a correlation between natural light and job satisfaction, and that study then led the owner to conclude that natural light results in better job satisfaction. So the first half of the first sentence is background, and the second half is the final conclusion.

The structure is **Background – Conclusion – Premise – Intermediate Conclusion**.

1

Takeaways

A **premise** is a piece of evidence (fact or claim) that supports the author's conclusion.

A (**final**) **conclusion** is the author's main claim.

An **intermediate conclusion** is both a conclusion and a premise; it supports the final conclusion.

Background information helps to set the context for an argument.

A **counterpoint** or **counterpremise** goes against the author's conclusion.

We can use these building blocks to understand the structure of an argument. Understanding the structure will help us to answer the question.

When we have more than one conclusion, we can use the **Therefore Test** to find the final conclusion. Either "A is true, THEREFORE B is true" or "B is true, THEREFORE A is true."

MANHATTAN
GMAT

Answer Key

1.

Budget Fitness will grow its membership base by 10% in the next six months.	*This is a prediction about the future, so it is a claim, not a fact. This is a good candidate to be the conclusion.*
Budget Fitness has recently crafted a clever ad campaign that it plans to air on several local radio stations.	*Budget Fitness already crafted the campaign—this is a fact. It is also a fact that the company currently "plans" to air the campaign (though whether it will actually air is uncertain, since that is a future event). This information supports the claim in the first sentence, so it is a premise.*

(Task 1) The structure is **Conclusion – Premise**. (Task 2) The author claims that the gym *will* increase its membership in the future *because* the company will implement a strategy (ad campaign) that may help attract new customers.

2.

Last year, the Hudson Family Farm was not profitable.	*This is a fact; it already occurred in the past. This may be background info, though it may also be a premise or counterpoint.*
However, the farm will be profitable this year.	*The word "however" indicates a change in direction. This prediction is the <u>opposite</u> of what happened last year. This future prediction is a good candidate to be the conclusion, in which case the previous sentence would be a counterpoint.*
The farm operators have planted cotton, rather than corn, in several fields.	*Hmm, why do we care which crop the farm is planting?*
Because cotton prices are expected to rise dramatically this year, the farm can expect larger revenues from cotton sales than it previously earned from corn.	*Okay, now we can see that planting cotton will lead to more revenue than last year. The author is using this information to support his conclusion.*

(Task 1) The structure is **Counterpoint – Conclusion – Premise – Premise**. (Task 2) The argument predicts that an unprofitable farm *will* become profitable *because* a change in crops will result in higher revenues.

Did you spot any flaws in the author's reasoning? There are several, but the biggest one is the fact that revenues and profits are not the same thing! A company can have lots of revenue and zero profit—or even lose money.

Problem Set

Read the argument and try to identify the role of each sentence or major piece of information. Use that information to write out the building block structure.

1. A program instituted by a state government to raise money allows homeowners to prepay their future property taxes at the current rate. Even if the government were to raise the tax rate in a subsequent year, any prepaid taxes would allow the homeowner to maintain taxes at the lower rate, lowering the overall property tax burden over time. For this reason, homeowners should participate in the program.

2. Tay Sachs disease, a usually fatal genetic condition caused by the build-up of gangliocides in nerve cells, occurs more frequently among Ashkenazi Jews than among the general population. The age of onset is typically six months and generally results in death by the age of four.

3. Some critics have argued that the price of food and drink at Ultralux, a restaurant, is too high, given its quality. However, Ultralux features a beautiful interior and comfortable seating, and research has shown that consumers actually enjoy food and drink more in such a setting, even when the food and drink is of comparable quality to that served elsewhere. Thus, the food and drink at Ultralux is reasonably priced.

4. Editorial: To stem the influx of illegal immigrants, the government is planning to construct a wall along our entire border with Country Y. This wall, however, will do little to actually reduce the number of illegal immigrants. Because few economic opportunities exist in Country Y, individuals will simply develop other creative ways to enter our nation.

5. The cutback in physical education is the primary contributing factor to North High School's increasing failure rate on the year-end physical fitness examination. Last year, when students participated in gym class on a daily basis, 85 percent of the school's seniors passed the exam. This year, students had gym class twice weekly, and only 70 percent of seniors passed the test. Clearly, fewer sessions of gym class lead to reduced fitness.

Solutions

1.

A program instituted by a state government to raise money allows homeowners to prepay their future property taxes at the current rate.	*This is a fact. It sounds like background, though it could be a premise—I'm not sure yet. People can choose to pay future taxes right now at the current tax rate. [I'd only want to do this if it saved me money.]*
Even if the government were to raise the tax rate in a subsequent year, any prepaid taxes would allow the homeowner to maintain taxes at the lower rate, lowering the overall property tax burden over time.	*Ah, here's how it could save me money. This is a premise. If taxes go up but I've already pre-paid, I don't have to pay more; I got to pay at the lower rate. [What if tax rates go down? What if I sell my house?]*
For this reason, homeowners should participate in the program.	*Conclusion: people should participate. I've already thought of a couple of reasons why it could NOT be a good idea.*

The structure is **Background – Premise – Conclusion**. The author concludes that people should participate *because* they would save money *if* taxes go up.

2.

Tay Sachs disease, a usually fatal genetic condition caused by the build-up of gangliocides in nerve cells, occurs more frequently among Ashkenazi Jews than among the general population.	*This is a fact. It's so general that it sounds like background info, though it could be a premise.*
The age of onset is typically six months and generally results in death by the age of four.	*This is also a fact—just more information about this disease. That's interesting. There's no conclusion here, just two facts. Both are premises.*

The structure is **Premise – Premise**. The argument concludes nothing. (Note: two types of questions lack conclusions: Inference and Explain a Discrepancy. We'll discuss these later in the book.)

3.

Some critics have argued that the price of food and drink at Ultralux, a restaurant, is too high, given its quality.	*"Some critics" criticize the restaurant Ultralux for being too expensive. The language "some critics" is often used in counterpoints; later, the author will often tell us something else that the author or others believe instead.*
However, Ultralux features a beautiful interior and comfortable seating,	*This seems to be pointing out a good thing about Ultralux.*

P

and research has shown that consumers actually enjoy food and drink more in such a setting, even when the food and drink is of comparable quality to that served elsewhere.	*And this tells us why the beautiful interior and comfortable seating are beneficial. If we enjoy the food and drink more, then perhaps we're willing to pay more money?*
Thus, the food and drink at Ultralux is reasonably priced.	*This looks like a conclusion. In fact, it directly contradicts the critics' argument in the first sentence, which we now are sure is a counterpoint.*

The structure is **Counterpoint – Premise – Premise – Conclusion**. The author concludes that Ultralux is reasonably priced *because* research demonstrates that certain beneficial aspects provided by the restaurant are valuable to the consumer.

4.

Editorial: To stem the influx of illegal immigrants, the government is planning to construct a wall along our entire border with Country Y.	*The government plans to construct a wall and claims that this will reduce the number of illegal immigrants. This could be the conclusion, but the sentence also starts with the word "Editorial," implying that someone with a point of view is writing this argument. I'll have to see whether that person gives a different opinion or claim.*
This wall, however, will do little to actually reduce the number of illegal immigrants.	*"However!" Okay, whoever's writing the editorial thinks that the government's plan is not going to achieve its objective. This is the conclusion, so the previous sentence must be a counterpremise.*
Because few economic opportunities exist in Country Y, individuals will simply develop other creative ways to enter our nation.	*"Because"—and here's the reason why the Editorial writer thinks this: these illegal immigrants have no real opportunities in their own country, so they will just search for other ways to get into the neighboring country.*

The structure is **Counterpoint – Conclusion – Premise**. The author concludes that the government's plan won't work *because* the people trying to immigrate illegally will just search for other ways to do so, since they don't have many opportunities in their home country.

5.

The cutback in physical education is the primary contributing factor to North High School's increasing failure rate on the year-end physical fitness examination.	*This is an opinion, so it could be the conclusion. The school isn't offering as much physical education as it used to, and the author claims that this is causing more students to fail a physical fitness exam.*
Last year, when students participated in gym class on a daily basis, 85 percent of the school's seniors passed the exam.	*Fact. Last year, they had gym class daily, and the vast majority of students passed the exam.*

MANHATTAN
GMAT

This year, students had gym class twice weekly, and only 70 percent of seniors passed the test.	*Fact. This year, they had gym class less frequently, and a smaller percentage of students passed the exam.*
Clearly, fewer sessions of gym class lead to reduced fitness.	*Here's another claim. Having fewer gym classes causes reduced fitness levels. Is this the conclusion? What about the first sentence?*

I need to use the Therefore Test. A = cutback in gym is causing more kids to fail the fitness exam. B = cutback in gym causes reduced fitness.

Is it the case that cutbacks in gym are causing kids to fail the exam, THEREFORE those cutbacks are causing reduced fitness?

Or is it the case that cutbacks in gym are causing reduced fitness, THEREFORE those cutbacks are causing more kids to fail the fitness exam?

It's the second option—first, the kids have reduced fitness, and then that causes them to fail the fitness exam. So the first sentence is the final conclusion, and the last sentence is just an intermediate conclusion.

The structure is **Final Conclusion – Premise – Premise – Intermediate Conclusion**. The author concludes that gym cutbacks are causing kids to fail the fitness exam *because* this year's seniors had fewer gym classes, leading to reduced fitness levels which, in turn, caused more kids to fail the exam.

Chapter 2

of

Critical Reasoning

Methodology

In This Chapter...

Chapter 2:
Methodology

In Chapter 1, we introduced arguments, discussed their building blocks, and examined how to "deconstruct" an argument in order to understand how the pieces of information are related. These tasks represent the first two steps of our overall 4-step approach for any Critical Reasoning problem.

Before we dive into our 4-step process, let's discuss what we *don't* want to do. While there is a lot of flexibility in how different people can work their way through the same problem, there are some approaches that are downright bad, such as this one:

1. Read the argument pretty quickly, don't take notes, don't understand the "big picture"
2. Read the question
3. Realize need to read the argument again in order to answer; re-read argument
4. Re-read question
5. Examine answers, eliminating one or several
6. Read the argument yet again
7. Eliminate another answer
8. Start checking each answer against the argument and re-reading argument
9. Repeat until one answer is left

What's the problem? That's incredibly inefficient! Inefficiency both wastes time and makes it harder for us to answer the question correctly. There's too much going on, and that can distract us from our goal. So what do we do instead?

Here's our 4-step approach for all CR questions:

Step 1: Identify the question.
Step 2: Deconstruct the argument.
Step 3: State the Goal.
Step 4: Work from wrong to right.

2

Step 1: Identify the Question

Most arguments are followed by a question (there is actually one exception; we'll discuss this later). There are several different types of CR questions, and the wording of the question stem (the part below the argument itself) allows us to identify which type of CR question we're about to have to answer. It's critically important to identify that question type right away because we need to employ different kinds of reasoning depending upon the type of question we have. We want to know, right from the start, how best to work through the current problem.

There are three broad categories of CR questions: the Structure-based family, the Assumption-based family, and the Evidence-based family. Each of these families contains a few distinct question types. We also have one minor category, the Complete the Argument question type.

The Structure-Based Family

These questions all depend upon a solid understanding of the structure of the argument, similar to what we discussed in Chapter 1. What pieces do we have and how do they fit together? There are two types of Structure questions, both of which we'll discuss in Chapter 3:

Question Type	Sample Question Phrasing	Goal
Describe the Role	In the argument given, the two boldface portions play which of the following roles?	Identify the roles of the boldface portions.
Describe the Argument	In the passage, the mayor challenges the councilmember's argument by doing which of the following?	Describe the structure of the argument.

The Assumption-Based Family

These questions all depend upon an understanding of the assumptions made by the author to reach a certain conclusion. What is an assumption?

First, an assumption is something that the author *does not state* in the argument; for this reason, we call assumptions *unstated*. An assumption is, however, something that the author *must believe to be true* in order to draw the given conclusion.

We'll go into much more detail on assumptions in chapter 4 but let's look at a short example:

> That car is green. Therefore, that car cannot belong to Dan.

If we're only told that the car is green, how can we know for sure that it doesn't belong to Dan? Clearly, there's some information missing. What is the author assuming here?

> The assumption: Dan does not have a green car.

If we were to insert the assumption into the argument, it would make the argument stronger:

> That car is green. Dan does not have a green car. Therefore, that car cannot belong to Dan.

In this case, it not only makes the argument stronger, it makes the argument "air tight"—we can't argue with it! That won't always happen, but the assumption should make the argument significantly stronger.

There are five types of Assumption questions, which we'll cover in chapters 4 and 5.

Question Type	Sample Question Phrasing	Goal
Assumption	The argument depends on which of the following assumptions?	Identify an unstated assumption.
Evaluate	Which of the following must be studied in order to evaluate the argument above?	Identify a piece of information that would help to determine the soundness of the conclusion.
Flaw	Which of the following indicates a flaw in the reasoning above?	Identify something illogical in the argument.
Strengthen	Which of the following, if true, provides the most support for the argument above?	Strengthen the author's conclusion.
Weaken	Which of the following, if true, most seriously weakens the argument?	Attack the author's conclusion.

The Evidence-Based Family

These questions all lack conclusions; they consist entirely of premises! We're then asked to find something that *must be true* or something that *eliminates a discrepancy* in order to answer the question. We'll discuss both of these question types in Chapter 6.

Question Type	Sample Question Phrasing	Goal
Inference	Which of the following can be logically concluded from the passage above?	Identify something that must be true based upon the given information
Explain a Discrepancy	Which of the following, if true, most helps to explain the surprising finding?	Identify something that eliminates some discrepancy or paradox given in the argument.

There is also a minor type called Complete the Argument. We'll discuss this type in its own separate chapter; for now, know that you want to prioritize the three major families during your study.

As we go through each of the families and their question types, we will learn what kind of language signals specific question types—and that's our first big step in our 4-step approach.

Step 2: Deconstruct the Argument

Now that we've identified the family and question type, we can use that to help us deconstruct the argument. We began to learn how to do this in the previous chapter when we labeled arguments using the building block components. We'll learn even more about how to do this in later chapters, when we begin discussing each question type in detail.

In order to accomplish this argument deconstruction, many people take some light notes. Some people are able to deconstruct the argument and remember the pieces without taking notes, but most people do take some notes. If you aren't sure which way is best for you, try taking notes for a couple of weeks; you need some time to develop a good method and learn to work efficiently. Most people find that, the more they practice, the less they have to write, and some people even get to the point where they only have to write notes on the longest, most convoluted arguments.

In other words, you don't have to take notes, but don't underestimate the value of learning to take good notes—this is a powerful tool that can help us accomplish our main goal: deconstructing arguments efficiently and effectively.

These notes need to be neat enough to read quickly and easily, but they are also going to be heavily abbreviated. These are *not* the kind of notes you take during a class, when you have to write everything down thoroughly so that you can study for the test 3 weeks from now.

Rather, these notes will actually help us to *think our way through* the problem—we want to use them to understand the structure and flow of the information. By the time we're done reading and taking notes, we have maybe 60 to 90 seconds left. We can abbreviate extremely heavily and still remember what those abbreviations mean in another 60 to 90 seconds.

Let's revisit the first argument that we did in Chapter 1. What might the notes look like?

> The expansion of the runways at the Bay City Airport will allow for larger planes to travel to and from Bay City. These new planes will create a large amount of noise, a nuisance for residents who live near the airport. However, many of the residents in this neighborhood work in construction, and the contract to expand the runways has been awarded to a local construction company. Thus, the expansion of the runways will lead to an increased quality of life for the residents of this neighborhood.

Here's one method, idea by idea:

> BC rnwy ↑ → bigger planes → ↑ noise, bad for res
>
> BUT res = constr work, local com doing work
>
> ⓒ rnwy ↑ → better life for res

The first line encompasses the first *two* sentences of the argument. Most people would probably write down only the first sentence first:

> BC rnwy ↑ → bigger planes

Then, as we continue reading, we realize that the second sentence followed on from the first: those bigger planes then cause more noise. As a result, we can just continue that same line, even though the additional information is given in a new sentence.

If someone who hasn't read the original argument looks at our notes, then our notes would look like nonsense—and, in fact, they should be abbreviated enough that, if we were to re-read just the notes in a week or two (after forgetting the argument), we should *not* be able to tell what the full argument was. If, a week later, we can reconstruct the entire argument just from our notes, then we wrote too much down.

Let's try two more. Give yourself about 30 to 45 seconds to create notes for the below arguments that we saw in chapter 1, incorporating the techniques you've learned in this chapter.

> **TIP**
>
> When first learning this method, most people do write too much. As part of your review of problems, ask yourself, "Did I write this down in the most efficient and effective way? Did my notes make sense for short-term use? Did I write down something that I could've just skipped, or did I use too many words to write something down when I could've abbreviated more?" If you were really off the mark, make yourself write out the notes again in a more ideal way — and ask yourself why this new way is better than the old way. Now you're learning how to do a better job on the next new problem!

1. Budget Fitness will grow its membership base by 10% in the next six months. Budget Fitness has recently crafted a clever ad campaign that it plans to air on several local radio stations.

2. Last year, the Hudson Family Farm was not profitable. However, the farm will be profitable this year. The farm operators have planted cotton, rather than corn, in several fields. Because cotton prices are expected to rise dramatically this year, the farm can expect larger revenues from cotton sales than it previously earned from corn.

Answer Key

Below are sample representations of notes for the two given arguments. Your notes might differ quite a bit from the samples shown below. That's fine as long as your notes accomplish the following purposes:

- clearly delineate a conclusion (if there is one)
- demonstrate the "flow" of information (how one piece of info relates to the next, where applicable)
- indicates contrasts or changes of direction

1. Budget Fitness will grow its membership base by 10% in the next six months. Budget Fitness has recently crafted a clever ad campaign that it plans to air on several local radio stations.

Sample 1	BF new ad camp to air → BF member ↑ 10% in 6 mo. Ⓒ
Sample 2	Ⓒ BF mbrs > 10% 6 mos. BF to put new ads on radio

In this argument, the conclusion was in the first sentence, so we may write down that info before we know that it is the conclusion. The second sentence actually leads to the first sentence, so if we have room to do so on our scrap paper, we could just write that information to the left of the conclusion. If so, we might end up with something that looks like Sample 1. Alternatively, we might write down each "big idea" on its own line, and then use an arrow to show that the second line leads to the first one, similar to Sample 2.

In both cases, we label the conclusion clearly once we've found it (and, again, you can use any "this is my conclusion" label that you want, as long as you consistently use the same label every time).

2. Last year, the Hudson Family Farm was not profitable. However, the farm will be profitable this year. The farm operators have planted cotton, rather than corn, in several fields. Because cotton prices are expected to rise dramatically this year, the farm can expect larger revenues from cotton sales than it previously earned from corn.

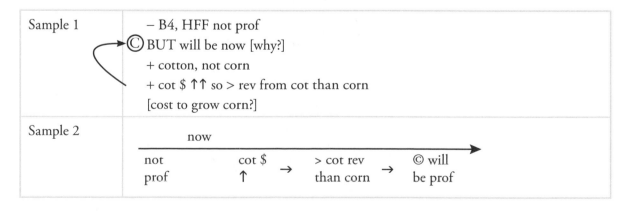

Sample 1	– B4, HFF not prof Ⓒ BUT will be now [why?] + cotton, not corn + cot $ ↑↑ so > rev from cot than corn [cost to grow corn?]
Sample 2	

In Sample 1, we've used some pluses and minuses, along with the usual conclusion symbol, to classify each line. A "plus" indicates a premise: something the author is using to support the conclusion. A "minus" indicates a counterpremise: something that does not support the conclusion.

Sample 2 shows us a timeline. If we've got a future prediction, along with some past background info, this can be an effective way to show the sequence of events. The first two sentences tell us that we've got a past/future situation in this argument, so we can tell at the beginning that a timeline might work.

Notice that we also added one new type of note to Sample 1: the bracketed notes [why?] and [cost to grow corn?]. As we take notes on the argument itself, we might also want to jot down notes about what we're thinking. It wasn't profitable before, but it will be now? Why? So we're already thinking about that as we continue to read the argument. Later, the argument says the farmers can earn more *revenue* from the cotton, but the conclusion said something about profits. Profit equals revenue minus costs. We've been given some evidence that we may be able to make more money from cotton (and even that's debatable), but we've been told nothing about costs, so how can the argument conclude anything about profits?

The argument told us that cotton prices are going up; it follows then, that farmers will make more money on the same amount of cotton this year than they did on the same amount of *cotton* last year. How do the prices of cotton and corn compare? We have no idea. It's entirely possible that cotton prices have increased but are still lower than corn prices. That's a subtle point, but if you noticed that, you might have wanted to jot down a note so that you wouldn't forget as you continued through the problem.

2

Step 3: State the Goal

This is a short but often overlooked step: what exactly am I trying to do when I answer this question? What's my goal? I know what kind of question I have, I understand the argument and how it fits together now, I know my conclusion (if there is one)… now what?

At this stage, we need to remind ourselves what it is we're actually trying to do when we start attacking the answers, and this goal depends upon the type of question that we have. Each question type requires a certain kind of reasoning and demands certain characteristics from the correct answer. There are also common types of wrong answer traps. Before we dive into the answers, we want to remind ourselves (briefly) of our goal and any traps that we want to avoid. We'll learn all about these things in later chapters.

Step 4: Work from Wrong to Right

Finally, the answer choices! On verbal in general, we're asked to find the "best" answer. We're going to use a two-step process in order to accomplish this. First, we look through all five answers and eliminate as many "definitely wrong" answers as we can. On this first pass through the answers, we're <u>not</u> actually trying to decide which is the *right* one, only which ones are definitely wrong.

If we only have one answer left, great; we're done. If we have two or more answers left, then we compare those remaining answers.

Why do we do it this way? By definition, finding the *best* answer is a comparison; if I spot a tempting answer, I can't know whether it's the best one until I've seen all of the others. It's most efficient to dump all of the "no way" answers as fast as we can, and then directly compare the remaining, more tempting answers.

Finally, we have one last important rule to remember for verbal questions: when we've narrowed down to two answers, we should look at each answer and compare the two once more, but then we should pick and move on. Going back and forth multiple times is a waste of time—either we know it after comparing the first time or we don't.

As we go through and assess these answers, it's critical to keep track of our thinking—we're actually going to track what we think about each of the five answers as we go. There are two big decisions to make in terms of how you choose to do this.

Decision #1: How do I write down ABCDE?

What to Do	Pros	Cons
Write ABCDE for each question	Can write directly on each letter; can keep letters with notes about argument	Have to write 41 separate times
Write ABCDE at the top of the page, then move to a new line for each question	Only have to write once for each page (several times for entire test)	Have to keep track "below" each letter; notes for problem might not be right next to answer tracking row

Option 1 (write for each question) might look like this:

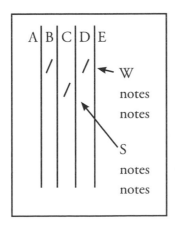

Option 2 (write once per page) might look like the below, where the first question (a Weaken) is answered in the first row and the second question (a Strengthen) is answered in the second row. Remember that the scrap paper will be graph paper, so there will already be lines built-in to separate the five answer choices.

2

Decision #2: What symbols will I use to keep track of my thoughts?

We need four symbols in order to keep track of our thoughts on the answers; you can use any symbols you prefer as long as you consistently use the same symbols to mean the same things:

✕ or /	Definitely wrong
⁓	Maybe
?	I have no idea
○	This is it!

Let's try all of this on an actual problem.

> Over the past decade, many companies have begun using automated telephone services; callers hear a machine-generated voice and are able to select options using the numbers on the telephone keypad. Research shows that callers are more patient when the machine-generated voice is that of a woman. Thus, smaller companies that cannot afford an automated service should consider hiring women, rather than men, to interact with customers by phone.
>
> Which of the following, if true, would be most damaging to the conclusion above?
>
> (A)   Automated telephone services are becoming cheaper and cheaper every year.
>
> (B)   Patient customers tend to order more products and return fewer products than impatient customers.
>
> (C)   A separate study indicated that the extra patience exhibited by callers is limited to interactions with an automated system.
>
> (D)   Some customers prefer automated systems to talking with a live person.
>
> (E)   On average, callers are only slightly more patient when interacting with a female voice, rather than a male voice, in an automated telephone system.

How did you do with each step? Did you identify the question type? Do you feel comfortable with your notes, and did you identify the conclusion (if there is one)? Did you remember to state the goal (briefly) before looking at the answers? Did you use the 2-pass process to assess the answer choices?

Here's how someone might work through the above problem. We'll show each of the four steps separately. The first column will show the relevant text from the problem. The second column will show what we might write on the scrap paper. The third column will show what we might be thinking while working on the problem.

Step 1: Identify the Question

Which of the following, if true, would be most damaging to the conclusion above?	W A B C D E	*"most damaging to the conclusion"* means this is a Weaken. I need to find the conclusion, and I need to think about what flaws or gaps might exist between the premises and the conclusion.

Step 2: Deconstruct the argument.

Over the past decade, many companies have begun using automated telephone services;	**10y: coms use auto phone**	*Sounds like background, but I'll jot down a note anyway.*
callers hear a machine-generated voice and are able to select options using the numbers on the telephone keypad.		*This is describing what an automated phone system is; I probably don't need to write that down.*
Research shows that callers are more patient when the machine-generated voice is that of a woman.	**R: female = ↑ patience**	*This is a fact, not a claim, so it has to be either a premise or counterpremise. It's probably a premise, since there's only one sentence left.*
Thus, smaller companies that cannot afford an automated service should consider hiring women, rather than men, to interact with customers by phone.	**Small com → use women phone**	This is the only claim, so it's the conclusion. Now I can go back and add a © to the conclusion in my notes and a + to the premise.

The final notes might look something like this:

W A B C D E

10y: coms use auto phone

+ R: female = ↑ patience

© Small com → use women phone

Your notes might look very different from the above notes. That's perfectly fine as long as your notes convey the basic flow of information clearly and concisely. Your notes also need to identify the question type, and you need some mechanism by which to track your answers.

Step 3: State the Goal.

The conclusion is that small companies should hire women to answer the phones, because callers are more patient when hearing automated female voices.

I need to weaken the conclusion, so that would mean there's some reason why companies might not be better off hiring women to answer the phones.

[Hmm. The evidence is about automated female voices, while the conclusion is about real women. Is there any kind of disconnect there?]

First, we briefly restate the core of the argument—the conclusion and the main reasoning that supports that conclusion. Then we articulate what kind of answer would accomplish our goal—in this case, to weaken the conclusion. We may also happen to notice significant discrepancies, and we can articulate those at this stage as well.

Step 4: Work from wrong to right.

Now, we're ready to attack the answers.

(A) Automated telephone services are becoming cheaper and cheaper every year.	A B C D E	*The conclusion discusses what companies should do when they can't afford automated services. If the service becomes cheap enough that a particular company can buy it, that company no longer has to worry about whether to hire women or men to answer the phones.*
(B) Patient customers tend to order more products and return fewer products than impatient customers.	A B C D E	*This is a good reason for the company to do whatever it can to keep its customers in a patient mood. If anything, that would strengthen the argument.*
(C) A separate study indicated that the extra patience exhibited by callers is limited to interactions with an automated system.	A B C̲ D E	*Hmm. This creates a distinction between automated and live voices… I was wondering earlier whether that might be the disconnect. There doesn't seem to be any evidence now that a live female voice will make callers more patient. Keep this one in.*
(D) Some customers prefer automated systems to talking with a live person.	A B C̲ D̶ E	*Presumably these customers would be more patient with an automated system… oh, but this argument is only about those companies who can't afford the system and are using real people. Nope, this isn't it.*

MANHATTAN
GMAT

| (E) On average, callers are only slightly more patient when interacting with a female voice, rather than a male voice, in an automated telephone system. | A B Ⓒ Đ E | *This one seems to be telling me there isn't a huge difference between male and female voices—but there is still a small positive effect for female voices. If anything, this strengthens the argument; after all, as a small business owner, I'll take any necessary steps that will get me more business! I only have one answer left, so C is the answer.* |

How to Abbreviate

A clear, consistent shorthand (abbreviation) method will help us to take notes efficiently and spend more of our mental energy focused on how the argument works (rather than how to write down a particular piece of information).

The chart below contains some symbols and abbreviations that are especially useful for Critical Reasoning. As you study, make sure to develop your own.

Increase / more / high	↑	Decrease / less / low	↓
Causes / leads to / results in	→	Was caused by	←
Greater than / more than / majority	>	Less than / smaller than / minority	<
Equals / correlates with	−	Number	#
Price / dollar amount	$	Percent	%
Change	Δ	Women / Men	W / M
Best / most effective	★	Worst / least effective	✕
Attribution (e.g. the Mayor said…)	: e.g. M:	Like / dislike	☺ / ☹
Future / prediction (something will happen, someone plans to do something)	F	Century (e.g., 20th century)	c e.g. 20c
Time	t	However / although / etc	BUT
years	y	conclusion	Ⓒ
your own thoughts (not in the argument)	[your own thoughts in brackets]	Profit, Revenue, Cost	P = R − C
premise	+ (plus)	counterpremise	− (minus)

2

For very large increases or decreases, a very large majority or very small minority, and so on, double the symbol. For example, for a very large increase in the number of employees, write ↑↑ # emp.

For the profit formula, do write out the whole formula even if the argument mentions only profit, or only profit and either revenues or costs. All three variables go together (and that fact is often the weak point for a question that mentions profit).

For any names, unfamiliar "big" words, or other unusual words, simply use the first letter of the name or word. In traditional note-taking, that wouldn't be adequate, but we only need to remember for about 90 seconds, and a single-letter abbreviation is sufficient to remember for 90 seconds.

Takeaways

Our 4-step approach for all CR Questions is:

Step 1: Identify the question.

- we'll learn how to do this in later chapters
- the question type tells us what kind of information we expect to find in the argument and what kind of reasoning help to answer the question

Step 2: Deconstruct the argument.

- break the argument down into its building blocks
- take very abbreviated notes showing both the details and the "flow" of the information

Step 3: State the Goal.

- very briefly articulate your goal based upon this question type (again, we'll learn the goals for each type in later chapters)

Step 4: Work from wrong to right.

- plan to go through the answers twice
- on the first pass, focus on eliminating anything that is definitely wrong; leave everything else in
- on the second pass, compare any choices that remain, then pick

Know how you're going to keep track of your answers on your scrap paper. First, decide whether to have a separate ABCDE grid for each problem or whether to use the "write once per page" method described earlier in the chapter. Second, make sure you have four consistent symbols for these four labels: definitely wrong; maybe; I have no idea; and this is it!

Problem Set

Read the argument and try to identify the role of each sentence or major piece of information. Take abbreviated notes for the argument. Use that information to write out the building block structure.

1. A series of research studies has reported that flaxseed oil can have a beneficial effect in reducing tumor growth in mice, particularly the kind of tumor found in human postmenopausal breast cancer. Thus, flaxseed oil should be recommended as an addition to the diets of all postmenopausal women.

2. During the past thirty years, the percentage of the population that smokes cigarettes has consistently declined. During the same time period, however, the number of lung cancer deaths attributed to smoking cigarettes has increased.

3. The Chinese white dolphin is a territorial animal that rarely strays far from its habitat in the Pearl River Delta. In recent years, increasing industrial and agricultural runoff to the Delta's waters has caused many white dolphins to perish before they reach breeding age. Unless legislation is enacted to ensure there is no further decline in the Delta's water quality, the Chinese white dolphin will become extinct.

4. Most doctors recommend consuming alcohol only in moderation, since the excessive intake of alcohol has been linked to several diseases of the liver. Drinking alcohol is no more dangerous for the liver, however, than abstaining from alcohol entirely. Last year, more nondrinkers than drinkers were diagnosed with liver failure

5. To increase the productivity of the country's workforce, the government should introduce new food guidelines that recommend a vegetarian diet. A study of thousands of men and women revealed that those who stick to a vegetarian diet have IQs that are around five points higher than those who regularly eat meat. The vegetarians were also more likely to have earned advanced degrees and hold high-paying jobs.

Solutions

Note: the sample notes show in the answer key represent only one example of how someone might take ntoes. Just make sure that your notes are legible, very concise, and convey the main points in a manner that makes sense to you.

P

1.

Argument	Notes	Thoughts
A series of research studies has reported that flaxseed oil can have a beneficial effect in reducing tumor growth in mice, particularly the kind of tumor found in human postmenopausal breast cancer.	R: Flax helps ↓ tumor mice esp PM BC	*This is a fact. It's either background or a premise.*
Thus, flaxseed oil should be recommended as an addition to the diets of all postmenopausal women.	R: flax helps ↓ tumor mice esp BC Ⓒ PM women shd take flax	*Definitely the conclusion.*

The structure of this argument is **Premise – Conclusion**.

2.

Argument	Notes	Thoughts
During the past thirty years, the percentage of the population that smokes cigarettes has consistently declined.	30y: % pop smoke cig ↓ steady	*This is a fact. It's either background or a premise.*
During the same time period, however, the number of lung cancer deaths attributed to smoking cigarettes has increased.	30y: % pop smoke cig ↓ steady same P: # LC dead from cig ↑	*Another fact, so another premise. There isn't a conclusion.*

The structure of this argument is **Premise – Premise**.

3.

Argument	Notes	Thoughts
The Chinese white dolphin is a territorial animal that rarely strays far from its habitat in the Pearl River Delta.	CWD stays in PRD	*This is a fact. It's either background or a premise.*
In recent years, increasing industrial and agricultural runoff to the Delta's waters has caused many white dolphins to perish before they reach breeding age.	CWD stays in PRD rcnt: ind + ag in PRD → CWD die b4 breed	*This is also a fact but is more like a premise because it feels like it could build to a conclusion.*
Unless legislation is enacted to ensure there is no further decline in the Delta's water quality, the Chinese white dolphin will become extinct.	CWD stays in PRD rcnt: ind + ag in PRD → CWD die b4 breed IF govt doesn't fix H2O → CWD extinct	*And here's the conclusion.* *[Note: H2O here is an abbreviation for water, based on the chemical formula H_2O.]*

The structure of this argument is **Premise – Premise – Conclusion**.

4.

Argument	Notes	Thoughts
Most doctors recommend consuming alcohol only in moderation, since the excessive intake of alcohol has been linked to several diseases of the liver.	Drs rec ↓ alc bc ↑ alc → liver dis	*This is a fact. It's either background or a premise.*
Drinking alcohol is no more dangerous for the liver, however, than abstaining from alcohol entirely.	Drs rec ↓ alc bc ↑ alc → liver dis © drink not worse than abstain	*Oh, this has the word "however!" The last sentence was a counterpremise, and this one sounds like the conclusion.*
Last year, more nondrinkers than drinkers were diagnosed with liver failure.	Drs rec ↓ alc bc ↑ alc → liver dis drink not ↑ bad than abstain 1y: >nondrink had liv dis	*This supports the previous sentence; it's a premise. [It also seems pretty flawed. What **percentage** of nondrinkers vs. drinkers had liver disease?]*

The structure of this argument is **Counterpremise – Conclusion – Premise**.

5.

Argument	Notes	Thoughts
To increase the productivity of the country's workforce, the government should introduce new food guidelines that recommend a vegetarian diet.	govt shd rec veg to ↑ wrkr prod	*This is definitely a claim. It sounds like a conclusion, though I don't know for sure yet.*
A study of thousands of men and women revealed that those who stick to a vegetarian diet have IQs that are around five points higher than those who regularly eat meat.	govt shd rec veg to ↑ wrkr prod S: veg ↑ IQ than non-veg	*This is a fact—the results of a study. It also supports the claim above, so it's a premise.*
The vegetarians were also more likely to have earned advanced degrees and hold high-paying jobs.	govt shd rec veg to ↑ wrkr prod S: veg ↑ IQ than non-veg veg > better schl and high pay	*This is another premise supporting the first sentence.*

The structure of this argument is **Conclusion – Premise – Premise**.

P

Chapter 3 of Critical Reasoning

Structure-Based Family

In This Chapter...

Describe the Role

Describe the Argument

Chapter 3:
Structure-Based Family

In the first two chapters, we introduced arguments, examined the building blocks used to construct them, and learned the overall 4-step approach to tackling any Critical Reasoning question. We also introduced the main types of questions found on the test. Here's our 4-step approach:

Step 1: Identify the question.

Step 2: Deconstruct the argument.

Step 3: State the Goal.

Step 4: Work from wrong to right.

Now, we're going to begin tackling the first of our three main Critical Reasoning Families: the Structure-Based questions. As the name implies, these questions depend upon our ability to understand the structure of the argument. What kinds of building blocks are present in the argument? Which piece leads to which piece? What is the purpose of each piece of info—what role does it play?

There are two main Structure question types: **Describe the Role** and **Describe the Argument**.

Describe the Role

Of the two types, Describe the Role (or Role, for short) is more common. These questions present a standard argument, but one or two portions of that argument are presented in **boldface** font. We are asked to describe the *role* each portion of boldface font plays.

What does "role" mean? We actually already studied this. The "role" is just another name for *building block*. A particular bolded portion could be a premise, a conclusion, a counterpremise, an intermediate conclusion, or background information. It could also be a counter-conclusion or opposing conclusion,

3

something we didn't discuss earlier. An opposing conclusion is simply a conclusion that goes against the author's main conclusion.

These question types are easy to identify because one or two statements (usually two) will be presented in bold font, and the question stem will include the word "boldface."

Our task here is to determine the role that each boldface statement plays in the argument. We're going to discuss two possible methods. The Primary Method will always work, but it's more complicated and time-consuming to use. The Secondary Method will allow us to narrow down answer choices more easily but may not allow us to get all the way to one answer—that is, we may have to guess from a narrowed set of answers.

Primary Method
There are three possible roles: (C) The statement in boldface is the author's CONCLUSION. (P) The statement in boldface is a PREMISE (it supports the author's conclusion) (X) The statement in boldface is SOMETHING ELSE (this might be a counterpremise, background information, acknowledgement of a weakness in the argument…)
Strategy Tip: Labels C and P are considered to be "on the same side" (because both are part of the author's argument).
Strategy Tip: Label X is considered to be "on the opposite side" of labels C and P, because label X does not support the author's argument.

In our notes, we'll classify each statement using the labels C, P, or X, as described above. When we evaluate the answer choices, we'll look for matching language based upon our labels.

How would that work? Let's say that we've decided to label the first boldface statement with an X and the second boldface with a C. Then we check our answers for an XC pattern.

The answer choices are the most difficult part of Structure questions in general because they are written in an abstract form. For example, an answer might read:

(A)   The first **[boldface statement]** is evidence that has been used to weaken a claim made by the argument; the second **[boldface statement]** is that claim.

The first half of that sentence is quite convoluted. Let's start with the most basic piece: a building block. There is a claim made by the argument; the claim is the conclusion. This first half says that the first boldface weakens the conclusion. Something used to weaken the conclusion is a counterpremise. If we labeled the first boldface statement with an X, then this might be the right answer.

The second half of the sentence is more straightforward but includes a structure that is commonly used to try to confuse us. It refers back to something that was said in the first half of the answer choice. In this case, the second half refers to "*that* claim." It's not just talking about any claim here; it's talking about the *same* claim that was mentioned in the first half of the sentence. The second half is describing the conclusion; if we labeled the second boldface statement a C, then this might be the right answer.

Great! We wanted an XC combo (in that order), and we just found an answer choice that gives us an XC combo. We're done!

If we can use the above method accurately, we will be able to eliminate the 4 wrong answers and get to the right answer. We might struggle to do that, though, or it might take too much time. Our Secondary Method allows us to get rid of some answers more quickly before taking a guess from among the remaining answers.

Secondary Method
There are three possible roles: (C) The statement in boldface is the author's CONCLUSION.   (F) The statement in boldface is a FACT.   (O) The statement in boldface is an OPINION (but not the conclusion).
Strategy Tip: Check for the conclusion first. Only label something an O if it is NOT the conclusion.

How would this work on our answer choice from above? This time, let's say that we have labeled the first boldface from our argument with an F and the second boldface with a O (opinion but not conclusion). Next, we check the answers.

> (A)   The first [**boldface statement**] is evidence that has been used to weaken a claim made by the argument; the second [**boldface statement**] is that claim.

The word "evidence" typically indicates a fact, not an opinion, so the first half is likely describing an F label. The second half is still describing the conclusion, so it would receive a label of C.

That doesn't match. We're looking for an FO combo, but this answer gives us an FC combo. Eliminate it.

Common Trap Answers

The most tempting trap answers on Role questions tend to be "off" by just one word, and that word is usually at the end of the sentence. For instance, let's imagine that we've decided the first boldface is a premise in support of the author's conclusion—in other words, a P. A tempting wrong answer might read:

(A)   The first **[boldface statement]** provides evidence in support of the position that the argument seeks to reject.

Every word of that answer matches what we want to find with the exception of the very last word, "reject." In fact, if we changed that one word, the answer would be correct:

(A)   The first **[boldface statement]** provides evidence in support of the position that the argument seeks to *establish.*

The first version of the answer choice says that the first boldface is a premise in support of some *counter*conclusion. That's an X label, not a P. The second version says that the first boldface is a premise in support of the author's conclusion, and that is, indeed, a P label. If we're not reading every word very carefully, we may pick the first version without even realizing that it's an X, not a P!

Putting It All Together

Let's try a full example:

> Mathematician: Recently, Zubin Ghosh made headlines when he was recognized to have solved the Hilbert Conjecture. Ghosh posted his work on the internet, rather than submitting it to established journals. In fact, **he has no job, let alone a university position**; he lives alone and has refused all acclaim. In reporting on Ghosh, the press unfortunately has reinforced the popular view that mathematicians are antisocial loners. But **mathematicians clearly form a tightly knit community**, frequently collaborating on important efforts; indeed, teams of researchers are working together to extend Ghosh's findings.
>
> In the argument above, the two portions in boldface play which of the following roles?
>
> (A)   The first is an observation the author makes to illustrate a social pattern; the second is a generalization of that pattern.
>
> (B)   The first is evidence in favor of the popular view expressed in the argument; the second is a brief restatement of that view.
>
> (C)   The first is a specific example of a generalization that the author contradicts; the second is a reiteration of that generalization.
>
> (D)   The first is a specific counterexample to a generalization that the author asserts; the second is that generalization.
>
> (E)   The first is a judgment that counters the primary assertion expressed in the argument; the second is a circumstance on which that judgment is based.

Step 1: Identify the question.

In the argument above, the two portions in boldface play which of the following roles?	R A B C D E	*This is a Role question. The argument contains bold font, and the question stem contains the words "boldface" and "role."*

Step 2: Deconstruct the argument.

3

Mathematician: Recently, Zubin Ghosh made headlines when he was recognized to have solved the Hilbert Conjecture.	R A B C D E M: ZG slvd HC	*A past fact—this is likely background. Still, I'll jot down a note.*
Ghosh simply posted his work on the internet, rather than submitting it to established journals.	R A B C D E M: ZG slvd HC ZG pub Int	*Sounds like more background.*
In fact, **he has no job, let alone a university position**; he lives alone and has refused all acclaim.	R A B C D E M: ZG slvd HC ZG pub Int no job, not math guy	*Here's the first boldface. He's not a mathematician; that's surprising. Still, I don't know what the conclusion is, so I don't know what role this sentence is playing.*
In reporting on Ghosh, the press unfortunately has reinforced the popular view that mathematicians are antisocial loners.	R A B C D E M: ZG slvd HC ZG pub Int no job, not math guy R: ZG, math = loners	*So the first boldface is "evidence" of "the popular view" that mathematicians are loners… but the sentence also uses the word "unfortunately" so it sounds like the author doesn't agree…*
But **mathematicians clearly form a tightly knit community**, frequently collaborating on important efforts; indeed, teams of researchers are working together to extend Ghosh's findings.	R A B C D E M: ZG slvd HC ZG pub Int no job, not math guy R: ZG, math = loners ⓒ BUT math = commun, collab	*I was right; the author disagrees. The author's conclusion is this second boldface statement, so I can label it with a ⓒ.*
	R A B C D E M: ZG slvd HC ZG pub Int Ⓧ no job, not math guy R: ZG, math = loners ⓒ BUT math = commun, collab	*Now, what about that first boldface statement? It's not the conclusion, and it doesn't support the conclusion, so it must be an X: Something Else.*

Step 3: State the Goal.

The first boldface statement is an X; that is, it is neither the conclusion nor a premise. In this case, it supports the alternate point of view, so we can call it a counterpremise. It goes against the conclusion. The second boldface statement is a C; it is the author's conclusion.

Whatever answer I find should describe the first statement as something consistent with an X label and should describe the second statement as something consistent with a C label. I'm looking for an XC combo, and those two labels are on "opposite sides."

Step 4: Work from wrong to right.

(A) The first is an observation the author makes to illustrate a social pattern; the second is a generalization of that pattern.	R A̶ B C D E M: ZG slvd HC ZG pub Int Ⓧ no job, not math guy R: ZG, math = loners Ⓒ BUT math = commun, collab	*Hmm. I'm not 100% sure what they mean by "illustrate a social pattern," but I can tell that the description of the two statements here makes them sound like they're on the same "side"—the first illustrates something, and the second generalizes that same thing. I want an "opposite sides" answer.*
(B) The first is evidence in favor of the popular view expressed in the argument; the second is a brief restatement of that view.	R A̶ B̶ C D E M: ZG slvd HC ZG pub Int Ⓧ no job, not math guy R: ZG, math = loners Ⓒ BUT math = commun, collab	*The first supports a popular view… okay, maybe. You could call the press view the popular view. Oh, but the second doesn't restate that view; the second goes against that view. These two are on the same side again, and I want an "opposite sides" answer.*
(C) The first is a specific example of a generalization that the author contradicts; the second is a reiteration of that generalization.	R A̶ B̶ C̶ D E M: ZG slvd HC ZG pub Int Ⓧ no job, not math guy R: ZG, math = loners Ⓒ BUT math = commun, collab	*"The first is a <something> that the author contradicts." The <something> part confuses me, but I agree that the author contradicts the first one; this is a good description of this "label X" statement. Hmm. The second repeats "that generalization"—the same one mentioned for the first statement? No, I'm looking for opposite sides.*

(D) The first is a specific counterexample to a generalization that the author asserts; the second is that generalization.	R A B ~~C~~ <u>D</u> E M: ZG slvd HC ZG pub Int Ⓧ no job, not math guy R: ZG, math = loners Ⓒ BUT math = commun, collab	*The first is a counterexample to something the author says? Yes, that accurately describes a "label X." The second is "that generalization?" I crossed off the last one for this same language. But wait… which generalization is this referring to this time? Oh, a generalization that the author <u>asserts</u>; that's the conclusion, which is a "label C." Leave this answer in.*
(E) The first is a judgment that counters the primary assertion expressed in the argument; the second is a circumstance on which that judgment is based.	R A B ~~C~~ Ⓓ E M: ZG slvd HC ZG pub Int Ⓧ no job, not math guy R: ZG, math = loners Ⓒ BUT math = commun, collab	*"Counters" language—yes, the first statement does counter the conclusion, which is consistent with the label X. "That judgment" = the first boldface. The second is not something on which the first one is based—that would be same side, and I want opposite sides.*

Takeaways for Describe the Role Questions

We recognize this question type by the boldface font in the argument and the use of the word "boldface" in the question stem. The question stem will also typically use the word "role" or a synonym. We will usually have two boldface statements, but sometimes there will be only one.

Our goal is to identify the specific role, or building block category, of each boldface statement. Our primary method involves splitting the building blocks into three categories:

> C: The conclusion
> P: A premise supporting the conclusion
> X: Something other than C or P

If needed, we can also try a secondary method that will allow us to make an educated guess if we're short on time or get stuck:

> C: The conclusion
> F: A fact
> O: An opinion that is *not* the conclusion

The most tempting trap answers will be "off" by just one or two words, often at the end of the sentence or phrase. We have to read very carefully all the way to the end in order not to fall for this trap.

Describe the Argument

Describe the Argument questions can be similar to Role questions in that Describe the Argument questions usually also offer "abstract" answer choices that explicitly discuss the *structure* of the argument, including referring to the various building blocks (conclusions, premises, and so on). The majority of these Argument questions will offer two competing points of view and ask us, for example, how one person responds to the argument made by the other person.

Important note: other question types can also be presented in this "two people speaking" format—the mere existence of two speakers does not make the problem a Describe the Argument problem. *It's always necessary to identify the question type based upon the question stem.*

A minority of these questions will instead offer just one point of view and ask us how the author of that argument develops his or her point of view.

Common question formulations include:

> Bill responds to Sally's argument by

> Bill challenges Sally's argument by

> The author develops the argument by doing which of the following?

These all indicate that we have a Develop the Argument question.

Our task here is to determine the manner in which a particular part of the text was constructed. If the second person disagrees with the first person, for example, we may be asked to explain *how* the second person disagrees, and possible answers might involve providing alternate evidence that contradicts the first person's claim, demonstrating that some evidence used by the first person is invalid or flawed (or simply questioning the accuracy of that evidence), introducing a new piece of information that the first person failed to consider, and so on.

If the argument is presented in two parts, with one person presenting an argument and the second replying, then the first person's text is a complete argument that we need to read and diagram just as we do any argument. It's critically important to label each piece of information in the first speaker's argument. Next, we examine the response and figure out which piece of the argument the response attacks. Ultimately, the attack is designed to find fault with the conclusion, but don't assume that the second person is attacking the conclusion directly. Tearing down any piece of the argument would ultimately undermine the conclusion, so find the piece that the second person most directly attacks.

Here's an example:

> Bill: I need to learn the names of 100 muscles for the anatomy exam in two hours. I've just memorized 5 of them in 5 minutes, so I only need 95 more minutes to study. Therefore, I'll have plenty of time to memorize everything and get a perfect score on the test.
>
> Sally: Are you sure? Perhaps the more you memorize, the harder it gets.
>
> Sally responds to Bill by

We're not going to look at answer choices yet for this one. What is Bill's argument? What is his conclusion, and how does he support it?

   must learn 100 names in 2h

   mem 5 in 5m, so need 95m

   [have >95m]

   ⓒ will get 100%

Which part does Sally attack? Does she attack the conclusion directly? No, but her words certainly cast doubt on Bill's eventual conclusion. She attacks Bill's assumption that he can maintain the same rate of learning, 1 name every minute, for all 100 words. He doesn't explicitly state that he can maintain that rate, but he clearly believes it to be true in order to say that he needs only 95 more minutes. The correct answer might read something like:

> Sally calls into question an assumption Bill makes about the efficacy of his plan.

This answer addresses the appropriate part of the argument—an assumption that Bill makes about his plan. An incorrect answer might look something like:

> Sally introduces new evidence that contradicts one of Bill's premises.

Sally does say something new, but does it rise to the level of evidence? She only suggests that his memorization rate might not be constant; she doesn't prove that it is not. While we might be able to argue that the word "evidence" is okay, the word "contradicts" clearly takes things too far. Sally does not definitively contradict Bill's premise that he will need only 95 more minutes; rather, she raises a question as to *whether* he really can memorize the words in only 95 minutes.

We probably won't be able to anticipate the exact abstract language of the correct answer, but if we can identify the part of the argument addressed, then we are in a much better position to find the appropriate "matching" language in the correct answer.

Common Trap Answers

The most tempting trap answers on Describe the Argument questions will be similar to those on Role questions: most of the answer is fine, but one or two words will throw the answer "off."

In addition, because most of these arguments will consist of a second person objecting to something the first person says, it will always be tempting to choose an answer that indicates that Sally rejects Bill's conclusion. It is the case, ultimately, that Sally's comment is going to weaken Bill's conclusion somehow, but she may not directly attack the conclusion—and the question asks us to articulate what she attacks directly.

Let's try a full example:

> Mayor: The recycling program costs us nearly $1 million to operate every year, and our budget shortfall this year is projected to be $5 million. We need to cut the recycling program in order to help balance the budget.
>
> Consumer Advocate: It costs the city more to throw something out than to recycle it.
>
> The consumer advocate responds to the mayor by

(A)   establishing that the mayor's figures were incorrectly calculated
(B)   accepting the mayor's conclusion but questioning the legality of the plan
(C)   interpreting the mayor's evidence in a way that reduces the validity of the mayor's claim
(D)   introducing a new piece of information that calls into question the validity of the mayor's conclusion
(E)   pointing out that the mayor has not adequately considered the potential causes and effects of the budget shortfall

Step 1: Identify the question.

The consumer advocate responds to the mayor by	DA A B C D E	*This is a Describe the Argument question. Two people are talking, and I have to explain how one responds to the other.*

Step 2: Deconstruct the argument.

Mayor: The recycling program costs us nearly $1 million to operate every year, and our budget shortfall this year is projected to be $5 million.	DA A B C D E M: R cost $1m; this yr $5m short	*The mayor is stating a couple of facts—recycling costs $1m and they're going to miss their budget by $5m.*
We need to cut the recycling program in order to help balance the budget.	DA A B C D E M: R cost $1m; this yr $5m short → cut R → bal budg Ⓒ	*So the mayor suggests that they should cut the R program in order to help balance the budget.*
Consumer Advocate: It costs the city more to throw something out than to recycle it.	DA A B C D E M: R cost $1m; this yr $5m short → cut R → bal budg Ⓒ CA: throw away costs > R	*That's interesting. The CA says that it costs even more to throw something out. Why does this matter? If you can't recycle something, what are you going to do with it instead? Probably throw it out.*

Step 3: State the Goal.

For Describe the Argument questions I have to address how some part of the argument is made. In this case, I have to describe how the CA responds to the M. First, it sounds like the CA thinks that the M's plan isn't going to work. The CA doesn't say so directly, but does say that throwing stuff out is more costly than recycling it. If that's true, then the plan to cut the recycling program just got a bit worse—it might not actually achieve the ultimate goal, which is to save money (to help balance the budget).

The answer I find should indicate that the CA disagrees with the M, and specifically the CA disagrees as to whether the suggested action (cutting the R program) will result in the desired outcome (saving money, helping to balance the budget).

MANHATTAN
GMAT

Step 4: Work from wrong to right.

(A) establishing that the mayor's figures were incorrectly calculated	DA A̶ B C D E M: R cost $1m; this yr $5m short → cut R → bal budg © CA: throw away costs > R	The CA doesn't say anything about the mayor's figures—in fact, the CA doesn't dispute the mayor's evidence at all. Rather, the CA attacks the mayor's assumption that cutting the program will lead to balancing the budget.
(B) accepting the mayor's conclusion but questioning the legality of the plan	DA A̶ B̶ C D E M: R cost $1m; this yr $5m short → cut R → bal budg © CA: throw away costs > R	The CA doesn't accept the conclusion, nor does the CA say anything about legality. Rather, the CA questions whether the plan will really lead to saving money.
(C) interpreting the mayor's evidence in a way that reduces the validity of the mayor's claim	DA A̶ B̶ C̲ D E M: R cost $1m; this yr $5m short → cut R → bal budg © CA: throw away costs > R	Hmm. Maybe. The CA does reduce the validity of the mayor's claim. I'm not 100% sure what "interpreting the evidence" means. I'll leave this in for now.
(D) introducing a new piece of information that calls into question the validity of the mayor's conclusion	DA A̶ B̶ C̶ D̲ E M: R cost $1m; this yr $5m short → cut R → bal budg © CA: throw away costs > R	The CA does call the mayor's conclusion into question, yes. Oh, I see—this one is better than answer C because the CA does introduce a new piece of info (that it costs more to throw something away).
(E) pointing out that the mayor has not adequately considered the potential causes and effects of the budget shortfall	DA A̶ B̶ C̲ Ⓓ E M: R cost $1m; this yr $5m short → cut R → bal budg © CA: throw away costs > R	This one is tricky. It's true that the mayor hasn't fully considered the potential effects of the plan to cut the recycling program—but that's not what this choice says. It talks about the causes and effects of the budget shortfall.

Takeaways for Describe the Argument Questions

We recognize this question type by the question stem (most commonly asking us how one person "responds" or "objects" to something that another person said), and by the "abstract" answer choices that address the role of the information (claim or conclusion, evidence or premise, and so on). We will be asked to address the role of a particular sentence or statement within the conversation (usually the respondent's statement, if there are two people talking).

Our goal is to identify the specific role played by the statement about which we're asked. Most of the time, that role will have something to do with calling into question a premise, assumption, or conclusion made by the first person. That can be done by directly attacking what the first person said, or by introducing new information that undermines the first person's argument.

3

Problem Set

1. *Ad Revenues*

Media Critic: Network executives allege that television viewership is decreasing due to the availability of television programs on other platforms, such as the internet and mobile devices. These executives claim that **declining viewership will cause advertising revenue to fall and networks will thus be unable to spend the large sums necessary to produce high-quality programming**. That development, in turn, will lead to a dearth of programming for the very devices that cannibalized television's audience. However, research shows that users of alternative platforms are exposed to new programs and, **as a result, actually increase the number of hours per week that they watch television**. This demonstrates that alternative platforms will not prevent networks from increasing advertising revenue.

The portions in boldface play which of the following roles in the media critic's argument?

(A) The first is an inevitable trend that weighs against the critic's claim; the second is that claim.

(B) The first is a prediction that is challenged by the argument; the second is a finding upon which the argument depends.

(C) The first clarifies the reasoning behind the critic's claim; the second demonstrates why that claim is flawed.

(D) The first acknowledges a position that the network executives accept as true; the second is a consequence of that position.

(E) The first opposes the critic's claim through an analogy; the second outlines a scenario in which that claim will not hold.

P

2. *Renaissance Masters*

Many people praise High Renaissance painting for creating very realistic images from observation, but **scholars have documented that some High Renaissance painters used pinhole cameras to project the likeness of their subjects onto the canvas and painted from there**. Thus, people who credit High Renaissance painters with superior artistic skills are misguided. **Painting from a projected image requires only an insignificant amount of additional skill beyond that needed to copy a picture outright**.

In the argument given, the two boldfaced portions play which of the following roles?

(A)   The first is a finding that has been used to support a conclusion that the argument rejects; the second is a claim that supports that conclusion.

(B)   The first is a finding that has been used to support a conclusion that the argument rejects; the second is that conclusion.

(C)   The first is a claim put forth to support a conclusion that the argument rejects; the second is a consideration that is introduced to counter the force of that evidence.

(D)   The first is evidence that forms the basis for the position that the argument seeks to establish; the second is a claim presented to solidify that position.

(E)   The first is evidence that forms the basis for the position that the argument seeks to establish; the second is that position.

3. *Democracy*

As the United States demonstrated during its early development, it is not enough for citizens simply to have rights; the successful functioning of a democracy requires that they also know how to exercise those rights. Access to formal education was one necessary component that helped the U.S. citizenry to learn how to exercise its rights. Therefore, in order for a democracy to function successfully, its citizens must have access to a formal education.

The author develops the argument by

(A)   using an analogy to establish a precedent for a planned future event

(B)   illustrating differences in the requirements for the functioning of a democracy depending upon the democracy in question

(C)   introducing an example that illustrates a common principle

(D)   forming a hypothesis that explains apparently contradictory pieces of evidence

(E)   supplying an alternate explanation for a known phenomenon

4. *Malaria*

In an attempt to explain the cause of malaria, a deadly infectious disease, early European settlers in Hong Kong attributed the malady to poisonous gases supposedly emanating from low-lying swampland. In the 1880s, however, doctors determined that Anopheles mosquitoes were responsible for transmitting the disease to humans after observing that **the female of the species can carry a parasitic protozoan that is passed on to unsuspecting humans when a mosquito feasts on a person's blood**.

What function does the statement in boldface fulfill with respect to the argument presented above?

(A) It provides support for the explanation of a particular phenomenon.
(B) It presents evidence that contradicts an established fact.
(C) It offers confirmation of a contested assumption.
(D) It identifies the cause of an erroneous conclusion.
(E) It proposes a new conclusion in place of an earlier conjecture.

5. *Digital Marketing*

Sania: The newest workers in the workforce are the most effective digital marketing employees because they are more likely to use social networking websites and tools themselves.

Carlos: But effective digital marketing also requires very technical expertise, such as search engine optimization, that is best learned on the job via prolonged exposure and instruction.

Carlos responds to Sania by

(A) demonstrating that Sania's conclusion is based upon evidence that is not relevant to the given situation
(B) questioning the accuracy of the evidence presented by Sania in support of her conclusion
(C) reinforcing Sania's argument by contributing an additional piece of evidence in support of her conclusion
(D) pointing out differences in the qualifications desired by different employers seeking digital marketing employees
(E) providing an additional piece of evidence that undermines a portion of Sania's claim

6. *Innovative Design*

Products with innovative and appealing designs relative to competing products can often command substantially higher prices in the marketplace. **Because design innovations are quickly copied by other manufacturers**, many consumer technology companies charge as much as possible for their new designs to extract as much value as possible from them. But large profits generated by the innovative designs give competitors stronger incentives to copy the designs. Therefore, **the best strategy to maximize overall profit from an innovative new design is to charge less than the greatest possible price**.

In the argument above, the two portions in boldface play which of the following roles?

(A)   The first is an assumption that supports a described course of action; the second provides a consideration to support a preferred course of action.

(B) The first is a consideration that helps explain the appeal of a certain strategy; the second presents an alternative strategy endorsed by the argument.

(C) The first is a phenomenon that justifies a specific strategy; the second is that strategy.

(D) The first is a consideration that demonstrates why a particular approach is flawed; the second describes a way to amend that approach.

(E) The first is a factor used to rationalize a particular strategy; the second is a factor against that strategy.

7. Gray Wolf Population

Government representative: Between 1996 and 2005, the gray wolf population in Minnesota grew nearly 50 percent; the gray wolf population in Montana increased by only 13 percent during the same period. Clearly, the Minnesota gray wolf population is more likely to survive and thrive long term.

Environmentalist: But the gray wolf population in Montana is nearly 8 times the population in Minnesota; above a certain critical breeding number, the population is stable and does not require growth in order to survive.

The environmentalist challenges the government representative's argument by doing which of the following?

(A) introducing additional evidence that undermines an assumption made by the representative

(B) challenging the representative's definition of a critical breeding number

(C) demonstrating that the critical breeding number of the two wolf populations differs significantly

(D) implying that the two populations of wolves could be combined in order to preserve the species

(E) suggesting that the Montana wolf population grew at a faster rate than stated in the representative's argument

P

Solutions

1. Ad Revenues: The correct answer is **B**.

<u>Step 1: Identify the question.</u>

The portions in boldface play which of the following roles in the media critic's argument?	R A B C D E	*This is a Role question. The question contains the word "boldface," and I'm asked to find the "role" of each bold statement.*

<u>Step 2: Deconstruct the argument.</u>

Media Critic: Network executives allege that television viewership is decreasing due to the availability of television programs on other platforms, such as the internet and mobile devices.	R A B C D E MC: NE say TV ↓ b/c use other Ps	*The word "allege" tells me this is a claim. Also, the critic is talking about what other people claim, so I'm guessing the critic is going to contradict what they claim—so this is probably a counterpremise.*
These executives claim that **declining viewership will cause advertising revenue to fall and networks will thus be unable to spend the large sums necessary to produce high-quality programming**.	R A B C D E MC: NE say TV ↓ b/c use other Ps NE: TV ↓ → ad ↓ → no $ for qual prog	*More from the NEs. More claims about bad things happening. Is the last thing the NEs conclusion? This is the 1st boldface. If the MC does contradict the NEs later, then this first boldface will be labeled an X.*
That development, in turn, will lead to a dearth of programming for the very devices that cannibalized television's audience.	R A B C D E MC: NE say TV ↓ b/c use other Ps NE: TV ↓ → ad ↓ → no $ for qual prog → no prog for other Ps	*Ah, I see. Ironic. The fact that people are watching on other platforms will eventually lead to not having enough programming for those other platforms. Conclusion of the NEs.*
However, research shows that users of alternative platforms are exposed to new programs and, as a result, actually increase the number of hours per week that they watch television.	R A B C D E MC: NE say TV ↓ b/c use other Ps NE: TV ↓ → ad ↓ → no $ for qual prog → no prog for other Ps BUT alt P users watch MORE TV	*Here's the contradiction! I'll wait till I find the conclusion for sure, but the first boldface is probably an X.*

| This demonstrates that alternative platforms will not prevent networks from increasing advertising revenue. | R   A B C D E

MC: NE say TV ↓ b/c use other Ps

Ⓧ NE: TV ↓ → ad ↓ → no $ for qual prog → no prog for other Ps

Ⓟ BUT alt P users watch MORE TV

Ⓒ ad rates

I want this combo: X P | *Hmm. I didn't think of that. The recyclable materials still have to go somewhere. Okay, the MC is concluding the opposite: that ad rates will go up. And if that's my conclusion, then the first boldface is indeed an X and the second one supports the conclusion, so it's a P.* |

Step 3: State the Goal.

The question asks me to find the role of two boldface statements. The MC's conclusion is in the last line, and the second boldface, right before it, supports that conclusion. The second boldface is a P. The first boldface is part of the NE's argument, which is the opposite of the MC's argument, so the first boldface is an X. I want to find the combo X P (in that order) in an answer choice.

Step 4: Work from wrong to right.

| (A) The first is an inevitable trend that weighs against the critic's claim; the second is that claim. | R   A̶ B C D E

MC: NE say TV ↓ b/c use other Ps

Ⓧ NE: TV ↓ → ad ↓ → no $ for qual prog → no prog for other Ps

Ⓟ BUT alt P users watch MORE TV

Ⓒ ad rates

I want this combo: X P | *"Weighs against the MC's claim"—yes, that's consistent with an X label. The second is "that" claim, meaning the MC's claim. No. the second one is a P, not a C.*

(Note: the word "inevitable" can also be considered incorrect. The trend described in the first statement says that ad rates will go down, but the MC provides a reason why ad rates wouldn't go down… so the trend isn't necessarily inevitable.) |

(B) The first is a prediction that is challenged by the argument; the second is a finding upon which the argument depends.	R A B̲ C D E MC: NE say TV ↓ b/c use other Ps Ⓧ NE: TV ↓ → ad ↓ → no $ for qual prog → no prog for other Ps Ⓟ BUT alt P users watch MORE TV Ⓒ ad rates I want this combo: X P	*That's true, the MC does challenge the first one. That's an X. And the second one is a P, so we can describe that as something upon which the MC's argument depends. Keep this one in.*
(C) The first clarifies the reasoning behind the critic's claim; the second demonstrates why that claim is flawed.	R A B̲ C̶ D E MC: NE say TV ↓ b/c use other Ps Ⓧ NE: TV ↓ → ad ↓ → no $ for qual prog → no prog for other Ps Ⓟ BUT alt P users watch MORE TV Ⓒ ad rates I want this combo: X P	*Clarifies the <u>MC's</u> claim? No. The first one is something the NE's claim. I don't even need to read the second half of the answer.*
(D) The first acknowledges a position that the network executives accept as true; the second is a consequence of that position.	R A B̲ C̶ D̶ E MC: NE say TV ↓ b/c use other Ps Ⓧ NE: TV ↓ → ad ↓ → no $ for qual prog → no prog for other Ps Ⓟ BUT alt P users watch MORE TV Ⓒ ad rates I want this combo: X P	*Yes, the <u>NEs</u> do accept the first boldface as true—it's their premise. And they're on the opposite side of the MC, so something they think is an X. Okay, that's fine. "The second is a consequence of that position." What position? Oh, they use "position" in the first half of the sentence... the NE's position. The second isn't something about the NE's position. It goes against the NE's position. No.*

P

| (E) The first opposes the critic's claim through an analogy; the second outlines a scenario in which that claim will not hold. | R ⠀⠀A Ⓑ C̶ D̶ E̶

MC: NE say TV ↓ b/c use other Ps

Ⓧ NE: TV ↓ → ad ↓ → no $ for qual prog → no prog for other Ps

Ⓟ BUT alt P users watch MORE TV

Ⓒ ad rates

I want this combo: X P | *The first one does oppose what the MC concludes. I'm not quite sure whether it does so "through an analogy." Let's look at the second half. A scenario in which the MC's claim won't hold—meaning something that's on the opposite side of what the MCs say. No! The second one outlines a scenario in which the NE's claim won't hold, not the MC's claim.* |

2. Renaissance Masters: The correct answer is **D**.

Step 1: Identify the question.

| In the argument given, the two boldfaced portions play which of the following roles? | R ⠀⠀A B C D E | *The word "boldfaced," along with the boldface font in the argument, indicates that this is a Role question.* |

Step 2: Deconstruct the argument.

Many people praise High Renaissance painting for creating very realistic images from observation,	R ⠀⠀A B C D E ppl like HR pntg b/c realstc	*The "many people" intro feels like there's a contrast coming… and there is! Okay, let's just get this piece down first.*
but scholars have documented that some High Renaissance painters used pinhole cameras to project the likeness of their subjects onto the canvas and painted from there.	R ⠀⠀A B C D E ppl like HR pntg b/c realstc BUT some HR pntrs just project / trace	*Okay, so people think the HR painters can paint realistically just by observing, but actually some were just projecting the images onto a canvas and sort of tracing the image.*
Thus, people who credit High Renaissance painters with superior artistic skills are misguided.	R ⠀⠀A B C D E ppl like HR pntg b/c realstc BUT some HR pntrs just project / trace ppl who like HR = misguided	*The word "thus" might mean this is the conclusion. Hmm. The previous sentence only said that "some" HR painters did the tracing thing, not all of them. But this sentence seems to be condemning all of them.*

Painting from a projected image requires only an insignificant amount of additional skill beyond that needed to copy a picture outright.	R A B C D E ppl like HR pntg b/c realstc BUT some HR pntrs just project / trace Ⓒ ppl who like HR = misguided project / trace = ↓ skill	*Okay, the last sentence was definitely the conclusion. This sentence is supporting the conclusion. If this is true, then yes, painters who use this technique aren't that great.*
n/a	R A B C D E ppl like HR pntg b/c realstc BUT some HR pntrs just project / trace Ⓒ ppl who like HR = misguided project / trace = ↓ skill	*I'm not 100% sure how to label the first boldface, but I did notice that the first one was a fact and the second one was a claim. I could use that alternate conclusion / fact / opinion strategy.*

P

Step 3: State the Goal.

I need to identify the role of the two boldfaced statements as they relate to the conclusion—which was that people who think HR painters are really skilled are misguided. The first one is a fact, and the second one is an opinion. I'm going to try to fact / opinion strategy and see how that works.

Step 4: Work from wrong to right.

(A) The first is a finding that has been used to support a conclusion that the argument rejects; the second is a claim that supports that conclusion.	R <u>A</u> B C D E ppl like HR pntg b/c realstc BUT some HR pntrs just project / trace Ⓒ ppl who like HR = misguided project / trace = ↓ skill	*A "finding" could be a fact, and a claim is an opinion, so this one is okay so far.*

(B) The first is a finding that has been used to support a conclusion that the argument rejects; the second is that conclusion.	R A̲ B C D E ppl like HR pntg b/c realstc BUT some HR pntrs just project / trace ©ppl who like HR = misguided project / trace = ↓ skill	*A "finding" could be a fact, but the conclusion is the conclusion; it doesn't fit into the "opinion" category. (Recall that an opinion is any claim that is NOT the conclusion.) This one's wrong.*
(C) The first is a claim put forth to support a conclusion that the argument rejects; the second is a consideration that is introduced to counter the force of that evidence.	R A̲ B ∈ D E ppl like HR pntg b/c realstc BUT some HR pntrs just project / trace ©ppl who like HRR = misguided project / trace = ↓ skill	*A "claim" is not a fact. I can eliminate this one.*
(D) The first is evidence that forms the basis for the position that the argument seeks to establish; the second is a claim presented to solidify that position.	R A̲ B ∈ D̲ E ppl like HR pntg b/c realstc BUT some HR pntrs just project / trace ©ppl who like HRR = misguided project / trace = ↓ skill	*"Evidence" can be a fact, and a claim is a claim. This one has to stay in, too.*
(E) The first is evidence that forms the basis for the position that the argument seeks to establish; the second is that position.	R A̲ B ∈ D̲ E ppl like HR pntg b/c realstc BUT some HR pntrs just project / trace ©ppl who like HR = misguided project / trace = ↓ skill	*"Evidence" can be a fact, but the second boldface is a claim, while this choice says that the second boldface is the "position," or conclusion. I can eliminate this one.*

MANHATTAN
GMAT

| compare A and D | R   A B C Ⓓ E

ppl like h-R pntg b/c realstc

BUT some h-R pntrs just project / trace

Ⓒppl who like h-R = misguided

project / trace = ↓ skill | *Based on the fact / opinion guessing technique, I can't get any further; I just have to guess between B and D. Using the regular technique, both boldfaces are Premises used to support the author's conclusion. Answer A says that the first boldface is used "to support a conclusion that the argument rejects." Eliminate answer A.* |

3. Democracy: The correct answer is **C**.

<u>Step 1: Identify the question.</u>

| The author develops the argument by | DA   A B C D E | *The wording is similar to a Describe the Argument question, though it doesn't have the "two people talking" feature. This might be one of the rare variants that doesn't have two people talking. A quick glance at the abstract wording of the answer choices confirms: this is a Describe Arg question.* |

Step 2: Deconstruct the argument.

| As the United States demonstrated during its early development, it is not enough for citizens simply to have rights; the successful functioning of a democracy requires that they also know how to exercise those rights. | DA   A B C D E

Ex: US Cit have rights and exercise rights → success democ | *Okay, specific example of a principle: the US showed that citizens need to have rights AND know how to exercise those rights.* |
| Access to formal education was one necessary component that helped the US citizenry to learn how to exercise its rights. | DA   A B C D E

Ex: formal edu → US Cit have rights and exercise rights → success democ | *More detail on the US example. Formal education was needed to know how to exercise those rights.* |

Therefore, in order for a democracy to function successfully, its citizens must have access to a formal education.	DA A B C D E Ex: formal edu → US Cit have rights and exercise rights → success democ ⓒ formal edu nec for success democ	*Conclusion. The author's just sort of putting together the two "end" pieces of the argument here.*

P

Step 3: State the Goal.

The author concludes that formal education is necessary in general for a democracy to be successful. The evidence: it happened this way in one country (the US).

Step 4: Work from wrong to right.

(A) using an analogy to establish a precedent for a planned future event	DA A̶ B C D E Ex: formal edu → US Cit have rights and exercise rights → success democ ⓒ formal edu nec for success democ	*The argument used an example. Is that they same thing as an analogy? Maybe. Oh, but what's the "planned future event"? There isn't anything; rather, the author concluded with a general statement, not a discussion of an event.*
(B) illustrating differences in the requirements for the functioning of a democracy depending upon the democracy in question	DA A̶ B C D E Ex: formal edu → US Cit have rights and exercise rights → success democ ⓒ formal edu nec for success democ	*I can imagine that it would be true that there are different requirements for different governments… but that's not what this argument says. The author only mentions the US and then concludes something in general about that.*
(C) introducing an example that illustrates a common principle	DA A̶ B C̲ D E Ex: formal edu → US Cit have rights and exercise rights → success democ ⓒ formal edu nec for success democ	*This looks decent. The argument did introduce an example and then used that to conclude a general principle.*
(D) forming a hypothesis that explains apparently contradictory pieces of evidence	DA A̶ B̶ C̲ D̶ E Ex: formal edu → US Cit have rights and exercise rights → success democ ⓒ formal edu nec for success democ	*It would be reasonable to describe the conclusion as a hypothesis… but there aren't any contradictory things in the argument. Rather, the example given does illustrate the conclusion.*

MANHATTAN
GMAT

(E) supplying an alternate explanation for a known phenomenon	DA A̶ B̶ Ⓒ D̶ E̶ Ex: formal edu → US Cit have rights and exercise rights → success democ Ⓒformal edu nec for success democ	*The author doesn't supply an "alternate" explanation; he isn't arguing against anyone. He just concludes something from the US example.*

P

4. Malaria: The correct answer is **A**.

Step 1: Identify the question.

What function does the statement in boldface fulfill with respect to the argument presented above?	R A B C D E	*This is a Role question. The question contains the word "boldface," and I'm asked to find the "function" of each bold statement.*

Step 2: Deconstruct the argument.

In an attempt to explain the cause of malaria, a deadly infectious disease, early European settlers in Hong Kong attributed the malady to poisonous gases supposedly emanating from low-lying swampland.	R A B C D E ES: Pgas → M	*This is a fact. Likely either background or premise.*
In the 1880s, however, doctors determined that Anopheles mosquitoes were responsible for transmitting the disease to humans after observing that **the female of the species can carry a parasitic protozoan that is passed on to unsuspecting humans when a mosquito feasts on a person's blood.**	R A B C D E ES: Pgas → M 1880: mosq → M by blood I want this combo: P	*Okay, this is still a fact, but it's the conclusion of the story. They used to think it was one thing, and then they figured out it was really the mosquitoes. The boldface language, in particular, is the evidence used to show that it was mosquitoes. That's a Premise.*

(Note: our "combo" in this case consists of only one label because we only have one boldface statement.)

Step 3: State the Goal.

The question specifically asks me what role this information plays: "the female carries a PP that is passed to humans when a mosquito <bites someone>." Because of that, the scientists decided that the mosquitoes were transmitting the disease. That's the most like a P—a premise that supports some further conclusion.

I need to find the abstract language that indicates some kind of premise or support.

Step 4: Work from wrong to right.

(A) It provides support for the explanation of a particular phenomenon.	R A̲ B C D E ES: Pgas → M 1880: mosq → M by blood I want this combo: P	*"Support"—that's good—for a "phenomenon." Okay, that's just fancy-speak for: provides support for something that happened. That sounds okay. Leave it in.*
(B) It presents evidence that contradicts an established fact.	R A̲ B̶ C D E ES: Pgas → M 1880: mosq → M by blood I want this combo: P	*"Evidence"—that's also good. And that evidence does "contradict" what the earlier settlers thought! Oh, wait—was that an established fact? Let me look at the first sentence again. No, they thought that, but the argument doesn't say it was an "established fact." Cross this one off.*
(C) It offers confirmation of a contested assumption.	R A̲ B̶ C̶ D E ES: Pgas → M 1880: mosq → M by blood I want this combo: P	*"Confirmation" is also good… of a "contested assumption." I'm not quite sure what they're referring to when they say "assumption," but nothing was contested here. First, some people thought one thing, and later, new evidence led some doctors to conclude something else. No.*
(D) It identifies the cause of an erroneous conclusion.	R A̲ B̶ C̶ D̶ E ES: Pgas → M 1880: mosq → M by blood I want this combo: P	*No—the only thing we <u>might</u> be able to describe as an erroneous conclusion is what the early settlers thought. But the bold stuff supports the doctors' conclusion.*
(E) It proposes a new conclusion in place of an earlier conjecture.	R Ⓐ B̶ C̶ D̶ E̶ ES: Pgas → M 1880: mosq → M by blood I want this combo: P	*Oh, yes, a new conclusion. Yes, that's exactly what the argument says! Oh, wait—I labeled the boldface stuff a P, not a C. Why was that? Oh, I see—tricky. The first half of the sentence, the non-bold part, is the new conclusion. The bold part is the evidence supporting that. This isn't it after all!*

5. Digital Marketing: The correct answer is **E**.

Step 1: Identify the question.

Carlos responds to Sania by	DA A B C D E	*The "two person" structure and the focus on how Carlos responds indicate that this is a Describe the Argument question.*

Step 2: Deconstruct the argument.

Sania: The newest workers in the workforce are the most effective digital marketing employees because they are more likely to use social networking websites and tools themselves.	DA A B C D E S: new empl use soc nw → most eff dig mktg empl Ⓒ	*Sania claims that the workers who use certain online tools are also the most effective at digital marketing, and that those people are the newest workers. In order to conclude that they're the MOST effective, she must be assuming that this is the most important criterion by which to judge such employees.*
Carlos: But effective digital marketing also requires very technical expertise, such as search engine optimization, that is best learned on the job via prolonged exposure and instruction.	DA A B C D E S: new empl use soc nw → most eff dig mktg empl Ⓒ C: SE opt learn on job over long time → eff dig mktg	*Carlos doesn't dispute Sania's evidence, but he brings up a new point: you also need these other skills to be a good digital marketer… and those skills are learned on the job over a long time ("prolonged")… which hurts Sania's claim that the <u>newest</u> workers are the most effective.*

Step 3: State the Goal.

I need to articulate <u>how</u> Carlos responds to Sania. He doesn't say that she's wrong about the newest workers using social networking tools. Rather, he says that digital marketers also need this other skill that takes a long time to learn on the job. If that's the case, then this weakens Sania's claim that the <u>newest</u> workers are the most effective.

Step 4: Work from wrong to right.

(A) demonstrating that Sania's conclusion is based upon evidence that is not relevant to the given situation	DA A̶ B C D E S: new empl use soc nw → most eff dig mktg empl Ⓒ C: SE opt learn on job over long time → eff dig mktg	*Carlos doesn't say anything negative about Sania's evidence; rather, he introduces new evidence that attacks Sania's assumption that her piece of evidence is the most important thing to consider.*
(B) questioning the accuracy of the evidence presented by Sania in support of her conclusion	DA A̶ B̶ C D E S: new empl use soc nw → most eff dig mktg empl Ⓒ C: SE opt learn on job over long time → eff dig mktg	*Carlos doesn't attack Sania's evidence; rather, he introduces new evidence that attacks Sania's assumption that her piece of evidence is the most important thing to consider.*
(C) reinforcing Sania's argument by contributing an additional piece of evidence in support of her conclusion	DA A̶ B C̶ D E S: new empl use soc nw → most eff dig mktg empl Ⓒ C: SE opt learn on job over long time → eff dig mktg	*Carlos does contribute an additional piece of evidence, but his new evidence hurts Sania's argument. Carlos doesn't support Sania's conclusion.*
(D) pointing out differences in the qualifications desired by different employers seeking digital marketing employees	DA A̶ B C̶ D̶ E S: new empl use soc nw → most eff dig mktg empl Ⓒ C: SE opt learn on job over long time → eff dig mktg	*Carlos does point out a different way to assess the effectiveness of digital marketing employees, but he doesn't mention employers at all or differences among different employers.*
(E) providing an additional piece of evidence that undermines a portion of Sania's claim	DA A̶ B C̶ D̶ Ⓔ S: new empl use soc nw → most eff dig mktg empl Ⓒ C: SE opt learn on job over long time → eff dig mktg	*Bingo. This is exactly what Carlos does—a new piece of information that hurts the "newest workers" portion of Sania's claim.*

6. Innovative Design: The correct answer is **C**.

Step 1: Identify the question.

In the argument above, the two portions in boldface play which of the following roles?	R A B C D E	*This is a Role question. The question contains the word "boldface," and I'm asked to find the "role" of each bold statement.*

MANHATTAN
GMAT

Step 2: Deconstruct the argument.

Products with innovative and appealing designs relative to competing products can often command substantially higher prices in the marketplace.	R A B C D E ID → ↑↑ $	*Sort of between a fact and a claim. Probably a premise.*
Because design innovations are quickly copied by other manufacturers, many consumer technology companies charge as much as possible for their new designs to extract as much value as possible from them.	R A B C D E ID → ↑↑ $ others copy, so COs charge ↑↑ $	*Getting more towards claim-based material, but I'm not sure this is the conclusion.*
But large profits generated by the innovative designs give competitors stronger incentives to copy the designs.	R A B C D E ID → ↑↑ $ others copy, so COs charge ↑↑ $ BUT ↑↑ prof → faster copy	*BUT signals a contrast. Oh, so there's actually a drawback to making a lot of money: competitors will copy even faster so I guess that could hurt market share. That's interesting.*
Therefore, **the best strategy to maximize overall profit from an innovative new design is to charge less than the greatest possible price**.	R A B C D E ID → ↑↑ $ others copy, so COs charge ↑↑ $ BUT ↑↑ prof → faster copy Ⓒ to max prof, charge < than max price I want this combo: P C	*Here we go, the conclusion. The person's claiming that companies actually <u>shouldn't</u> charge the largest possible price and this will actually help maximize profits in the end. The second boldface is the conclusion; that gets a C. And the first is a Premise that supports this conclusion.*

Step 3: State the Goal.

The question asks me to determine the role played by each of 2 boldface statements. I've decided the second one is the conclusion and the first is a premise supporting that conclusion, so I want to find an answer that gives this combo: P C (premise, then conclusion).

Step 4: Work from wrong to right.

(A) The first is an assumption that supports a described course of action; the second provides a consideration to support a preferred course of action.	R A̶ B C D E ID → ↑↑ $ others copy, so COs charge ↑↑ $ BUT ↑↑ prof → faster copy Ⓒ to max prof, charge < than max price I want this combo: P C	*Hmm, they call the first an assumption, not a premise, but I suppose that's okay; they do say it "supports" something. The second, though, is the actual conclusion—but this answer choice makes the second sound like another premise. I don't think so.*
(B) The first is a consideration that helps explain the appeal of a certain strategy; the second presents an alternative strategy endorsed by the argument.	R A̶ B C D E ID → ↑↑ $ others copy, so COs charge ↑↑ $ BUT ↑↑ prof → faster copy Ⓒ to max prof, charge < than max price I want this combo: P C	*The wording for the first statement is a little strange, but I suppose that could be considered a premise. Okay. The wording for the second definitely doesn't work, though—the second isn't discussing an "alternative" strategy compared to the first. The first one actually supports the second!*
(C) The first is a phenomenon that justifies a specific strategy; the second is that strategy.	R A̶ B C̲ D E ID → ↑↑ $ others copy, so COs charge ↑↑ $ BUT ↑↑ prof → faster copy Ⓒ to max prof, charge < than max price I want this combo: P C	*Something that "justifies" something else… yes, this could be a way to describe something that supports something else. That part's okay. And the second part "is that strategy"—yes, strategy could be a synonym for conclusion. Keep this one in.*
(D) The first is a consideration that demonstrates why a particular approach is flawed; the second describes a way to amend that approach.	R A̶ B C̲ D̶ E ID → ↑↑ $ others copy, so COs charge ↑↑ $ BUT ↑↑ prof → faster copy Ⓒ to max prof, charge < than max price I want this combo: P C	*No, the first supports the conclusion—it doesn't illustrate a flaw. I don't even need to read the second half of this choice.*

| (E) The first is a factor used to rationalize a particular strategy; the second is a factor against that strategy. | R   A̶ B̶ Ⓒ D̶ E̶

ID → ↑↑ $

others copy, so COs charge ↑↑ $

BUT ↑↑ prof → faster copy

Ⓒ to max prof, charge < than max price

I want this combo: P C | *Something used to "rationalize" a "strategy"? Yes, that could be describing a premise that supports a conclusion. Oh, but the second goes against the strategy? No! The second is actually the strategy, or conclusion.* |

P

7. Gray Wolf Population: The correct answer is **A**.

Step 1: Identify the question.

| The environmentalist challenges the government representative's argument by doing which of the following ? | DA   A B C D E | *We have a 2-person-talking structure, and we're asked how the second person responds; this is a Describe the Argument question.* |

Step 2: Deconstruct the argument.

| Government representative: Between 1996 and 2005, the gray wolf population in Minnesota grew nearly 50 percent; the gray wolf population in Montana increased by only 13 percent during the same period. | DA   A B C D E

GR: 96-05, Min GW ↑ 50%, Mon GW ↑ 13% | *This is just a straight fact. The Minnesota wolf population grew a lot faster in that time period than the Montana wolf population.* |
| Clearly, the Minnesota gray wolf population is more likely to survive and thrive long term. | DA   A B C D E

GR: 96-05, Min GW ↑ 50%, Mon GW ↑ 13%

Ⓒ Min > likely to survive/thrive | *Conclusion! Claiming that Minnesota wolves are more likely to survive and thrive. Certainly, the Minnesota wolf population grew more... but does that automatically mean they're more likely to survive and thrive?* |

Environmentalist: But the gray wolf population in Montana is nearly 8 times the population in Minnesota; above a certain critical breeding number, the population is stable and does not require growth in order to survive.	DA A B C D E GR: 96-05, Min GW ↑ 50%, Mon GW ↑ 13% Ⓒ Min > likely to survive/thrive E: BUT Mon 8x Min; when ↑ enough, already stable	*Ah, okay. The environmentalist is pointing out that they're not necessarily the same thing. Once the population is large enough, it's already stable, so growth isn't necessarily critical to survival.*

P

Step 3: State the Goal.

The GR concludes that the Min wolves are more likely to survive and thrive because the growth rate was a lot higher, but the E responded that the Mon population was already a lot larger, so growth might not have been necessary to keep the population thriving. The Mon population might already have been stable in the first place.

I need to find something that explains this is a more abstract way: a new piece of evidence changes the way we think about the issue addressed in the conclusion (surviving and thriving).

Step 4: Work from wrong to right.

(A) introducing additional evidence that undermines an assumption made by the representative	DA A̲ B C D E GR: 96-05, Min GW ↑ 50%, Mon GW ↑ 13% Ⓒ Min > likely to survive/thrive E: BUT Mon 8x Min; when ↑ enough, already stable	*This sounds pretty good. The E's statement is a new piece of evidence, and it does undermine the R's assumption that growth is a good indicator of likelihood to survive and thrive.*
(B) challenging the representative's definition of a critical breeding number	DA A̲ B̶ C D E GR: 96-05, Min GW ↑ 50%, Mon GW ↑ 13% Ⓒ Min > likely to survive/thrive E: BUT Mon 8x Min; when ↑ enough, already stable	*The E does challenge the R's assumption about what it takes to survive and thrive, but the E can't challenge the R on "critical breeding number," because the R never mentions this concept.*

P

(C) demonstrating that the critical breeding number of the two wolf populations differs significantly	DA A̲ B E̶ D E GR: 96–05, Min GW ↑ 50%, Mon GW ↑ 13% ⓒMin > likely to survive/ thrive E: BUT Mon 8x Min; when ↑ enough, already stable	*The E does mention the concept of "critical breeding number" but establishes only that the number of wolves in each population differs significantly, not that the number of wolves needed to achieve the "critical breeding number" is different.*
(D) implying that the two populations of wolves could be combined in order to preserve the species	DA A̲ B E̶ D̶ E GR: 96–05, Min GW ↑ 50%, Mon GW ↑ 13% ⓒMin > likely to survive/ thrive E: BUT Mon 8x Min; when ↑ enough, already stable	*This might be an interesting strategy, but the E doesn't actually mention it.*
(E) suggesting that the Montana wolf population grew at a faster rate than stated in the representative's argument	DA Ⓐ B E̶ D̶ E̶ GR: 96–05, Min GW ↑ 50%, Mon GW ↑ 13% ⓒMin > likely to survive/ thrive E: BUT Mon 8x Min; when ↑ enough, already stable	*This is tricky if we're not reading very carefully. The E does introduce a new figure, but that figure has to do with the size of the two populations, not the rate of growth. The E does not dispute the R's figures for rate of growth.*

Chapter 4

of

Critical Reasoning

Assumptions

In This Chapter...

Chapter 4:
Assumptions

We briefly introduced **assumptions** in chapter 2, but we haven't done much yet with this concept. Assumptions are the key to the largest family of questions, the Assumption Family; all questions in this family require us to identify and conduct some reasoning using some assumption made by the author. (When we refer to the "author," we're referring to a hypothetical person who is "speaking" the argument and believes the argument to be valid. We're not referring to the test writer.)

An assumption is something that *the author must believe to be true* in order to draw a certain conclusion; however, the author *does not state* the assumption in the argument. The assumption itself might not necessarily be true in the real world; the only requirement is that the *author* has to believe it's true in order to make his or her claim.

For example, what is the author of the below argument assuming must be true?

Amy got an A on the test. Therefore, Amy must have studied for a long time.

The author assumes that, in order to get an A on the test, it is absolutely required to study for a long time. Note that the author is not just assuming that studying for a long time is one way to get an A on the test. The author concludes that Amy must have studied for a long time, so that is the *only* way.

The diagram above represents the **core** of the argument; we previously discussed the core in Chapter 1. The core consists of the conclusion and the main premise or premises that lead to that conclusion, as well as the *assumption*.

Assumptions fill a gap in the argument; the gap is represented by the arrow in the diagram above. If we insert a correct assumption into the argument, it makes the argument stronger:

Amy got an A on the test. *Studying for a long time is the only way to get an A.* Therefore, Amy must have studied for a long time.

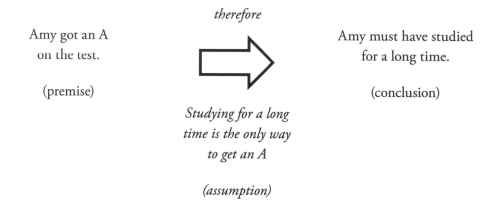

therefore

Amy got an A
on the test.

(premise)

Amy must have studied
for a long time.

(conclusion)

*Studying for a long
time is the only way
to get an A*

(assumption)

Most GMAT arguments will contain multiple assumptions. Any one assumption will not automatically make the argument air-tight, but it will make the conclusion more likely to be true. Brainstorm some assumptions for this argument:

> Thomas's football team lost in the championship game last year. The same two teams are playing in the championship game again this year, and the players on Thomas's team have improved. Therefore, Thomas's team will win the championship game this year.

The author is making multiple assumptions here. Thomas's team has improved enough to be better than last year's winner. Last year's winning team has not also improved enough to keep them ahead of Thomas's team.

This brings us to a couple of important strategies for dealing with assumptions on the test.

Do		Don't
do brainstorm assumptions you can think of relatively easily	**but**	don't spend more than about 20 seconds brainstorming up front
do look for your brainstormed assumptions in the answers	**but**	don't eliminate answers because they don't match any of your brainstormed assumptions
do find something that the author must believe to be true in order to draw the conclusion	**but**	don't hold out for something that makes the conclusion "perfect" or definitely true

Let's insert an assumption into our football argument and see how it works:

> Thomas's football team lost in the championship game last year. The same two teams are playing in the championship game again this year, and the players on Thomas's team have improved *enough to be better than the players on the defending champion team.* Therefore, Thomas's team will win the championship game this year.

That assumption does make the argument stronger, but we could easily argue that Thomas's team still might not win. There are too many other potential factors involved; the author is making many assumptions, not just one, in order to draw this conclusion.

Let's try another. On your scrap paper, draw out the core for the following argument, then try to brainstorm some assumptions.

> Charles is a sculptor. Therefore, he does not work in a practical field.

The first sentence offers a fact; the second offers a conclusion. Those are the two halves of our core, but what is the gap in between?

therefore

Charles is a sculptor. He does not work
in a practical field.

Sculpting is not practical.
Sculpting is not just a hobby
done in his spare time.
He does not hold a different
job in a practical field.

The author is making a number of assumptions here; three are shown in the diagram above. Different people will brainstorm different assumptions; any are valid assumptions as long as the author *must* believe them to be true in order to draw that conclusion.

Drill: Brainstorm Assumptions

Draw out the "core," and brainstorm at least one assumption that must be true in order to draw each conclusion.

1. Chocolate is Prabha's favorite flavor of ice cream. Therefore, she also likes chocolate candy bars.

2. The employees of Quick Corp's accounting department consistently show a significant jump in productivity in the two weeks before taking vacation. Clearly, the knowledge that they are about to go on vacation motivates the employees to maximize their productivity.

3. Mayor: The Acme Factory has developed a new manufacturing process that uses chemical Q, the residue of which is toxic to babies. In order to protect our children, we need to pass a law banning the use of this chemical.

Answer Key for Drill: Brainstorm Assumptions

The assumption is noted in italics below the arrow. You may brainstorm different assumptions from the one shown. Other assumptions are acceptable as long as they represent something that MUST be true in order to draw the given conclusion.

1.

The author assumes that Prabha will definitely like chocolate in at least one other form (candy bars). The author assumes that it's not true that she likes chocolate only in the form of ice cream.

2.

therefore

2 wks b4 vaca:
↓ prod

emp choose to max
prod b4 vaca

*"sig. jump" is the same thing
as "max prod"
They didn't plan vacation to
occur right after a big dead-
line or other busy time.*

The author assumes a couple of things here. First, the premise mentions only a "significant jump" in productivity; it does not say that this productivity represents the employees' maximum productivity. So the author is assuming that this significant jump does, in fact, represent the maximum productivity.

Second, the author concludes that employees *decide* to be more productive because they'll be taking vacation soon. Perhaps it's the case, instead, that the employees choose to take vacation right after they know they'll be *forced* to work harder for some other reason. This author is assuming that this is NOT the case—that employees are NOT choosing to take vacation after what they know will be a busy time at work.

3.

therefore

Acme using Q,
toxic baby

to protect kids,
ban Q

*If Acme uses Q, then kids will
somehow come into contact
with Q*

The author assumes that use of chemical Q in the production process will somehow eventually expose babies to the chemical residue. Maybe it's the case that the chemical is used only for something that never comes into contact with the final product and will never come into contact with kids.

Assumption Family Questions

As we discussed earlier, there are 5 different types of assumption questions. We'll cover three, Find the Assumption, Evaluate, and Flaw, in this chapter. In the next chapter, we'll learn about Strengthen and Weaken questions. (Note: Find the Assumption *Questions* are one type of question in the overall Assumption Family.)

Each type of question has its own key characteristics and goals, but there are some commonalities across all five types. There will be a conclusion, so we need to make sure to find it. In addition, *while* we read, we also try to brainstorm any gaps, or assumptions, that we can in a short amount of time (but we don't take very much longer than we take to read the argument itself).

4

Find the Assumption (FA) Questions

Find the Assumption questions ask us to find an assumption that the author must believe to be true in order to draw the conclusion. The correct answer should make the argument stronger. In addition, if the correct answer were *not* necessarily true, that would significantly harm the argument.

Our task is to figure out which answer choice represents something that must hold true according to the author. Note one especially tricky aspect of these problems: the assumption itself might be flawed. We might think, "Well, is that really true in the real world? I don't think that's necessarily true." Don't ask that question! The only issue is whether the *author* must believe it to be true in order to arrive at his or her conclusion. In our chocolate ice cream example from the last problem set, the author had to believe that Prabha liked at least one other form of chocolate (other than ice cream), but that assumption could be false. Perhaps Prabha really does like chocolate only in the form of ice cream.

Identifying the Question

Most of the time, these questions are easy to identify because the question stem will use some form of the noun "assumption" or the verb "to assume." Occasionally, the question will be worded differently. It may ask for a new premise, or piece of information, that is "required" or a new premise that will help the conclusion to be "more properly drawn" (or similar language). Here are a couple of examples:

> Which of the following is an assumption on which the argument depends?

> The conclusion above would be more properly drawn if it were established that

Let's look at a sample argument:

> When news periodicals begin forecasting a recession, people tend to spend less money on non-essential purchases. Therefore, the perceived threat of a future recession decreases the willingness of people to purchase products that they regard as optional or luxury goods.

Which of the following is an assumption on which the argument depends?

We'll look at the answers in a moment. Let's do our first couple of steps:

Step 1: Identify the question.

Which of the following is an assumption on which the argument depends?	FA A B C D E	The question stem uses the word "assumption," so it is the Assumption type. Write "FA" on the scrap paper and then the 5 answer choice letters.

Step 2: Deconstruct the argument.

When news periodicals begin forecasting a recession, people tend to spend less money on non-essential purchases.	FA A B C D E news Ps fore rec → ppl spend ↓ $	This sounds like a premise, though I suppose it could be a conclusion. The news Ps predict a recession, and then people spend less money.
Therefore, the perceived threat of a future recession decreases the willingness of people to purchase products that they regard as optional or luxury goods.	FA A B C D E news Ps fore rec → ppl spend ↓ $ ©prcvd fut thrt → ppl spend ↓ $ lux	This is the conclusion. The premise just tells us what people do — spend less money. The conclusion tries to claim <u>why</u> they do it — a perceived future threat.
n/a	FA A B C D E news Ps fore rec → ppl spend ↓ $ ©prcvd fut thrt → ppl spend ↓ $ lux	What is the author assuming? That people are actually reading or hearing about the news P forecasts. That the recession hasn't already started and <u>that's</u> why people are spending less money — maybe the news Ps are just slow in "forecasting" something that has already started.

Did you come up with any other assumptions? The key is to get our brains thinking about these things, but there are almost always multiple possible assumptions; we may not be able to brainstorm the exact one that will show up in the answers.

Step 3: State the Goal.

My core is:

therefore

News Ps:
rec!
↓ spend & ↓

Prcvd threat → spend $ ↓

*Ppl reading / hearing info
from News Ps
Threat only prcvd today;
hasn't actually started*

I'll look for the assumptions I brainstormed, but I'll also be flexible; I might not have thought of the assumption in the correct answer. On FA questions, traps often involve going too far out of scope (the answer is not tied to the conclusion), using reverse logic (the answer makes the argument weaker, not stronger), or making an irrelevant distinction or comparison. (Note: we'll discuss more about trap answers a bit later in the chapter.)

Let's take a look at the full problem now.

> When news periodicals begin forecasting a recession, people tend to spend less money on non-essential purchases. Therefore, the perceived threat of a future recession decreases the willingness of people to purchase products that they regard as optional or luxury goods.
>
> Which of the following is an assumption on which the argument depends?
>
> (A) People do not always agree as to which goods should be considered luxury goods.
> (B) People are more likely to have read a news periodical recently because more and more periodicals are being published.
> (C) Most people do not regularly read news periodicals.
> (D) The consumer perception of the threat of recession increases when news periodicals begin forecasting a recession.
> (E) At least some of the biggest-spending consumers prior to the recession were among those who curtailed their spending after the recession began.

Step 4: Work from wrong to right.

(A) People do not always agree as to which goods should be considered luxury goods.	FA A B C D E news Ps fore rec → ppl spend ↓ $ ⒸprⒸvd fut thrt → ppl spend ↓ $ lux	*I can believe that this is true in the real world, but this is irrelevant to the conclusion. The argument is not based upon whether people agree as to how to classify certain goods.*
(B) People are more likely to have read a news periodical recently because more and more periodicals are being published.	FA A̶ B̲ C D E news Ps fore rec → ppl spend ↓ $ Ⓒprcvd fut thrt → ppl spend ↓ $ lux	*This sounds a little bit like one of my brainstormed assumptions—the argument is assuming that people are actually reading those periodicals. I'm not so sure about the "more periodicals are being published" part, though. You don't absolutely have to believe that in order to draw that conclusion. I'll keep it in for now, but maybe I'll find something better.*
(C) Most people do not regularly read news periodicals.	FA A̶ B̲ C̶ D E news Ps fore rec → ppl spend ↓ $ Ⓒprcvd fut thrt → ppl spend ↓ $ lux	*This is also about reading the periodicals... but it's the opposite of what I want! The argument needs to assume that people DO read the Ps; if they don't, then how can they be influenced by what the Ps forecast!*
(D) The consumer perception of the threat of recession increases when news periodicals begin forecasting a recession.	FA A̶ B̲ C̶ D̲ E news Ps fore rec → ppl spend ↓ $ Ⓒprcvd fut thrt → ppl spend ↓ $ lux	*Let's see. News Ps begin forecasting, then perception of threat increases, then people spend less $. If that's true, then it IS the case that the perception of the threat leads people to spend less $. This one is looking better than B. I can cross off B now.*
(E) At least some of the biggest-spending consumers prior to the recession were among those who curtailed their spending after the recession began.	FA A̶ B̲ C̶ Ⓓ E̶ news Ps fore rec → ppl spend ↓ $ Ⓒprcvd fut thrt → ppl spend ↓ $ lux	*Hmm. This one sounds good, too. Maybe if the biggest spenders keep spending during the recession, then the overall amount of money being spent won't go down that much... although the argument doesn't really seem to depend on how much it goes down. Oh, and this says "after the recession began"—that doesn't make sense with this conclusion. The conclusion is about a "perceived threat of a future recession." Nice trap!*

We had a couple of good brainstormed assumptions ahead of time, but it turns out that we didn't brainstorm the assumption contained in the correct answer, D. We did, however, see an "opposite" answer in choice C; it contained information that was the opposite of one of our brainstormed assumptions, and that made it easier for us to know that C was wrong.

The Negation Technique

On harder questions, we might find ourselves stuck between two answer choices. What can we do to distinguish between tempting wrong answers and the right answer? We can try the Negation technique.

On Find the Assumption questions, the correct answer will be something that the author must believe to be true in order to draw his or her conclusion. Because that is the case, if we were to negate the correct answer—say that it isn't true—then the author's argument should be harmed. Negating the correct answer should actually weaken the author's conclusion.

The Negation technique takes a bit of time to implement, so we don't want to use it on all five answer choices, but the extra time needed might be worth it when we're stuck between two answers.

How do we do this? Let's try it out on the News Periodicals problem we just finished. Let's say that we narrowed our answers to B and D:

(B)   People are more likely to have read a news periodical recently because more and more periodicals are being published.

(D)   The consumer perception of the threat of recession increases when news periodicals begin forecasting a recession.

Recall the argument itself:

news Ps fore rec $\rightarrow$ ppl spend $\downarrow$ $

Ⓒ prcvd fut thrt $\rightarrow$ ppl spend $\downarrow$ $ lux

That is, the author claims that the news Ps forecast a recession, which causes people to perceive a future threat, and so people choose to spend less money on luxury goods.

What if answer choice B were NOT true? It would say something like:

(B)   People are NOT more likely to have read a news periodical recently

(and) more periodicals are NOT being published.

Does this tear down the author's conclusion? Not really. The number of periodicals being published is irrelevant to the argument.

Try negating answer D:

MANHATTAN
GMAT

(D)   The consumer perception of the threat of recession DOES NOT increase
        when news periodicals begin forecasting a recession.

Hmm. If the news Ps forecast a recession, but the consumers don't actually perceive any threat of recession… then how can the author claim that they change their buying behavior based on perceiving this
threat? Negating this answer does weaken the author's conclusion, so this one is the right answer.

Don't use this technique on every answer choice, or you'll be in danger of spending too much time on
CR questions—but, when you're stuck, try to unstick yourself using the Negation technique.

Common Trap Answers

Let's take a look at some of the trap answers we saw in that last question and discuss the kinds of traps
that they typically try to set for us on Assumption questions.

On many FA questions, a trap answer will go too far out of scope: it won't actually address the conclusion. Answer A in the above problem is a good example. The issue is not whether different people would
agree to classify the same item as a luxury good. Rather, the conclusion is about what causes someone to
spend less money on anything that that individual believes to be a luxury good.

Trap answers can also use reverse logic, which we see in answer choice C. Reverse logic does the opposite of what we want to do: in this case, answer C actually makes the argument worse, when we're
trying to articulate an assumption that would make the argument a bit stronger.

Answer E is an example of another trap: making an irrelevant distinction or comparison. The argument
does not hinge upon whether the highest-spending consumers do something different from the rest.
Rather, all consumers are lumped together in the argument.

Takeaways for Find the Assumption Questions

Most of the time, an FA question stem will contain some form of the word "assumption." Occasionally, the question may ask for a new premise that is "required" to draw the conclusion or will help the
conclusion to be "more properly drawn."

Our goal is to find the core (conclusion plus major premises) and brainstorm assumptions while laying
out the core.

Correct answers will represent something that the author must believe to be true in order to draw his or
her conclusion.

If we get stuck between two answers, we can try the Negation technique: negate each answer and see
whether doing so weakens the conclusion; the one that weakens the conclusion is the right answer.

Trap answer types include:

Out of Scope: goes beyond the scope of the argument, doesn't address or affect the conclusion

Reverse Logic: does the opposite of what we want (on FA questions, a reverse logic trap would make the conclusion weaker, not stronger)

Irrelevant Distinction or Comparison: makes a distinction or comparison that doesn't matter between two groups

4 Evaluate the Argument Questions

For Evaluate questions, our first step is still to find an assumption, but we have to do a little more work after finding the assumption. At heart, we are asked what additional information would help us to try to determine whether the assumption is valid or invalid.

Most Evaluate question stems will contain one of the following:

- some form of the word "evaluate"

- some form of the word "determine"

- language asking what would be "useful to know (or establish)" or "important to know"

For example, an Evaluate question stem might ask:

"Which of the following must be studied in order to evaluate the argument?"

"Which of the following would it be most useful to know in determining whether the mayor's plan is likely to be successful?"

Occasionally, an Evaluate question will use different wording from the above, but the question will still get at the same overall idea—what is relevant to consider or important to research or understand in making some decision or evaluating some claim?

The "Two Paths" Strategy

Evaluate answers will often be in the form of a question or in the form "Whether <a certain thing is one way or the other>." For example, let's say we're given this argument:

In order to increase its profits, MillCo plans to reduce costs by laying off any non-essential employees.

Let's see. According to the argument:

> MillCo will lay off non-essential employees → reduce costs → increase profits

Does that sound like a good plan? What is MillCo assuming in claiming that laying off non-essential employees will result in increased profits?

Profits are a measure of revenues minus costs so, for one thing, MillCo is assuming that revenues won't drop a lot as a result of these layoffs. If revenues dropped as much as or more than the expected cost savings, then MillCo's profits wouldn't increase.

An Evaluate question would ask us what would be most important to know in order to evaluate Mill-Co's plan. A correct answer might read:

> Whether revenues will be affected adversely enough to threaten MillCo's profit structure.

There are two possible paths to examine, yes or no:

> Yes, MillCo's revenues *will* be affected adversely enough. In this case, MillCo's argument is weakened—the plan to increase profits is less likely to work.

> No, MillCo's revenues won't be affected adversely enough. In this case, MillCo's argument is strengthened—the plan to increase profits might work.

This answer choice, then, is designed to *test* the assumption; it helps to determine whether the assumption is valid. The correct answer should be structured in such a way that there are at least two possible "paths"—one path will strengthen the argument, and the other will weaken it.

The incorrect answers will also be presented in this "two paths" format, with one key distinction: the two paths won't lead in two different directions (strengthening *and* weakening the argument). What if we had this answer choice?

> Whether MillCo might reduce its costs by eliminating some health insurance benefits.

Let's evaluate the two paths:

> Yes, MillCo can reduce costs by eliminating some health benefits. How will this affect the given plan to lay off employees? It doesn't—it isn't part of the plan at all.

> No, MillCo cannot reduce costs by eliminating some health benefits. Again, this doesn't affect the plan given in the argument.

This incorrect answer choice is trying to distract us by offering a different way to increase profits… but we aren't asked to find alternate ways to increase profits. We're asked to evaluate whether the *existing argument* is valid. We don't know any more than we did about whether MillCo's plan (reduce employees → reduce costs → increase profits) will work.

On Evaluate questions, we're going to do what we do on all Assumption Family questions:

(1)   find the core (conclusion plus major premises), noting this on our scrap paper

(2)   brainstorm any assumptions we can

Then we're going to look for an answer that addresses one of our assumptions (if we've been able to brainstorm the right one!). The correct answer should offer at least two different "paths," one that would make the argument stronger and one that would make the argument weaker.

Let's try a full example; set your timer for 2 minutes and pick an answer before you read the explanation!

> Editorial: In order to preserve the health of its local economy, Metropolis should not permit a CostMart warehouse department store to open within city limits. It has been demonstrated that when CostMart opens a warehouse department store within a city, the bankruptcy rate of local retailers increases in that city by twenty percent over the next several years.
>
> Which of the following questions would be most useful for evaluating the conclusion of the Editorial?
>
> (A)   Does the bankruptcy rate of local retailers in a city generally stabilize several years after a CostMart warehouse department store opens?
> (B)   Do most residents of Metropolis currently do almost all of their shopping at stores within the city limits of Metropolis?
> (C)   Have other cities that have permitted CostMart warehouse department stores within city limits experienced any economic benefits as a result?
> (D)   Is the bankruptcy rate for local retailers in Metropolis higher than in the average city that has permitted a CostMart warehouse department store within city limits?
> (E)   Does CostMart plan to hire employees exclusively from within Metropolis for the proposed warehouse department store?

Step 1: Identify the question.

Which of the following questions would be most useful for evaluating the conclusion of the Editorial?	Ev A B C D E	*The language "most useful" and "evaluating" tells me that this is an Evaluate question. I'll write down "Ev" to indicate that.*

Step 2: Deconstruct the argument.

Editorial: In order to preserve the health of its local economy, Metropolis should not permit a CostMart warehouse department store to open within city limits.	Ev A B C D E ⓒ M ban CM in city → help loc econ	*"In order to" means that something is going to cause this. Okay, the author is saying that M shouldn't let CM into the city so that M can preserve the health of the local economy. That's causation and kind of sounds like a conclusion.*
It has been demonstrated that when CostMart opens a warehouse department store within a city, the bankruptcy rate of local retailers increases in that city by twenty percent over the next several years.	Ev A B C D E ⓒ M ban CM in city → help loc econ if new CM store → bnkrpt locals ↑ 20% for years	*Okay, there's a bad economic outcome for local retailers when a new CM store opens. So certainly this is evidence that supports the author's claim that preventing CM from opening a store will preserve the local economy. This is a premise, so the previous sentence was the conclusion.*
(brainstorm assumptions)	Ev A B C D E ⓒ M ban CM in city → help loc econ if new CM store → bnkrpt locals ↑ 20% for years [any good results?]	Are there any good economic results when CM opens a store? Maybe there are some bad and good results… and maybe the good results could outweigh the bad.

Step 3: State the Goal.

When CM opens a new store, there's at least one bad economic outcome. The author concludes that preventing CM from opening a new store will preserve a good local economy.

I need to find an answer that will have two possible paths—one way will strengthen the author's claim, and the other way will weaken it. Possibly, the answer might have something to do with the assumption I brainstormed—could there be both good and bad possible results from a new CM store?

4

Step 4: Work from wrong to right.

(A) Does the bankruptcy rate of local retailers in a city generally stabilize several years after a CostMart warehouse department store opens?	Ev A B C D E ⓒ M ban CM in city → help loc econ if new CM store → bnkrpt locals ↑ 20% for years [any good results?]	*If yes, then the bad result wouldn't continue to happen over time… but it would still happen in the first place. If no, then the bad result would keep happening over time. Either way, there is a bad result for at least a few years, so both "paths" strengthen the author's conclusion.*
(B) Do most residents of Metropolis currently do almost all of their shopping at stores within the city limits of Metropolis?	Ev A B C D E ⓒ M ban CM in city → help loc econ if new CM store → bnkrpt locals ↑ 20% for years [any good results?]	*If yes, then… I'm not sure what this has to do with the conclusion. If some stores go out of business, then people will have to switch stores? Okay, but that doesn't impact the city's overall economic situation—either there are local retailers or there's the CM store in the city (or both).*
(C) Have other cities that have permitted CostMart warehouse department stores within city limits experienced any economic benefits as a result?	Ev A B C̲ D E ⓒ M ban CM in city → help loc econ if new CM store → bnkrpt locals ↑ 20% for years [any good results?]	*If yes, then that would be a reason to let CM open a store (because economic benefits would help to "preserve the health of the local economy"); that weakens the author's argument. If no, there are no benefits to a CM store, then this strengthens the author's claim. This one is looking pretty good.*
(D) Is the bankruptcy rate for local retailers in Metropolis higher than in the average city that has permitted a CostMart warehouse department store within city limits?	Ev A B C̲ D̶ E ⓒ M ban CM in city → help loc econ if new CM store → bnkrpt locals ↑ 20% for years [any good results?]	*If yes, then… would that make local stores even more likely to go out of business? I'm not sure—I don't know why they're going out of business now. This doesn't seem to affect the conclusion one way or the other.*
(E) Does CostMart plan to hire employees exclusively from within Metropolis for the proposed warehouse department store?	Ev A B C̲ D̶ E̲ ⓒ M ban CM in city → help loc econ if new CM store → bnkrpt locals ↑ 20% for years [any good results?]	*This one could be good, too. If yes, then that would be an economic benefit—jobs are good! If no, then… hmm… it's not bad necessarily but it's not good either.*

(compare C and E)	Ev A B Ⓒ Đ Ɇ Ⓒ M ban CM in city → help loc econ if new CM store → bnkrpt locals ↑ 20% for years [any good results?]	*Wait. For E, if some stores are going out of business, that means people losing jobs. There's only a benefit to the new CM store adding jobs if it adds even more jobs than are lost. So there's no definite benefit given in E, but there is in C. Tricky. C it is.*

Common Trap Answers

Answer choice E in the last question was a very tricky trap. How do they get us to pick wrong answers on Evaluate questions?

Out of Scope: don't make additional assumptions! Answer E presented us with something that seemed like a benefit at first, until we realized that we had to make an additional assumption in order to know that we definitely had a benefit. We shouldn't have to make additional assumptions; the answer should work "as is."

Irrelevant Distinction or Comparison: we saw this trap for the first time in our Find the Assumption example earlier in the chapter. In the above problem, Answer D does discuss something mentioned by the argument—bankruptcy—but tries to compare a no–CostMart-in-Metropolis scenario with a CostMart-in-other-cities scenario, both of which are not the scenario we want to discuss: the scenario in which CostMart does open up in Metropolis.

Takeaways for Evaluate Questions

As always, we use the question stem to identify the question type. On Evaluate questions, the question stem will likely contain some form of the word "evaluate," "determine," or "useful (or important) to know."

Our goal is to find a "two-path" answer: an answer that can be interpreted in two ways, one of which will strengthen the conclusion and the other of which will weaken the conclusion.

Trap answers will try to get us to make additional assumptions—these answers are actually out of scope—or to make an irrelevant distinction or comparison between two things that are not the focus of the argument's conclusion.

Flaw Questions

Flaw Questions are the least common of the five Assumption Family question types. The question stems will almost always contain some form of the word "flaw," but we have to be careful because Weaken the Conclusion questions can also contain the word "flaw" in the question stem.

Weaken questions will also contain "if true" language; Flaw questions will *not* contain this language.

Flaw	Weaken
Look for this first:	
contains the word "flaw" but NOT "if true" language	contains the word "flaw" AND the words "if true" (or an equivalent synonym)
If you're still not sure, try this:	
answer choices are a bit more abstract, similar to but not as abstract as Structure Family questions	answer choices represent a new piece of information (see next chapter for more)
Example	
Which of the following indicates a <u>flaw</u> in the reasoning above?	Which of the following, <u>if true</u>, would indicate a <u>flaw</u> in the teacher's plan?

On occasion, a Flaw question may not contain a synonym of the word "flaw," such as "vulnerable to criticism."

As with the other Assumption Family questions, Flaw questions will contain a conclusion, and we will want to brainstorm some assumptions if we can. The correct answer will have something to do with an assumption, but rather than articulating the assumption (which would help to strengthen the argument), we are looking for wording that indicates why it is flawed thinking to believe that this assumption is true.

For example:

> Pierre was recovering from the flu when he visited Shelley last week, and now
> Shelley is showing signs of the flu. If Pierre had waited until he was no longer
> contagious, Shelley would not have become ill.

The author is assuming that Pierre was the one to infect Shelley. The author is also assuming that there is no other way Shelley could have gotten sick. Perhaps it is flu season, and many people with whom Shelley comes in contact have the flu!

The correct answer might be something like:

> The author fails to consider that there are alternate paths by which Shelley could have
> become infected.

Contrast that language with the assumption itself: the author assumes that only Pierre could have infected Shelley. If that's true, then that piece of information strengthens the author's argument. When we take the same information, though, and flip it around into a flaw, we harm the author's argument:

Pierre was recovering from the flu when he visited Shelley last week, and now Shelley is showing signs of the flu. If Pierre had waited until he was no longer contagious, Shelley would not have become ill.	
Assumption	*Flaw*
Only Pierre could have infected Shelley.	The author fails to consider that there are alternate paths by which Shelley could have become infected.
The argument is made stronger.	*The argument is made weaker.*

In sum, we can think of Flaw questions as the "reverse" of Assumption questions. The answer still hinges on an assumption, but the correct answer will word that assumption in a way that hurts the argument.

In addition, the answer choice language may be a bit more abstract than the answer choices we see on other Assumption Family questions. Often, the answer choices will talk about what the author "fails to consider (or establish)," "does not specify (or identify)," or something along those lines.

Let's take a look at a full example.

> Environmentalist: Bando Inc's manufacturing process releases pollution into the atmosphere. In order to convince the company to change processes, we will organize a boycott of the product that represents its highest sales volume, light bulbs. Because Bando sells more light bulbs than any other product, a boycott of light bulbs will cause the most damage to the company's profits.
>
> The environmentalist's reasoning is flawed because it fails to
>
> (A)   allow for the possibility that Bando may not want to change its manufacturing process
> (B)   does not supply information about other possible ways for Bando to reduce pollution
> (C)   consider that the relative sales volumes of a company's products are not necessarily proportional to profits
> (D)   identify any alternative methods by which to convince Bando to change its manufacturing process
> (E)   consider that a boycott may take too long to achieve its purpose

Step 1: Identify the question.

The environmentalist's reasoning is flawed because it fails to	Fl A B C D E	*The word "flawed" tells me this is either a Flaw or Weaken question. "If true" does not appear, so this is a Flaw question. I'll write down "Fl" on my scrap paper.*

Step 2: Deconstruct the argument.

Environmentalist: Bando Inc's manufacturing process releases pollution into the atmosphere.	Fl A B C D E E: B MP → atmo poll	*This is a fact (we'll assume the E is telling the truth).*
In order to convince the company to change processes, we will organize a boycott of the product that represents its highest sales volume, light bulbs.	Fl A B C D E E: B MP → atmo poll boyc LB (↑ sales) → conv B Δ MP	*Okay, here's a plan, so it's likely a conclusion. They think if they boycott something, B might change its MP. So they're going to boycott LBs because B sells more LBs than anything else.*

Because Bando sells more light bulbs than any other product, a boycott of light bulbs will cause the most damage to the company's profits.	Fl A B C D E E: B MP → atmo poll Ⓒ boyc LB (↑ sales) → conv B Δ MP B sells ↑ LBs → boyc → ↑ damage to prof	*Another claim. Because they sell more LBs than anything else, the E figures that a boycott of LBs will do the most damage to profits. Profits? How profitable are the LBs?* *Okay, the conclusion was the previous sentence, because all of this is designed to convince B to change its MP.*

Step 3: State the Goal.

Long one. Okay, E doesn't like that B pollutes. B sells more LBs than any other product, so E wants to boycott the LBs because that will do the most damage to B's profits (according to E, anyway…), and then E hopes this will all cause B to change its MP.

I need to find an answer that will articulate a flaw in that reasoning. I've already thought of one. The E is assuming that just because B sells more LBs than anything else, B is also earning the most profits from LB. But there's no evidence there to support that. Another might be that consumers might not actually agree to boycott B.

Step 4: Work from wrong to right.

(A) allow for the possibility that Bando may not want to change its manufacturing process	Fl ~~A~~ B C D E E: B MP → atmo poll Ⓒ boyc LB (↑ sales) → conv B Δ MP B sells ↑ LBs → boyc → ↑ damage to prof	*If anything, you could argue that the E is assuming B <u>will not</u> want to change —that's why the E thinks he has to organize a boycott to change B's mind!*
(B) does not supply information about other possible ways for Bando to reduce pollution	Fl ~~A~~ ~~B~~ C D E E: B MP → atmo poll Ⓒ boyc LB (↑ sales) → conv B Δ MP B sells ↑ LBs → boyc → ↑ damage to prof	*In the real world, I agree that E should explore all possible ways… but the question asks me to find a flaw in this particular plan about the boycott. This doesn't apply to that plan.*

(C) consider that the relative sales volumes of a company's products are not necessarily proportional to profits	Fl A B C̲ D E E: B MP → atmo poll Ⓒ boyc LB (↑ sales) → conv B Δ MP B sells ↑ LBs → boyc → ↑ damage to prof	*This sounds kind of like what I said before. It's a little abstract, so I'm not sure I fully understand all of it, but it does say that sales aren't necessarily proportional to profits, so I'll keep this one in.*
(D) identify any alternative methods by which to convince Bando to change its manufacturing process	Fl A B C̲ D̶ E E: B MP → atmo poll Ⓒ boyc LB (↑ sales) → conv B Δ MP B sells ↑ LBs → boyc → ↑ damage to prof	*This is like answer B. It'd be good in general for E to do this… but this doesn't help us figure out a flaw in the boycott plan specifically.*
(E) consider that a boycott may take too long to achieve its purpose	Fl A B Ⓒ D̶ E E: B MP → atmo poll Ⓒ boyc LB (↑ sales) → conv B Δ MP B sells ↑ LBs → boyc → ↑ damage to prof	*I think what really matters is whether the plan is going to work at all, not how long it takes. The argument doesn't have any requirements about how long it will take to get B to change its process.*

Common Trap Answers

The most common trap on Flaw questions involves making an irrelevant distinction or comparison:

- discussing alternate plans or paths when we were asked to comment on the given plan (similar to answers B and D in the above example)

- brings up a detail or distinction that does not actually affect the conclusion; similar to choice E in the above problem

Flaw questions may also occasionally use Reverse Logic, similar to answer choice A in the above example.

Takeaways for Flaw Questions

We recognize Flaw Questions by use of the word "flaw" and *the absence of* any "if true" language. On occasion, the word "flaw" may be replaced by a synonym, such as "vulnerable to criticism."

On Flaw Questions, we want to find the conclusion and quickly brainstorm any assumptions we can. The correct answer will be tied to an assumption, but it will be worded to highlight the *flaw* in assuming something to be true; it will hurt the argument.

The most common trap answers typically involve making some kind of irrelevant distinction or comparison. The answer might address something in a premise that doesn't affect the conclusion, or it may go down a different path entirely when we were asked to comment on a specific plan.

4

Problem Set

Answer each question using the 4-step CR process. Check your answer after each question. As you improve, consider timing yourself; critical reasoning questions need to be completed in an average of 2 minutes.

1. *MTC & Asthma*

Methyltetrachloride (MTC) is a chemical found in some pesticides, glues, and sealants. Exposure to MTC can cause people to develop asthma. In order to halve the nation's asthma rate, the government plans to ban all products containing MTC.

The government's plan to halve the nation's asthma rate relies on which of the following assumptions?

(A) Exposure to MTC is responsible for no less than half of the nation's asthma cases.
(B) Products containing MTC are not necessary to the prosperity of the American economy.
(C) Asthma has reached epidemic proportions.
(D) Exercise and proper nutrition are helpful in maintaining respiratory health.
(E) Dust mites and pet dander can also cause asthma.

2. *Tuition*

Recently, the tuition at most elite private colleges has been rising faster than inflation. Even before these increases, many low and middle income families were unable to afford the full tuition costs for their children at these institutions of higher learning. With the new tuition increases, these colleges will soon cater solely to students with affluent family backgrounds.

Which of the following would it be most useful to determine in order to evaluate the argument?

(A) Whether students from affluent families are more likely to prefer public or private colleges
(B) Whether students from low and middle income families are qualified to attend elite private colleges
(C) Whether low income families are less likely to be able to afford tuition costs than middle income families
(D) Whether tuition costs at elite public colleges have also been rising faster than inflation
(E) Whether grants or scholarships are earmarked for students from economically disadvantaged families

3. *Charity*

Studies show that impoverished families give away a larger percentage of their income in charitable donations than do wealthy families. As a result, fundraising consultants recommend that charities direct their marketing efforts toward individuals and families from lower socioeconomic classes in order to maximize the dollar value of incoming donations.

Which of the following best explains why the consultants' reasoning is flawed?

(A)   Marketing efforts are only one way to solicit charitable donations.
(B)   Not all impoverished families donate to charity.
(C)   Some charitable marketing efforts are so expensive that the resulting donations fail to cover the costs of the marketing campaign.
(D)   Percentage of income is not necessarily indicative of absolute dollar value.
(E)   People are more likely to donate to the same causes to which their friends donate.

4. *Oil and Ethanol*

Country N's oil production is not sufficient to meet its domestic demand. In order to sharply reduce its dependence on foreign sources of oil, Country N recently embarked on a program requiring all of its automobiles to run on ethanol in addition to gasoline. Combined with its oil production, Country N produces enough ethanol from agricultural by-products to meet its current demand for energy.

Which of the following must be assumed in order to conclude that Country N will succeed in its plan to reduce its dependence on foreign oil?

(A)   Electric power is not a superior alternative to ethanol in supplementing automobile gasoline consumption.
(B)   In Country N, domestic production of ethanol is increasing more quickly than domestic oil production.
(C)   Ethanol is suitable for the heating of homes and other applications aside from automobiles.
(D)   In Country N, gasoline consumption is not increasing at a substantially higher rate than domestic oil and ethanol production.
(E)   Ethanol is as efficient as gasoline in terms of mileage per gallon when used as fuel for automobiles.

5. *Exchange Student*

Student Advisor: One of our exchange students faced multiple arguments with her parents over the course of the past year. Not surprisingly, her grade point average (GPA) over the same period showed a steep decline. This is just one example of a general truth: problematic family relationships can cause significant academic difficulties for our students.

The claim by the Student Advisor would be more properly drawn if which of the following were inserted into the argument as an additional premise?

(A) Last year, the exchange student reduced the amount of time spent on academic work, resulting in a lower GPA.

(B) The decline in the GPA of the exchange student was not the reason for the student's arguments with her parents.

(C) School GPA is an accurate measure of a student's intellectual ability.

(D) If proper measures are not taken, the decline in the student's academic performance may become irreversible.

(E) Fluctuations in academic performance are typical for many students.

6. *Food Allergies*

Food allergies account for more than thirty thousand emergency department visits each year. Often, victims of these episodes are completely unaware of their allergies until they experience a major reaction. Studies show that ninety percent of food allergy reactions are caused by only eight distinct foods. For this reason, individuals should sample a minuscule portion of each of these foods to determine whether a particular food allergy is present.

Which of the following must be studied in order to evaluate the recommendation made in the argument?

(A) The percentage of allergy victims who were not aware of the allergy before a major episode

(B) The percentage of the population that is at risk for allergic reactions

(C) Whether some of the eight foods are common ingredients used in cooking

(D) Whether an allergy to one type of food makes someone more likely to be allergic to other types of food

(E) Whether ingesting a very small amount of an allergen is sufficient to provoke an allergic reaction in a susceptible individual

P

7. *News War*

For several years, Nighttime News attracted fewer viewers than World News, which broadcasts its show at the same time as Nighttime News. Recently, the producers of Nighttime News added personal interest stories and increased coverage of sports and weather. The two programs now have a roughly equal number of viewers. Clearly, the recent programming changes persuaded viewers to switch from World News to Nighttime News.

The conclusion above is properly drawn if which of the following is assumed?

A)   Viewers are more interested in sports and weather than in personal interest stories.

(B)   The programming content of Nighttime News is more closely aligned with the interests of the overall audience than is the content of World News.

(C)   Some World News viewers liked the new Nighttime News programming better than they liked the World News programming.

(D)   There are other possible causes for an increase in the number of viewers of Nighttime News, including a recent ad campaign that aired on many local affiliates.

(E)   The quality of World News will remain constant even if Nighttime News improves.

8. *Five-Step Process*

Manager: the new manufacturing process should save us time overall, even though the first step of the five-step process will take twice as long as it does under the old process. Under the new process, far fewer of the components will be found defective, and the sole purpose of steps two and three under the old process is to weed out defective components. As a result, we should be able to eliminate two of the five steps in the existing manufacturing process.

Which of the following would be most useful in evaluating the claim made in the argument?

(A)   Whether factory workers will require training in order to use the new manufacturing process

(B)   Whether the new process is likely to introduce deficiencies or imperfections that must be corrected

(C)   Whether defective components can be fixed or must be thrown out

(D)   Whether a third manufacturing process would save even more time than both the old and new manufacturing processes

(E)   Whether saving time with the new manufacturing process will ultimately lead to cost savings for the company

9. *Genetics*

Two genes, BRCA1 and BRCA2, are linked to hereditary breast cancer. Therefore, in order to decrease the annual number of mammogram tests administered across a population and to more accurately assess a woman's individual risk of breast cancer, all women should be tested for these genes.

Which of the following is an assumption on which the argument depends?

(A)   Some of the women who are tested for the two genes will subsequently undergo mammograms on a less frequent basis than they used to.

(B)   The majority of breast cancer patients have no family history of the disease.

(C)   Researchers may have identified a third breast cancer gene that is linked with hereditary breast cancer.

(D)   Women who have these genes have an 80 percent chance of getting breast cancer, while women who do not have these genes have only a 10 percent chance of getting breast cancer.

(E)   The presence of BRCA1 and BRCA2 can explain up to 50 percent of hereditary cases.

P

Solutions

1. MTC & Asthma: The correct answer is **A**.

Step 1: Identify the question.

The government's plan to halve the nation's asthma rate relies on which of the following assumptions?	FA A B C D E	*Asks for the "assumption"; this is a Find the Assumption question.*

Step 2: Deconstruct the argument.

Methyltetrachloride (MTC) is a chemical found in some pesticides, glues, and sealants.	FA A B C D E MTC chem	*This is just a fact—background or maybe a premise.*
Exposure to MTC can cause people to develop asthma.	FA A B C D E MTC chem → asthma	*Another fact but it's specifically a bad fact. This is likely a premise.*
In order to halve the nation's asthma rate, the government plans to ban all products containing MTC.	FA A B C D E MTC chem → asthma ⓒban MTC → ½ asthma rate	*Okay, the government has a plan to ban MTC ,and the result will be (they claim) that the asthma rate will be cut in half. There are no numbers or anything to support that. Are a lot of people exposed now? What percentage of those who develop asthma were exposed? Etc.*

Step 3: State the Goal.

The government claims that it can halve the asthma rate by banning MTC, but it gives absolutely no evidence or numbers to support <u>halving</u> the rate.

I need to find an answer that supports the idea that they can halve the asthma rate—maybe that a very large percentage of people who develop asthma were exposed to MTC or something like that.

Step 4: Work from wrong to right.

(A) Exposure to MTC is responsible for no less than half of the nation's asthma cases.	FA A̲ B C D E MTC chem → asthma Ⓒban MTC → ½ asthma rate	*This sounds similar to what I said. Let's see. If MTC actually is responsible for at least half of asthma cases, then getting rid of it would get rid of all those cases as well. This one looks pretty good.*
(B) Products containing MTC are not necessary to the prosperity of the American economy.	FA A̲ B C D E MTC chem → asthma Ⓒban MTC → ½ asthma rate	*Prosperity of the economy? They're just trying to distract me by making me think of a reason why we might want to use MTC. The conclusion is about halving the asthma rate, and this doesn't affect that conclusion.*
(C) Asthma has reached epidemic proportions.	FA A̲ B C̶ D E MTC chem → asthma Ⓒban MTC → ½ asthma rate	*If asthma rates are really high, then that supports the idea of wanting to lower them. But that's not what I'm trying to do—the author doesn't HAVE to believe this is true. Plus it says nothing about whether MTC is the cause.*
(D) Exercise and proper nutrition are helpful in maintaining respiratory health.	FA A̲ B C̶ D̶ E MTC chem → asthma Ⓒban MTC → ½ asthma rate	*Distraction! Nothing about how or whether MTC causes asthma, or whether getting rid of MTC will lower asthma rates.*
(E) Dust mites and pet dander can also asthma.	FA Ⓐ B C̶ D̶ E̶ MTC chem → asthma Ⓒban MTC → ½ asthma rate	*Distraction! Nothing about how or whether MTC causes asthma, or whether getting rid of MTC will lower asthma rates.*

2. Tuition: The correct answer is **E**.

Step 1: Identify the question.

Which of the following would it be most useful to determine in order to evaluate the argument?	Ev A B C D E	*Contains the words "evaluate" and "useful to determine"—this is an Evaluate question.*

Step 2: Deconstruct the argument.

Recently, the tuition at most elite private colleges has been rising faster than inflation.	Ev A B C D E EPC ↑ tuit > infl	*Fact: tuition at this specific type of school has been going up even faster than inflation.*

Even before these increases, many low and middle income families were unable to afford the full tuition costs for their children at these institutions of higher learning.	Ev A B C D E EPC ↑ tuit > infl B4: ↓ + mid inc fams can't afford	And people without much money already couldn't afford these schools, even before the tuition went up. Another fact.
With the new tuition increases, these colleges will soon cater solely to students with affluent family backgrounds.	Ev A B C D E EPC ↑ tuit > infl B4: ↓ + mid inc fams can't afford ⒸEPC will have only rich students	This must be the conclusion because the other two were facts. Basically, they're saying that only wealthy students are going to be able to afford these schools now.

P

Step 3: State the Goal.

This is an Evaluate question, so I need to find an answer that will help to determine whether or not the conclusion is likely to be valid. The correct answer will have "two paths": one path will make the conclusion a little more likely to be valid, and the other will make the conclusion a little less likely to be valid.

The conclusion is that only wealthy students are going to be able to go to these EPCs. What is the author assuming? Absolutely none of the low or middle income students can afford these schools. Non-wealthy students aren't going to be taking out loans, or working their way through school, or finding some other way to cover the tuition costs.

Step 4: Work from wrong to right.

(A) Whether students from affluent families are more likely to prefer public or private colleges	Ev A̶ B C D E EPC ↑ tuit > infl B4: ↓ + mid inc fams can't afford ⒸEPC will have only rich students	If affluent students prefer public colleges, that doesn't change the fact that the private colleges charge a lot of money and poorer students can't afford them. If affluent students prefer private colleges, that also doesn't change the same fact.
(B) Whether students from low and middle income families are qualified to attend elite private colleges	Ev A̶ B C D E EPC ↑ tuit > infl B4: ↓ + mid inc fams can't afford ⒸEPC will have only rich students	If these students are not qualified to attend the EPCs, that doesn't change anything about the tuition issue. If these students are qualified, that also doesn't change the tuition issue (though it makes it seem unfair that the EPCs charge so much money!).

P

(C) Whether low income families are less likely to be able to afford tuition costs than middle income families	Ev A̶ B C̶ D E EPC ↑ tuit > infl B4: ↓ + mid inc fams can't afford ⒸEPC will have only rich students	*This answer makes a distinction between low and middle income families, but the argument doesn't distinguish between these two groups—it combines them. Logically, it would make sense that the less money a family has, the less likely it could afford the tuition… but this doesn't change anything about the basic argument that low and middle income families can't afford the tuition.*
(D) Whether tuition costs at elite public colleges have also been rising faster than inflation	Ev A̶ B C̶ D̶ E EPC ↑ tuit > infl B4: ↓ + mid inc fams can't afford ⒸEPC will have only rich students	*If they have, then maybe that means lower-income students can't afford those schools either… but it might not mean anything, because perhaps the public schools have lower tuition fees in the first place. If rates have not been rising as fast at public colleges… that doesn't affect the argument's conclusion at all.*
(E) Whether grants or scholarships are ear-marked for students from economically disadvantaged families	Ev A̶ B C̶ D̶ Ⓔ EPC ↑ tuit > infl B4: ↓ + mid inc fams can't afford ⒸEPC will have only rich students	*If there are grants and scholarships for lower-income students, then perhaps they can afford to attend the EPCs—this hurts the argument's conclusion. If there are not grants and scholarships for these students, then the argument's conclusion is more likely to be true: these students won't be able to afford these colleges. The "two paths" on this answer do lead to strengthening the conclusion on one hand and weakening it on the other.*

3. Charity: The correct answer is **D**.

Step 1: Identify the question.

Which of the following best explains why the consultants' reasoning is flawed?	F A B C D E	*The word "flawed" indicates that this is either a Flaw or Weaken question. The lack of the words "if true" (or an equivalent) means that this is a Flaw question.*

MANHATTAN
GMAT

Step 2: Deconstruct the argument.

Studies show that impoverished families give away a larger percentage of their income in charitable donations than do wealthy families.	F A B C D E poor donate > % inc than rich	*This is a fact. It's impressive that the poor donate anything, but if they do donate anything, then this fact makes sense because donating $100 is a much greater percentage of your income if you don't have much income.*
As a result, fundraising consultants recommend that charities direct their marketing efforts toward individuals and families from lower socioeconomic classes in order to maximize the dollar value of incoming donations.	F A B C D E poor donate > % inc than rich ⓒFC: to get most $, char shld focus on ↓ inc ppl	*This is the conclusion. Based on the percentage info, the FCs are saying that the charities should focus on lower income people… but the FCs are assuming that "greater percentage" equals more money. A very rich person might donate $10 million, a small percentage of income but a very large sum.*

Step 3: State the Goal.

For flaw questions, it's important to find the conclusion and brainstorm any assumptions, if I can. I need to find an answer that hurts the argument or shows why the argument is not a good argument.

In this case, the FCs are recommending that the charities target lower income families in order to maximize the number of dollars they get in donations. I've identified one potential assumption: the FCs assume that donating a greater percentage of income also means donating a greater dollar amount collectively. If that's not actually the case, then that's a flaw.

Step 4: Work from wrong to right.

(A) Marketing efforts are only one way to solicit charitable donations.	F A̶ B C D E poor donate > % inc than rich ⓒFC: to get most $, char shld focus on ↓ inc ppl	*This might be true, but it just indicates that there might be other ways, in addition to marketing efforts, to raise money. That doesn't affect the FCs recommendation to target lower income families in particular.*
(B) Not all impoverished families donate to charity.	F A̶ B̶ C D E poor donate > % inc than rich ⓒFC: to get most $, char shld focus on ↓ inc ppl	*I'm sure this is true, but how does it affect the conclusion? It doesn't. The argument never claims that ALL impoverished families donate to charity—only that, in general, they donate a larger percentage of income to charity.*

(C) Some charitable marketing efforts are so expensive that the resulting donations fail to cover the costs of the marketing campaign.	F A̶ B̶ C̶ D E poor donate > % inc than rich Ⓒ FC: to get most $, char shld focus on ↓ inc ppl	*Oh, maybe this is it. If you spend more on the marketing than you make from donations, that can't be a very successful marketing campaign. What was the conclusion again? Oh, wait. "to maximize the dollar value of donations." Whether ther marketing covered costs isn't part of the conclusion—it just depended on how much money they get in donations. Tricky, but not correct.*
(D) Percentage of income is not necessarily indicative of absolute dollar value.	F A̶ B̶ C̶ D̲ E poor donate > % inc than rich Ⓒ FC: to get most $, char shld focus on ↓ inc ppl	*This is what I was saying before about the really rich person donating $10 million! You can have a bunch of low income people give 10% of their income and one billionaire give 9% of her income… and the billionaire could be giving more in terms of absolute dollars. This indicates the flawed assumption made by the FCs.*
(E) People are more likely to donate to the same causes to which their friends donate.	F A̶ B̶ C̶ Ⓓ E̶ poor donate > % inc than rich Ⓒ FC: to get most $, char shld focus on ↓ inc ppl	*I can believe that this is true, but the argument doesn't address which causes people choose for charity. Rather, the argument talks about amount of money donated.*

4. Oil and Ethanol: The correct answer is **D**.

Step 1: Identify the question.

Which of the following must be assumed in order to conclude that Country N will succeed in its plan to reduce its dependence on foreign oil?	FA A B C D E	*Contains the word "assumed"—this is a Find the Assumption question.*

Step 2: Deconstruct the argument.

Country N's oil production is not sufficient to meet its domestic demand.	FA A B C D E N oil prod ≠ dem	*They produce oil but can't make enough for their own needs. That must mean they have to import some oil.*

In order to sharply reduce its dependence on foreign sources of oil, Country N recently embarked on a program requiring all of its automobiles to run on ethanol in addition to gasoline.	FA A B C D E N oil prod ≠ dem N req cars eth → ↓ for. oil	They're requiring cars to use ethanol, and they think that'll lead to having to use less foreign oil. It sounds like the cars can still use gas, though…
Combined with its oil production, Country N produces enough ethanol from agricultural by-products to meet its current demand for energy.	FA A B C D E N oil prod ≠ dem N req cars eth → ↓ for. oil N eth + oil = N's dem now	Okay, so they do make enough ethanol PLUS oil combined to satisfy their own needs currently. The question is whether people are actually going to use ethanol for their cars or whether they'll want to keep using gasoline. And what if demand changes in future?

Step 3: State the Goal.

Country N thinks it can "sharply reduce" the amount of foreign oil it needs if it starts making people have cars that use ethanol. Will the plan really work that way? They're assuming people really will start to use the ethanol. They're also assuming they'll continue to produce enough oil and ethanol in the future.

I need to find an answer that must be true in order to allow the author to draw the above conclusion.

Step 4: Work from wrong to right.

(A) Electric power is not a superior alternative to ethanol in supplementing automobile gasoline consumption.	FA A̶ B C D E N oil prod ≠ dem N req cars eth → ↓ for. oil N eth + oil = N's dem now	*Electric power? That seems out of scope. We're supposed to find something that goes with the plan stated in the argument, and that plan mentions nothing about electric power.*
(B) In Country N, domestic production of ethanol is increasing more quickly than domestic oil production.	FA A̶ B̶ C D E N oil prod ≠ dem N req cars eth → ↓ for. oil N eth + oil = N's dem now	*If this is true, then switching stuff to ethanol seems like a good call. Does it HAVE to be true in order to draw the conclusion? What if the two were increasing at the same rate? That would be fine, actually. This doesn't have to be true—so it isn't a necessary assumption.*

(C) Ethanol is suitable for the heating of homes and other applications aside from automobiles.	FA A̶ B̶ ∈ D E N oil prod ≠ dem N req cars eth → ↓ for. oil N eth + oil = N's dem now	*If this is true, then switching stuff to ethanol seems like a good call. Does it HAVE to be true in order to draw the conclusion? No. The argument only talks about a plan to have cars start using ethanol.*
(D) In Country N, gasoline consumption is not increasing at a substantially higher rate than domestic oil and ethanol production.	FA A̶ B̶ ∈ D̲ E N oil prod ≠ dem N req cars eth → ↓ for. oil N eth + oil = N's dem now	*Hmm. The argument is assuming in general that the ethanol + oil production can keep up with the country's demand. So, yes, the author would have to assume that gas consumption isn't increasing at a much faster rate than production.* *Let's try negating this one: If gas consumption WERE increasing at a much higher rate, what would happen? Oh, they might have to get more from foreign sources—bingo! Negating this does weaken the conclusion.*
(E) Ethanol is as efficient as gasoline in terms of mileage per gallon when used as fuel for automobiles.	FA A̶ B̶ ∈ Ⓓ E N oil prod ≠ dem N req cars eth → ↓ for. oil N eth + oil = N's dem now	*It would be good to know how efficient ethanol is compared to gas… but does it HAVE to be true that they're __equally__ efficient? No. Even if ethanol were less efficient, it's possible that the country could still produce enough to meet its needs.*

5. Exchange Student: The correct answer is **B**.

<u>Step 1: Identify the question.</u>

The claim by the Student Advisor would be more properly drawn if which of the following were inserted into the argument as an additional premise?	FA A B C D E	*This is a tough one. They're asking me to find the answer that can be "inserted into the argument as a premise." Doing so makes the claim "more properly drawn." This is an example of unusual wording for a Find the Assumption question.*

<u>Step 2: Deconstruct the argument.</u>

Student Advisor: One of our exchange students faced multiple arguments with her parents over the course of the past year.	FA A B C D E SA: st arg par 1yr	*This is a fact—background or a premise.*

Not surprisingly, her grade point average (GPA) over the same period showed a steep decline.	FA A B C D E SA: st arg par 1yr GPA ↓↓	*Not only did the student's GPA go down, but the SA says "not surprisingly." Sounds like the SA is going to conclude something based on this.*
This is just one example of a general truth: problematic family relationships can cause significant academic difficulties for our students.	FA A B C D E SA: st arg par 1yr GPA ↓↓ ⓒfam prob → acad prob	*Here we go: the SA claims that this student's family problems <u>caused</u> the academic problems. Maybe there was a different cause.*

Step 3: State the Goal.

I need to find an answer that the author must believe to be true in order to draw this conclusion. The only thing I can think of right now is very general: if the SA is assuming the family problems were what caused the academic problems, then the SA is also assuming there wasn't something else causing the academic problems.

Step 4: Work from wrong to right.

(A) Last year, the exchange student reduced the amount of time spent on academic work, resulting in a lower GPA.	FA A̶ B C D E SA: st arg par 1yr GPA ↓↓ ⓒfam prob → acad prob	*This would explain why her GPA went down, which means maybe it didn't actually have to do with family problems. But I'm looking for something the author believes will HELP with the claim that it was family problems. This answer hurts that claim.*
(B) The decline in the GPA of the exchange student was not the reason for the student's arguments with her parents.	FA A̶ <u>B</u> C D E SA: st arg par 1yr GPA ↓↓ ⓒfam prob → acad prob	*Let's see. This is kind of what I said before—there is NOT a different cause for the decline of her GPA.* *Let's try negating this. If the student's GPA went down first and then her parents got mad at her for that reason, then you can't claim that the family problems caused the lower GPA. The SA's argument would fall apart. This one looks good.*
(C) School GPA is an accurate measure of a student's intellectual ability.	FA A̶ <u>B</u> C̶ D E SA: st arg par 1yr GPA ↓↓ ⓒfam prob → acad prob	*This doesn't matter. Either it's accurate or inaccurate. Regardless, it used to be higher and is now lower, and she and her parents have been arguing about something. Whether it's accurate doesn't come into consideration in the argument.*

(D) If proper measures are not taken, the decline in the student's academic performance may become irreversible.	FA A B̶ C̶ D̶ E SA: st arg par 1yr GPA ↓↓ Ⓒ fam prob → acad prob	*I could see how this might be true in general, but this doesn't support the idea that family problems can cause academic problems. If it doesn't support that idea, it can't possibly be the assumption.*
(E) Fluctuations in academic performance are typical for many students.	FA A̶ Ⓑ C̶ D̶ E̶ SA: st arg par 1yr GPA ↓↓ Ⓒ fam prob → acad prob	*I could see how this might be true in general, but this doesn't support the idea that family problems can cause academic problems. If it doesn't support that idea, it can't possibly be the assumption.*

P

6. Food Allergies: The correct answer is **E**.

Step 1: Identify the question.

Which of the following must be studied in order to evaluate the recommendation made in the argument?	Ev A B C D E	*The words "must be studied" and "evaluate" indicate that this is an Evaluate question.*

Step 2: Deconstruct the argument.

Food allergies account for more than thirty thousand emergency department visits each year.	Ev A B C D E FA → 30k ER/yr	*This is a fact.*
Often, victims of these episodes are completely unaware of their allergies until they experience a major reaction.	Ev A B C D E FA → 30k ER/yr ppl don't know till have rx	*Fact but more fuzzy. A lot of people don't know they're allergic till they have a major reaction.*
Studies show that ninety percent of food allergy reactions are caused by only eight distinct foods.	Ev A B C D E FA → 30k ER/yr ppl don't know till have rx only 8 foods → 90% FA rx	*More facts! That's interesting. Only 8 foods cause most allergic reactions.*
For this reason, individuals should sample a minuscule portion of each of these foods to determine whether a particular food allergy is present.	Ev A B C D E FA → 30k ER/yr ppl don't know till have rx only 8 foods → 90% FA rx Ⓒ ppl shld try tiny bit of 8 foods to see if FA	*This is the conclusion. The author's saying we should all try a tiny bit of these 8 foods to see what happens. That assumes that we'll actually have a reaction from a tiny amount. It also assumes we won't die from just a tiny amount (if we are allergic).*

Step 3: State the Goal.

This is an Evaluate question, so I need to find an answer that will help to determine whether or not the conclusion is likely to be valid. The correct answer will have "two paths": one path will make the conclusion a little more likely to be valid and the other will make the conclusion a little less likely to be valid.

In this case, the author recommends that we all try tiny bits of these 8 foods to see whether we're allergic. The author's assuming that we can tell whether we're allergic from trying just a tiny bit—and also that we won't die by trying a small amount if we are allergic.

Step 4: Work from wrong to right.

(A) The percentage of allergy victims who were not aware of the allergy before a major episode	Ev ~~A~~ B C D E FA → 30k ER/yr ppl don't know till have rx only 8 foods → 90% FA rx Ⓒppl shld try tiny bit of 8 foods to see if FA	*The argument told us that victims "often" aren't aware of the allergy beforehand. If I knew that 90% weren't aware, that would go along with what the argument already says. If I knew that 50% weren't aware... hmm, that wouldn't change the argument. In general, knowing the exact percentage doesn't change anything.*
(B) The percentage of the population that is at risk for allergic reactions	Ev ~~A~~ ~~B~~ C D E FA → 30k ER/yr ppl don't know till have rx only 8 foods → 90% FA rx Ⓒppl shld try tiny bit of 8 foods to see if FA	*If a really high percentage is at risk for allergies, then it's probably important to figure out whether people are allergic... but that doesn't mean that the specific recommendation in the conclusion here is a good or bad one. Also, this answer choice doesn't specifically limit itself to food allergies; it mentions all allergies in general.*
(C) Whether some of the eight foods are common ingredients used in cooking	Ev ~~A~~ ~~B~~ ~~C~~ D E FA → 30k ER/yr ppl don't know till have rx only 8 foods → 90% FA rx Ⓒppl shld try tiny bit of 8 foods to see if FA	*If yes, then many people may have already tried small amounts of these foods. That doesn't actually tell us, though, whether the recommendation is a good one. If no, then it doesn't affect the conclusion at all—we still don't know whether it's a good recommendation.*
(D) Whether an allergy to one type of food makes someone more likely to be allergic to other types of food	Ev ~~A~~ ~~B~~ ~~C~~ ~~D~~ E FA → 30k ER/yr ppl don't know till have rx only 8 foods → 90% FA rx Ⓒppl shld try tiny bit of 8 foods to see if FA	*If yes or if no, you'd still want to test people to see whether they're allergic to anything. This choice doesn't have "two paths" that lead to alternate outcomes.*

P

(E) Whether ingesting a very small amount of an allergen is sufficient to provoke an allergic reaction in a susceptible individual	Ev A̶ B̶ ∈ D̶ Ⓔ FA → 30k ER/yr ppl don't know till have rx only 8 foods → 90% FA rx Ⓒppl shld try tiny bit of 8 foods to see if FA	*This is one of the things that I said! If yes, then the author's plan will work: people will be able to try small amounts and determine whether they're allergic. If no, then the author's plan is not a good one: trying small amounts won't actually help us tell whether we're allergic.*

7. News War: The correct answer is **C**.

Step 1: Identify the question.

The conclusion above is properly drawn if which of the following is assumed?	FA A B C D E	*The word "assumed" tells me that this is a Find the Assumption question.*

Step 2: Deconstruct the argument.

For several years, Nighttime News attracted fewer viewers than World News, which broadcasts its show at the same time as Nighttime News.	FA A B C D E past: NN < WN	*NN and WN are competitors. In the past, WN got more viewers. Facts = premises.*
Recently, the producers of Nighttime News added personal interest stories and increased coverage of sports and weather.	FA A B C D E past: NN < WN rec: NN + pers, sp, weath	*NN added certain new things.*
The two programs now have a roughly equal number of viewers.	FA A B C D E past: NN < WN rec: NN + pers, sp, weath now: NN = WN	*Now, the two are about equal. Interesting. Why? So far, all premises.*
Clearly, the recent programming changes persuaded viewers to switch from World News to Nighttime News.	FA A B C D E past: NN < WN rec: NN + pers, sp, weath now: NN = WN Ⓒprog Δ → switch	*Conclusion! The author is claiming that the new programming things actually caused people to <u>switch</u> from one show to the other. Hmm—that would mean WN's numbers went down—did they? Or is it just that NN went up? Or maybe there's some other reason for the change entirely.*

Step 3: State the Goal.

The author is claiming specifically that people <u>switched</u> from WN to NN—but there's no evidence for that. The author is assuming that, if NN's numbers went up, then WN's numbers went down and that those people switched to NN (and didn't start watching something else or turn off their TVs entirely!).

The author's also assuming that the reason for the switch was NN's new programming and not something else.

I need to find an answer that represents something the author must believe to be true.

Step 4: Work from wrong to right.

(A) Viewers are more interested in sports and weather than in personal interest stories.	FA A̶ B C D E past: NN < WN rec: NN + pers, sp, weath now: NN = WN ©prog Δ → switch	*Hmm. NN added all 3 of these things. Does the author need to assume that two are more popular than the third? No—it doesn't matter as long as the programming in general did make people switch. Maybe they're trying to get me to think that the choice is comparing WN and NN—but that's not what this choice actually says.*
(B) The programming content of Nighttime News is more closely aligned with the interests of the overall audience than is the content of World News.	FA A̶ B̰ C D E past: NN < WN rec: NN + pers, sp, weath now: NN = WN ©prog Δ → switch	*This basically says that the audience likes NN's content better than WN's content. That could be a reason to switch. Does it absolutely have to be true? It also addresses the programming issue, so it does seem pretty good—I'll leave it in for now.*
(C) Some World News viewers liked the new Nighttime News programming better than they liked the World News programming.	FA A̶ B̰ C̰ D E past: NN < WN rec: NN + pers, sp, weath now: NN = WN ©prog Δ → switch	*This also talks about liking NN better than WN. In particular, it says that some WN viewers decided they liked the new NN stuff better. That also looks really good. Leave it in.*
(D) There are other possible causes for an increase in the number of viewers of Nighttime News, including a recent ad campaign that aired on many local affiliates.	FA A̶ B̰ C̰ D̶ E past: NN < WN rec: NN + pers, sp, weath now: NN = WN ©prog Δ → switch	*"Other possible causes"—oh, no, are all three of these choices good? Wait a second. I'm reading this backwards. This is saying there are other reasons why more people are watching NN, so that would actually hurt the author's claim that it's because WN viewers switched due to the programming.*

P

(E) The quality of World News will remain constant even if Night-time News improves.	FA A̶ B̲ C̶ D̶ E past: NN < WN rec: NN + pers, sp, weath now: NN = WN Ⓒprog Δ → switch	*If this were true, it might help explain why some people would switch, but does it HAVE to be true in order to claim that people already switched due to NN's new program-ming? No.*
compare B and C	FA A̶ B̲ Ⓒ D̶ E past: NN < WN rec: NN + pers, sp, weath now: NN = WN Ⓒprog Δ → switch	*Let's try negating B and C.* *B: NN content is not more closely aligned with audience than WN content. Maybe they're about the same? That doesn't really hurt the author's argument all that much.* *C: None of the WN viewers liked NN better than WN. Wait a second. If NONE of them liked NN better, why would they switch? Negating this definitely hurts the argument. C it is!*

8. Five-Step Process: The correct answer is **B**.

Step 1: Identify the question.

Which of the following would be most useful in evaluating the claim made in the argument?	Ev A B C D E	*The language "most useful in evaluating" indicates that this is an Evaluate question.*

Step 2: Deconstruct the argument.

Manager: the new manufactur-ing process should save us time overall, even though the first step of the five-step process will take twice as long as it does under the old process.	Ev A B C D E M: New MP faster but S1 = 2x longer	*This is a claim. It could be the conclusion—I'll have to keep reading to tell.*
Under the new process, far fewer of the components will be found defective, and the sole purpose of steps two and three under the old process is to weed out defective components.	Ev A B C D E M: New MP faster but S1 = 2x longer NMP = ↓ bad parts OMP S2+3 for bad parts	*This seems to be a combo of a claim and a fact, but both are supporting the first sentence.*

As a result, we should be able to eliminate two of the five steps in the existing manufacturing process.	Ev A B C D E M: New MP faster but S1 = 2x longer Ⓒ NMP = ↓ bad parts OMP S2+3 for bad parts so elim 2 steps for NMP	Yes, the first sentence was the con-clusion. If the other things are all true, then maybe the NMP will be faster than the old one.

Step 3: State the Goal.

This is an Evaluate question, so I need to find an answer that will help to determine whether or not the conclusion is likely to be valid. The correct answer will have "two paths": one path will make the conclusion a little more likely to be valid, and the other will make the conclusion a little less likely to be valid.

The manager is claiming that the new process will be faster than the old process. Although the 1st step will take twice as long under the new process, the manager claims they "should" be able to drop the second and third steps. If dropping the second and third steps saves even more time than is lost during the first step, then the manager might be right… but the manager is assuming that these other steps will save a lot more time.

Step 4: Work from wrong to right.

(A) Whether factory workers will require training in order to use the new manufacturing process	Ev A̶ B C D E M: New MP faster but S1 = 2x longer Ⓒ NMP = ↓ bad parts OMP S2+3 for bad parts so elim 2 steps for NMP	If they do… that may or may not affect how much time the process takes. If they don't, I still don't know anything more about how much time the new process is going to take versus the old process.
(B) Whether the new process is likely to introduce deficiencies or imperfections that must be corrected	Ev A̶ B̲ C D E M: New MP faster but S1 = 2x longer Ⓒ NMP = ↓ bad parts OMP S2+3 for bad parts so elim 2 steps for NMP	If the new process also introduces problems that then need to be fixed, then perhaps they can't drop steps two and three, or perhaps they have to introduce other new steps to fix the deficiencies… either of which would add time to the new process, making it less likely that the new process will save time. If the new process does not introduce new imperfections that need to be fixed, then that increases the likelihood that the new process will save time.

(C) Whether defective components can be fixed or must be thrown out	Ev A B̲ C̶ D E M: New MP faster but S1 = 2x longer Ⓒ NMP = ↓ bad parts OMP S2+3 for bad parts so elim 2 steps for NMP	*If defective components can be fixed, that would add time to the process. If defective components must be thrown out, that would also add manufacturing time, because they would have to make even more. This doesn't give us two different paths, one of which helps the conclusion and one of which hurts the conclusion.*
(D) Whether a third manufacturing process would save even more time than both the old and new manufacturing processes	Ev A B̲ C̶ D̶ E M: New MP faster but S1 = 2x longer Ⓒ NMP = ↓ bad parts OMP S2+3 for bad parts so elim 2 steps for NMP	*The conclusion focuses on whether the new process is faster than the old process. Introducing a third, different process tells us nothing about the first two processes or how long they are.*
(E) Whether saving time with the new manufacturing process will ultimately lead to cost savings for the company	Ev A Ⓑ C̶ D̶ E̶ M: New MP faster but S1 = 2x longer Ⓒ NMP = ↓ bad parts OMP S2+3 for bad parts so elim 2 steps for NMP	*The argument does not address anything about cost savings—the focus of the argument's conclusion is solely about saving time. Whether the company ultimately saves money does not tell us whether they'll save time.*

9. Genetics: The correct answer is **A**.

<u>Step 1: Identify the question.</u>

Which of the following is an assumption on which the argument depends?	FA A B C D E	*The word "assumption" indicates that this is a Find the Assumption question.*

<u>Step 2: Deconstruct the argument.</u>

Two genes, BRCA1 and BRCA2, are linked to hereditary breast cancer.	FA A B C D E G1 and G2 = BC	*Straight fact.*

Therefore, in order to decrease the current number of mammogram tests administered across a population and to more accurately assess a woman's individual risk of breast cancer, all women should be tested for these genes.	FA A B C D E G1 and G2 = BC Ⓒ test all W to ↓ M and assess risk	*Complicated. Okay, the author's recommending that all women be tested and claims this will do 2 things: decrease the # of Ms and better assess risk. So one assumption could be that those who test negatively won't get an M as frequently.*

Step 3: State the Goal.

The author claims that, if women are all tested for these genes, two things will happen: the number of Ms will go down __and__ they'll be able to assess risk more accurately.

I need to find an answer that the author must believe to be true in drawing this conclusion. That might have something to do with the number of Ms or with assessing risk.

Step 4: Work from wrong to right.

(A) Some of the women who are tested for the two genes will subsequently undergo mammograms on a less frequent basis than they used to.	FA A̲ B C D E G1 and G2 = BC Ⓒ test all W to ↓ M and assess risk	*If at least some women get tested and then get fewer Ms, then that would help to reduce the number of Ms. But does this HAVE to be true? Actually, I think so. It has to be the case that women who otherwise would've gotten Ms don't; otherwise, the number can't go down.*
(B) The majority of breast cancer patients have no family history of the disease.	FA A̲ B̶ C D E G1 and G2 = BC Ⓒ test all W to ↓ M and assess risk	*I'm not sure how this affects the "number of Ms" claim, but I think it actually hurts the "better assess risk" claim. It seems like the argument assumes that if you don't have the gene, you won't get Ms, but then this choice says a lot of women who do get BC don't have a family history. Also, someone can have a gene and not develop BC, so maybe that's why there's no family history. Too many "ifs" on this one.*
(C) Researchers may have identified a third breast cancer gene that is linked with hereditary breast cancer.	FA A̲ B̶ C̶ D E G1 and G2 = BC Ⓒ test all W to ↓ M and assess risk	*If so, then presumably the author of the argument might want to add this third one to the list. But that has nothing to do with the argument as it stands.*

P

(D) Women who have these genes have an 80 percent chance of getting breast cancer, while women who do not have these genes have only a 10 percent chance of getting breast cancer.	FA A̲ B̶ ∈ Đ E G1 and G2 = BC Ⓒ test all W to ↓ M and assess risk	*If that's true, then it does sound like knowing whether you have the gene would help more accurately assess your risk. Does this HAVE to be true? Not with those specific numbers, actually. Tricky. Maybe it's 70 percent or 90 percent instead of 80%; the message is still the same.*
(E) The presence of BRCA1 and BRCA2 can explain up to 50 percent of hereditary cases.	FA Ⓐ B̶ ∈ Đ E G1 and G2 = BC Ⓒ test all W to ↓ M and assess risk	*So, of the women who inherit BC, the genes account for about half of cases. This is kind of like the last one—that specific number doesn't have to be true.*

P

MANHATTAN
GMAT

Chapter 5
of
Critical Reasoning

Strengthen and Weaken

In This Chapter...

Chapter 5:
Strengthen and Weaken

In Chapter 4, we introduced the Assumption Family and discussed Assumption, Evaluate, and Flaw questions. If you haven't read chapter 4 yet, please do so before reading this chapter; we'll wait!

To recap briefly:

- assumptions are something an author must believe to be true in order to draw his or her conclusion; these assumptions are NOT stated explicitly in the argument

- all assumption arguments will contain a "core": a conclusion and the major premise or premises that lead to it

- all assumption arguments will contain at least one (and probably more than one) assumption

In this chapter, we'll address the remaining two Assumption Family question types: Strengthen the Conclusion and Weaken the Conclusion.

As we saw with the previous three question types, these last two question types also hinge upon identifying an assumption; each has certain characteristics, though, that warrant separating them into these different categories.

Strengthen and Weaken: The Basics

Both Strengthen and Weaken questions ask us to find a *new* piece of information that, if added to the existing argument, will make the conclusion either somewhat more likely to be true (Strengthen) or somewhat less likely to be true (Weaken). The fact that this information is new, or goes beyond what we already know from the argument, is the major difference between Strengthen and Weaken questions and the three question types we examined in the last chapter.

In the case of a Strengthen, the new piece of info will serve as evidence that some assumption is actually valid. In the case of a Weaken, the new piece of info will knock down some assumption: it will serve as evidence that the assumption is invalid.

How does that work? Let's look at one of our arguments from the last chapter again, about Thomas's football team:

therefore

Last year's 2nd place team has improved

(premise)

Team will win CH this year

(conclusion

If we were asked an Assumption question, the answer might be something like: Thomas's team has improved enough to be better than the defending champions. In order for the author to draw his conclusion, that must be true. If Thomas's team hasn't improved enough to be better than the first-place team, then how could we possibly conclude that Thomas's team will win this year?

If we're asked a Strengthen question, how does the answer change? A Strengthen answer provides us with some new piece of information that does not *have* to be true, but *if true*, it does make the conclusion more likely to be valid. For example:

> The star quarterback on the defending champion team will miss the game due to an injury.

Must it be true that the star quarterback will miss the game in order for Thomas's team to win? No. It's just a new piece of data, one we couldn't have anticipated, but if that information is true, then it also makes the conclusion more likely to be true. Thomas's team is more likely to win if a star player on the opposing team can't play.

What happens if we're asked a Weaken question? Similarly, a Weaken answer provides us with some new piece of information that does not *have* to be true but, *if true*, does make the conclusion a bit less likely to be valid. For example:

> The players on the defending champion team train more than the players on any other team.

MANHATTAN
GMAT

That specific fact does not have to be true in order for us to doubt the claim that Thomas's team will win — there are lots of reasons for us to doubt the claim — but if it is, indeed, true, that the defending champion team trains more than all the other teams, then the author's conclusion just got weaker.

Note that all Strengthen and Weaken question stems do include the words "if true" or an equivalent variation. In other words, we're explicitly told to accept the possibility that the information in the answer is actually true.

Finally, there are three possible ways that an answer choice could affect the conclusion on both Strengthen and Weaken questions: the answer *strengthens* the conclusion, the answer *weakens* the conclusion, or the answer *does nothing* to the conclusion. As we assess the answers, we'll be keeping these three categories in mind; we'll label Strengthen answers with an *S*, Weaken answers with a *W*, and "nothing" answers with an *n*. We'll discuss this in more detail later.

Strengthen the Conclusion Questions

As we discussed, Strengthen questions ask us to find a *new* piece of information that, if added to the existing argument, will make the conclusion somewhat more likely to be true.

Most often, Strengthen questions will contain some form of the words "strengthen" or "support," as well as the phrase "if true." Here are some typical examples:

> Which of the following, if true, most strengthens the argument above?

> Which of the following, if true, most strongly supports the mayor's claim?

Strengthen questions will sometimes use synonyms in place of the strengthen / support language; such synonyms might include:

- provides the best basis or the best reason for

- provides justification for

- provides a piece of evidence in favor of (a plan or a conclusion)

Strengthen questions may occasionally lack the exact phrase "if true" but, if so, some other wording will provide a similar meaning. That wording might be something quite similar, such as "if feasible." Alternatively, the wording might indicate that the answer can be "effectively achieved" or "successfully accomplished" (indicating that the information would become true).

Try out this short example:

> At QuestCorp, many employees have quit recently and taken jobs with a competitor. Shortly before the employees quit, QuestCorp lost its largest client. Clearly, the employees were no longer confident in QuestCorp's long-term viability.
>
> Which of the following, if true, most strengthens the claim that concerns about QuestCorp's viability caused the employees to quit?
>
> (A) Employees at QuestCorp's main competitor recently received a large and well-publicized raise.
>
> (B) QuestCorp's largest client accounted for 40% of sales and nearly 60% of the company's profits.
>
> (C) Many prospective hires who have interviewed with QuestCorp ultimately accepted jobs with other companies.

The question stem indicates that this is a strengthen question. Our core might look similar to this:

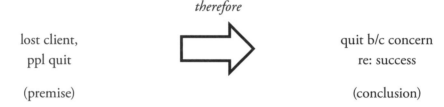

Note: you can write the core down as we did above, or you can articulate the core to yourself mentally (or both!). Whichever path works best for you is fine.

That's interesting. The author claims that, because the company lost its largest client, some employees lost confidence in the company, so they quit. The author assumes that losing that client will be a significant blow to the company. What if the company has many clients and the largest client only represented a very small fraction of the business? The author also assumes there aren't other reasons why employees would have quit.

This is a strengthen question, so I have to find some evidence that actually does support the claim that people quit specifically because they lost confidence in the company after it lost its largest client.

| (A) Employees at Quest-Corp's main competitor recently received a large and well-publicized raise. | S   A̶ B C
    W

lost client, ppl quit

ⓒbc concern re: success of com | *Wouldn't that make QC's employees jealous — maybe they'd expect more money? That'd make it more likely that they quit because of $ issues rather than a loss of confidence in the company. If anything, this actually weakens the conclusion; I want a strengthen answer.* |

(B) QuestCorp's largest client accounted for 40% of sales and nearly 60% of the company's profits.	S $\underset{W}{\text{A}}$ $\underset{S}{\text{B}}$ C lost client, ppl quit ©bc concern re: success of com	*Ouch. Then losing this client would be a pretty serious blow to the company. This is a fact that helps make the conclusion a little more likely; I'll keep it in.*
(C) Many prospective hires who have interviewed with QuestCorp ultimately accepted jobs with other companies.	S $\underset{W}{\text{A}}$ $\underset{S}{\text{Ⓑ}}$ $\underset{n}{\text{C}}$ lost client, ppl quit ©bc concern re: success of com	*Hmm. "Prospective hires" are not employees. I was asked to strengthen the part about* <u>employees</u> *losing confidence in QC. We could speculate that maybe something is wrong with QC if people take other jobs… but the answer doesn't even tell us* <u>why</u> *these people took other jobs. Maybe QC rejected them!*

Answer choice A represents one common trap on Strengthen questions: the answer does the opposite of what we want. That is, it weakens the conclusion rather than strengthening it.

Answer choice C represents another common trap: the answer addresses (and sometimes even strengthens) something other than what we were asked to address. In this case, the answer does seem to imply that there's something not so great about QuestCorp, but it discusses the wrong group of people (prospective hires) and doesn't actually provide any information that allows us to assess what they think of QuestCorp's viability. (Again, that last part doesn't matter in the end, because we're already talking about the wrong group of people in the first place.)

Putting It All Together

Let's try a full problem now.

> Donut Chain, wishing to increase the profitability of its new store, will place a coupon in the local newspaper offering a free donut with a cup of coffee at its grand opening. Donut Chain calculates that the cost of the advertisement and the free donuts will be more than recouped by the new business generated through the promotion.
>
> Which of the following, if true, most strengthens the prediction that Donut Chain's promotion will increase the new store's profitability?
>
> (A   Donut Chain has a loyal following in much of the country.
> (B)   Donut Chain has found that the vast majority of new visitors to its stores become regular customers.
> (C)   One donut at Donut Chain costs less than a cup of coffee.
> (D)   Most of the copies of the coupon in the local newspaper will not be redeemed for free donuts.
> (E)   Donut Chain's stores are generally very profitable.

Step 1: Identify the question.

Which of the following, if true, most strengthens the prediction that Donut Chain's promotion will increase the new store's profitability?	S　　A B C D E ⒸDC promo → ↑ prof	The language "if true" and "most strengthens the prediction that…" indicates that this is a strengthen the conclusion question. Also, the question stem tells me the conclusion I need to address: the plan will lead to better profitability.

Step 2: Deconstruct the argument.

Donut Chain, wishing to increase the profitability of its new store, will place a coupon in the local newspaper offering a free donut with a cup of coffee at its grand opening.	S　　A B C D E ⒸDC promo → ↑ prof promo = give free coupon	DC thinks that giving away a free donut will lead to increased profitability.
Donut Chain calculates that the cost of the advertisement and the free donuts will be more than recouped by the new business generated through the promotion.	S　　A B C D E ⒸDC promo → ↑ prof promo = give free coupon $ spent < $ made	It costs $ to place the ad and give away free donuts, but DC thinks it'll get enough new business to offset those costs. Still, does that lead to better profitability?
(brainstorm assumptions)	S　　A B C D E ⒸDC promo → ↑ prof promo = give free coupon $ spent < $ made	The argument isn't 100% clear that the profitability part is the conclusion, but the question stem also said so. I can label that info with my Ⓒ symbol. The author is assuming that giving away a free donut once will lead to increased revenues over time (what if they never come back?), and that will then lead to increase profits (> revenues don't necessarily equal > profitability).

Step 3: State the Goal.

I need to strengthen the claim that a particular plan is going to lead to increased profitability. The plan is to distribute coupons to give away free donuts.

I need to find an answer that makes it a little more likely that this plan will lead to more profits.

Step 4: Work from wrong to right.

(A) Donut Chain has a loyal following in much of the country.	S A B C D E _n_ ©DC promo → ↑ prof promo = give free coupon $ spent < $ made	*This is good for DC. Does that mean it will <u>increase</u> profitability though? No. It's already an established fact. Plus, it only says that DC enjoys a loyal following in "much" of the country, not absolutely everywhere.*
(B) Donut Chain has found that the vast majority of new visitors to its stores become regular customers.	S A B C D E _n_ _S_ ©DC promo → ↑ prof promo = give free coupon $ spent < $ made	*So if DC can get people to visit once, they'll usually keep coming back. That sounds pretty good for DC's plan, which is all about getting people to visit the first time for that free donut.*
(C) One donut at Donut Chain costs less than a cup of coffee.	S A B C̶ D E _n_ _S_ ©DC promo → ↑ prof promo = give free coupon $ spent < $ made	*This tells me nothing about profits or revenues or how much they could sell or anything, really. This doesn't address the conclusion.*
(D) Most of the copies of the coupon in the local newspaper will not be redeemed for free donuts.	S A B C̶ D̶ E _n_ _S_ _n_ _W_ ©DC promo → ↑ prof promo = give free coupon $ spent < $ made	*If this happens, then DC's plan is really unlikely to work—it spends money on the ads, but never gets the new customers to come in. That <u>weakens</u> the conclusion.*
(E) Donut Chain's stores are generally very profitable.	S A B C̶ D̶ E̶ _n_ _S_ _n_ _W_ ©DC promo → ↑ prof promo = give free coupon $ spent < $ made	*It's good that DC stores are usually profitable; that means this new one is likely to be profitable, too. The claim, though, specifically asks about <u>increasing</u> the store's profitability—and it specifically asks whether <u>this plan</u> will accomplish that goal. This choice looks tempting at first, but it doesn't address whether this plan will increase profitability.*

Common Trap Answers

One of the most common traps is the Reverse Logic answer: the question asks us to strengthen, but a trap answer choice weakens the conclusion instead. We saw an example of this with answer choice D in the last problem. These can be especially tricky if we misread the conclusion or otherwise get turned around while evaluating the argument.

Most of the wrong answers will have No Tie to the Conclusion—they will neither strengthen nor weaken the conclusion. Some of these will be more obviously wrong, but these answers can also be quite tricky. A No Tie trap might address something in a premise without actually affecting the conclusion, for example, as we saw with answer choice E in the last problem.

Takeaways for Strengthen Questions

The question stem will contain "if true" or a close synonym, as well as some form of the word "strengthen" or "support" (or a synonym). We will write down *S* to indicate that we have a Strengthen question.

On Strengthen questions, our goal is to find a new piece of information that makes the conclusion at least somewhat more likely to be valid.

The most common trap answers include the Reverse Logic trap (weakening the conclusion rather than strengthening it) and the No Tie trap (doesn't affect the specific conclusion).

Weaken the Conclusion Questions

As we discussed earlier, Weaken questions ask us to find a *new* piece of information that, if added to the existing argument, will make the conclusion somewhat less likely to be valid. Our goal, then, is to *attack* the conclusion. The correct answer will attack some assumption made by the author.

Most Weaken question stems contain the phrase "if true" (or an equivalent) and question stems similar to these examples:

- Which of the following, if true, most seriously weakens the conclusion? (variant: which is a weakness?)
- Which of the following, if true, would cast the most serious doubt on the validity of the argument? (variant: raise the most serious doubt regarding)
- Which of the following, if true, most strongly calls into question the author's conclusion?
- Which of the following, if true, most seriously undermines the mayor's claim?

Sometimes, the question stem will contain more unusual language, such as the words in quotes below:

- find a "disadvantage" or what is "damaging" to the argument
- a plan is "ill-suited" or otherwise unlikely to succeed
- find a "criticism" of the argument

Let's look at the same short example about QuestCorp, but with a different question and answers!

> At QuestCorp, many employees have quit recently and taken jobs with a competitor. Shortly before the employees quit, QuestCorp lost its largest client. Clearly, the employees were no longer confident in QuestCorp's long-term viability.
>
> Which of the following, if true, most seriously undermines the claim that concerns about QuestCorp's viability caused the employees to quit?
>
> (A)   A new competitor in the same town provides health insurance for its employees, a benefit that QuestCorp lacks.
> (B)   QuestCorp is unlikely to be able to replace the lost revenue via either an increase in existing client sales or the attraction of new clients.
> (C)   Many prospective hires who have interviewed with QuestCorp ultimately accepted jobs with other companies.

The question stem indicates that this is a Weaken question. Our core might look similar to this:

lost client,	*therefore*	quit b/c concern
ppl quit		re: success
(premise)		(conclusion)

Note: as we discussed on Strengthen question, you can write the core down as we did above, or you can articulate the core to yourself mentally (or both!). Whichever path works best for you is fine.

Hmm. The author claims that losing this client caused employees to lose confidence in QC, which then caused them to quit. The author is assuming that losing this one client was serious enough to result in a major problem for the company; is that necessarily the case? This is a Weaken question, so I have to find some evidence that makes it less likely that people quit for that reason. That could be because it wasn't really a big problem, or it could be that there was some other reason that people quit.

(A) A new competitor in the same town provides health insurance for its employees, a benefit that QuestCorp lacks.	S A B C W lost client, ppl quit ⓒbc concern re: success of com	*The argument claims that people left for one reason, but this answer actually provides an alternative. Maybe people quit because they could get better benefits at the other company. This would weaken the claim that people quit specifically because of concerns over QC's viability as a company.*

(B) QuestCorp is unlikely to be able to replace the lost revenue via either an increase in existing client sales or the attraction of new clients.	S A $\underset{W}{\text{B}}$ $\underset{S}{\text{C}}$ lost client, ppl quit Ⓒ bc concern re: success of com	*So QuestCorp lost its largest client, which means a loss of revenue, and the company probably can't find a way to make up that revenue through other sales. That definitely reinforces the problem described in the argument. This actually strengthens the conclusion; that's the opposite of what I want.*
(C) Many prospective hires who have interviewed with QuestCorp ultimately accepted jobs with other companies.	S A $\underset{W}{\text{B}}$ $\underset{S}{\text{B}}$ $\underset{n}{\text{C}}$ lost client, ppl quit Ⓒ bc concern re: success of com	*Hmm. "Prospective hires" are not employees. I was asked to weaken the part about <u>employees</u> losing confidence in QC. We could speculate that maybe something is wrong with QC if people take other jobs… but the answer doesn't even tell us <u>why</u> these people took other jobs. Maybe QC rejected them!*

Answer B repeats the common Reverse Logic trap we discussed earlier: it strengthens the conclusion but we want to weaken the conclusion. Answer C attempts to distract us by talking about a different part of the argument—perhaps we'll reason that, if interviewees took different jobs, that means they didn't believe QuestCorp was a good company. We have no idea why these prospective hires ended up working for another company, though—it's entirely possible that QuestCorp didn't extend a job offer to these people.

Note that we used the exact same answer choice C for both the Strengthen and Weaken versions of this QuestCorp problem. If a choice is irrelevant to the argument (as choice C was), then it doesn't matter whether we're asked to strengthen or weaken the conclusion. An irrelevant choice doesn't affect the conclusion at all.

Let's try a full example:

> The national infrastructure for airport runways and air traffic control requires immediate expansion to accommodate the increase in private, smaller planes. To help fund this expansion, the Federal Aviation Authority (FAA) has proposed a fee for all air travelers. However, this fee would be unfair, as it would impose costs on all travelers to benefit only the few who utilize the new private planes.
>
> Which of the following, if true, would cast the most doubt on the claim that the proposed fee would be unfair?
>
> (A)   The existing national airport infrastructure benefits all air travelers.
> (B)   The fee, if imposed, will have a negligible impact on the overall volume of air travel.
> (C)   The expansion would reduce the number of delayed flights resulting from small private planes congesting runways.
> (D)   Travelers who use small private planes are almost uniformly wealthy or traveling on business.
> (E)   A substantial fee would need to be imposed in order to pay for the expansion costs.

Step 1: Identify the question.

Which of the following, if true, would cast the most doubt on the claim that the proposed fee would be unfair?	W A B C D E ⒸΩfee = unfair	*The language "cast the most doubt on the claim" tells me that this is a weaken question. The specific claim I'm attacking is that the proposed fee would be unfair.*

Step 2: Deconstruct the argument.

The national infrastructure for airport runways and air traffic control requires immediate expansion to accommodate the increase in private, smaller planes.	W A B C D E Ⓒfee = unfair ↑ sm pl → must exp infra	*This is somewhat claim-like but it's written as a fact; I'm guessing it's just background info, not the conclusion, but I'm not 100% sure.*
To help fund this expansion, the Federal Aviation Authority (FAA) has proposed a fee for all air travelers.	W A B C D E Ⓒfee = unfair ↑ sm pl → must exp infra FAA: fee → fund exp	*Okay, here's a plan. It could be the conclusion. The FAA wants to charge a fee to pay for the expansion.*

However, this fee would be unfair, as it would impose costs on all travelers to benefit only the few who utilize the new private planes.	W A B C D E ⓒfee = unfair b/c all pay but few ben ↑ sm pl → must exp infra FAA: fee → fund exp	*Change of direction! The author disagrees with the fee plan, claiming it's unfair. Her reasoning is that everyone would have to pay the fee, but only a few people would benefit.*
	W A B C D E ⓒfee = unfair b/c all pay but few ben ↑ sm pl → must exp infra FAA: fee → fund exp	*Why wouldn't everyone benefit? If there's more space, then all the planes will be able to take off more quickly. The author is assuming the benefit is <u>only</u> for the people flying in small planes.*

Step 3: State the Goal.

The airports are congested because there are so many small planes, and the FAA wants to charge a fee to expand the airports. The author claims that this is unfair because the fee would be paid by all but the expansion would only benefit a few.

I want to weaken the author's conclusion, so I need to find some reason why it really isn't unfair. One possibility that I brainstormed: maybe everyone really will benefit, not just the "small plane" people.

Step 4: Work from wrong to right.

(A) The existing national airport infrastructure benefits all air travelers.	W A B C D E W ⓒfee = unfair b/c all pay but few ben ↑ sm pl → must exp infra FAA: fee → fund exp	*This sounds like what I was thinking before—everyone benefits, so why is it unfair for everyone to pay? Great; I'll leave it in.*
(B) The fee, if imposed, will have a negligible impact on the overall volume of air travel.	W A B C D E W ⓒfee = unfair b/c all pay but few ben ↑ sm pl → must exp infra FAA: fee → fund exp	*A "negligible impact" means it won't really change anything. The fee won't change the volume of planes trying to fly… but that was never the plan. The plan was to raise money to expand the infrastructure—then they'll be able to handle more volume. This answer doesn't address the right thing.*

(C) The expansion would reduce the number of delayed flights resulting from small private planes congesting runways.	W A B C D E W W Ⓒfee = unfair b/c all pay but few ben ↑ sm pl → must exp infra FAA: fee → fund exp	*Hmm. This is another potential benefit for everyone—a reduction in the number of flight delays. I'll leave this one in, too.*
(D) Travelers who use small private planes are almost uniformly wealthy or traveling on business.	W A B C Đ E W W Ⓒfee = unfair b/c all pay but few ben ↑ sm pl → must exp infra FAA: fee → fund exp	*That's nice for them, but what does it have to do with this argument? Maybe you could say "so they can afford to pay more," but that isn't the point of the argument. The point of the argument is that it's unfair to make the regular travelers pay for something that doesn't benefit them (according to the author).*
(E) A substantial fee would need to be imposed in order to pay for the expansion costs.	W A B C Đ E W W Ⓒfee = unfair b/c all pay but few ben ↑ sm pl → must exp infra FAA: fee → fund exp	*So the fee would have to be pretty large. If anything, doesn't that make it even more unfair? Though, actually, I don't think it really addresses the fairness at all. Either it is fair, in which case the size of the fee doesn't matter, or it isn't fair… in which case the size of the fee still doesn't matter.*
Examine A and C again	W A B Ⓒ Đ E W W Ⓒfee = unfair b/c all pay but few ben ↑ sm pl → must exp infra FAA: fee → fund exp	*Okay, I have to compare A and C now. Both say that this expansion would benefit everyone… wait a second. C does explicitly mention the expansion, but A says "the existing… infrastructure." Existing? Of course the existing structure benefits everyone who uses it—the argument isn't about that. It's about whether the <u>expansion</u> would benefit everyone. Only C actually says that; I missed that the first time around.*

Common Trap Answers

Weaken questions contain the same kind of common trap answers that we see on Strengthen questions.

One of the most tricky types is the Reverse Logic trap: the question asks us to weaken, but a trap answer choice strengthens the conclusion instead. We will also again see the No Tie traps—choices that might discuss something in a premise but don't affect the conclusion.

Our most tempting wrong answer in the last problem, answer choice A, is actually a No Tie trap. It was so tempting specifically because almost everything in the choice was addressing the right thing but one word made it wrong: "existing." The conclusion was about the future infrastructure, after an expansion, so limiting the answer to the existing infrastructure meant that the information didn't affect the conclusion after all.

Takeaways for Weaken Questions

The question stem will contain "if true" or a close synonym, as well as some form of the words "weaken," "doubt," "undermine," or a synonym. We will write down "W" to indicate that we have a Weaken question.

On Weaken questions, our goal is to attack the conclusion. The correct answer will be a new piece of information that makes the conclusion at least somewhat less likely to be valid.

The most common trap answers include the Reverse Logic trap (strengthening the conclusion rather than weakening it) and the No Tie trap (doesn't affect the specific conclusion).

EXCEPT Questions

Assumption Family questions may also be presented in a "negative" form that is commonly referred to as Except questions.

A regular Weaken question might read:

> Which of the following, if true, most seriously weakens the conclusion?

An Except Weaken question might read:

> Each of the following, if true, weakens the conclusion EXCEPT:

What is the difference in wording between those two questions?

The first one tells us that one answer choice, and only one, weakens the conclusion. That is the answer choice that we want to pick.

The second one tells us that four answer choices weaken the conclusion. These four are all wrong answers. What about the fifth answer—what does that one do?

Many people will assume that the fifth one must do the opposite: strengthen the conclusion. *This is not necessarily true.* Rather, the fifth one cannot weaken the conclusion but it may not strengthen the conclusion either. It might have no impact whatsoever on the conclusion.

For these negatively-worded questions, we're going to use the "odd one out" strategy. Four of the answers will do the same thing; in the case of the above example, four answers will weaken the conclusion. The fifth answer will do something else. It doesn't matter whether the fifth one strengthens the conclusion or does nothing—all that matters is that it is the "odd one out."

The four answers that do the same thing can be found by using the regular strategy that we would use for that question type. On a normal Weaken question, we want to choose the answer that makes the conclusion at least a little less valid. On an EXCEPT Weaken question, four answer choices will make the conclusion at least a little less valid, and we are going to cross those four choices off. The remaining answer will be the answer we pick.

Here's a full example.

> Supporters of a costly new Defense Advanced Research Projects Agency (DARPA) initiative assert that the project will benefit industrial companies as well as the military itself. In many instances, military research has resulted in technologies that have fueled corporate development and growth, and this pattern can be expected to continue.
>
> Each of the following, if true, serves to weaken the argument above EXCEPT:
>
> (A)   The research initiative will occupy many talented scientists, many of whom would otherwise have worked for private corporations.
> (B)   In the past decade, DARPA has adopted an increasingly restrictive stance regarding the use of intellectual property resulting from its research.
> (C)   If the DARPA initiative hadn't been approved, much of the funding would instead have been directed toward tax breaks for various businesses.
> (D)   At any given time, DARPA is conducting a wide variety of costly research projects.
> (E)   The research initiative is focused on defense mechanisms that will reduce injury to soldiers during combat, a need that is nonexistent for private corporations.

5

Step 1: Identify the question.

Each of the following, if true, serves to weaken the argument above EXCEPT:	WEx A B C D E	*The language "serves to weaken" tells me that this is a weaken question. The word EXCEPT tells me that the 4 wrong answers will weaken and I want to pick the "odd one out" answer.*

Step 2: Deconstruct the argument.

Supporters of a costly new Defense Advanced Research Projects Agency (DARPA) initiative assert that the project will benefit industrial companies as well as the military itself.	WEx A B C D E SD: ben ind coms & mil	*The SD's (Supporters of DARPA) think that this really costly project will be good for companies and the military.*
In many instances, military research has resulted in technologies that have fueled corporate development and growth, and this pattern can be expected to continue.	WEx A B C D E ©SD: ben ind coms & mil past: mil res → techs to help coms, will cont	*Research has helped coms in the past, and the author claims this will keep happening in the future. That all supports the claim of the SDs: that the specific D project will be beneficial for coms.*

Step 3: State the Goal.

In the past, military research has helped companies, and the claim is that this D project will also help companies.

I want to find four answers that weaken the conclusion (make it at least a little less likely to be valid). The answer that doesn't weaken—the odd one out—is the correct answer.

Step 4: Work from wrong to right.

(A) The research initiative will occupy many talented scientists, many of whom would otherwise have worked for private corporations.	WEx A̶ B C D E W ©SD: ben ind coms & mil past: mil res → techs to help coms, will cont	*This benefits the military and specifically does not benefit the companies. That does weaken the idea that companies will benefit.*

(B) In the past decade, DARPA has adopted an increasingly restrictive stance regarding the use of intellectual property resulting from its research.	WEx A̶ B C D E W W? Ⓒ SD: ben ind coms & mil past: mil res → techs to help coms, will cont	Hmm. "Restrictive" makes it sound like D doesn't let others use its research as much. If that's the case, then that would weaken the idea that companies will benefit. I'm not totally sure that's what this means though — the wording is tricky — so I'm not going to cross this one off yet.
(C) If the DARPA initiative hadn't been approved, much of the funding would instead have been directed toward tax breaks for various businesses..	WEx A̶ B C̶ D E W W? W Ⓒ SD: ben ind coms & mil past: mil res → techs to help coms, will cont	A tax break is a good thing, This choice is saying that the funding for the D project would instead have been spent on tax breaks, which is a definite benefit. So not giving those tax breaks is a bad thing for the companies; this does weaken the argument.
(D) At any given time, DARPA is conducting a wide variety of costly research projects.	WEx A̶ B C̶ D E W W? W n Ⓒ SD: ben ind coms & mil past: mil res → techs to help coms, will cont	This choice talks about all research projects D is conducting. Hmm. The argument makes a claim only about one specific project. Does this information make that claim more or less likely to be valid? I can't really see how it affects the argument's conclusion at all.
(E) The research initiative is focused on defense mechanisms that will reduce injury to soldiers during combat, a need that is nonexistent for private corporations.	WEx A̶ B C̶ D E̶ W W? W n W Ⓒ SD: ben ind coms & mil past: mil res → techs to help coms, will cont	The key here is the language "a need that is nonexistent for private corporations." If the private companies don't have any need for the results of this particular research, then that weakens the claim that the D research will benefit companies.
Examine B and D again	WEx A̶ B̶ C̶ Ⓓ E̶ W W? W n W Ⓒ SD: ben ind coms & mil past: mil res → techs to help coms, will cont	I need to compare B and D. I thought B might weaken a little bit, and I thought D didn't do anything to the conclusion. Between those two, I should choose the one that doesn't weaken at all, so I'm going to choose D.

The biggest "trap answer" on an EXCEPT question is simply to forget halfway through that we're working on an EXCEPT question. In other words, halfway through the above question, if I forget that it's a Weaken EXCEPT, I might accidentally pick a Weaken answer, or pick the answer that I think most weakens the conclusion.

Takeaways for EXCEPT Questions

Any of the five Assumption Family question types can be worded as an EXCEPT question. When that happens, the four wrong answers will be formulated in whatever way a right answer would have been written on a normally-worded question of that type. That is:

On _____ EXCEPT questions	Wrong answers will	Right answers will
Assumption	be an assumption on which the argument depends	NOT be an assumption on which the argument depends
Evaluate	help to tell us *whether* the conclusion may be valid	NOT help to tell us whether the conclusion may be valid
Flaw	represent a flaw in the reasoning	NOT represent a flaw in the reasoning
Strengthen	strengthen the conclusion at least a little	NOT strengthen the conclusion
Weaken	weaken the conclusion at least a little	NOT weaken the conclusion

On EXCEPT questions, we remind ourselves first what the usual goal is for a normal question of that type. The four wrong answers will follow that typical goal, and the right answer will be the "odd one out"—it will NOT do what we typically expect on a normal question of that type.

When writing down the question type, add the designation "Ex" to whatever you normally write down for that question type.

MANHATTAN
GMAT

Problem Set

1. *Digital Video Recorders*

Advertising Executive: More than 10 million households now own digital video recorders that can fast-forward over television commercials; approximately 75% of these households fast-forward over at least one commercial per 30-minute program. Because television commercials are not as widely watched as they used to be, they are much less cost-effective today.

Which of the following, if true, strengthens the claim that television commercials are less cost-effective than they used to be?

(A) Product placement within television programs is a viable alternative to traditional television commercials.

(B) The television programs preferred by consumers without digital video recorders are similar to those preferred by consumers with the devices.

(C) Prior to the advent of digital video recorders, very few television viewers switched channels or left the room when commercials began.

(D) The cost-effectiveness of television advertising is based less upon how many people watch a particular commercial and more upon the appropriateness of the demographic.

(E) Many companies find it difficult to determine the exact return on investment for television commercials.

2. *Smithtown Theatre*

The Smithtown Theatre, which stages old plays, has announced an expansion that will double its capacity along with its operating costs. The theatre is only slightly profitable at present. In addition, all of the current customers live in Smithtown, and the population of the town is not expected to increase in the next several years. Thus, the expansion of the Smithtown Theatre will prove unprofitable.

Which of the following, if true, would most seriously weaken the argument?

(A) A large movie chain plans to open a new multiplex location in Smithtown later this year.

(B) Concession sales in the Smithtown Theatre comprise a substantial proportion of the theatre's revenues.

(C) Many recent arrivals to Smithtown are students that are less likely to attend the Smithtown Theatre than are older residents.

(D) The expansion would allow the Smithtown Theatre to stage larger, more popular shows that will attract customers from neighboring towns.

(E) The Board of the Smithtown Theatre often solicits input from residents of the town when choosing which shows to stage.

3. *Books and Coffee*

The owners of a book store and a nearby coffee shop have decided to combine their businesses. Both owners believe that this merger will increase the number of customers and therefore the gross revenue, because customers who come for one reason may also decide to purchase something else.

Which of the following, if true, most weakens the owners' conclusion that a merger will increase revenue?

(A) Books and drinks can both be considered impulse purchases; often, they are purchased by customers without forethought.

(B) Profit margins at a coffee shop are generally significantly higher than profit margins at a book store.

(C) People who are able to read the first chapter of a book before buying are more likely to decide to buy the book.

(D) A large majority of the book store's current customer base already frequents the coffee shop.

(E) A combination book store and coffee shop that opened in a neighboring city last year has already earned higher than expected profits.

4. *Digital Coupons*

The redemption rate for e-mailed coupons is far lower than that for traditionally distributed paper coupons. One factor is the "digital divide"—those who might benefit the most from using coupons, such as homemakers, the elderly, and those in low-income households, often do not have the knowledge or equipment necessary to go online and receive coupons.

Which of the following, if true, does the most to support the claim that the digital divide is responsible for lower electronic coupon redemption rates?

(A) Computers are available for free in libraries, schools, and community centers.

(B) The redemption rate of ordinary coupons is particularly high among elderly and low income people that do not know how to use computers.

(C) Many homes, including those of elderly and low income people, do not have high-speed internet connections.

(D) More homemakers than elderly people would use computers if they had access to them.

(E) The redemption rate for coupons found on the internet has risen in the last five years.

5. *Teacher Compensation*

Traditionally, public school instructors have been compensated according to seniority. Recently, educational experts have criticized the system as one that rewards lackadaisical teaching and reduces motivation to excel. Instead, these experts argue that, to retain exceptional teachers and maintain quality instruction, teachers should receive salaries or bonuses based on performance rather than seniority.

Which of the following, if true, most weakens the argument of the educational experts?

(A)   Some teachers express that financial compensation is not the only factor contributing to job satisfaction and teaching performance.
(B)   School districts will develop their own unique compensation structures that may differ greatly from those of other school districts.
(C)   Upon leaving the teaching profession, many young, effective teachers cite a lack of opportunity for more rapid financial advancement as a primary factor in the decision to change careers.
(D)   In school districts that have implemented pay for performance compensation structures, standardized test scores have dramatically increased.
(E)   A merit-based system that bases compensation on teacher performance reduces collaboration, which is an integral component of quality instruction.

6. *The Gold Standard*

Brand X designs and builds custom sneakers, one sneaker at a time. It recently announced plans to sell "The Gold Standard," a sneaker that will cost five times more to manufacture than any other sneaker that has ever been created.

Which of the following, if it occurred, would cast the most serious doubt on the claim that The Gold Standard sneaker will be profitable?

(A)   The endorsement of The Gold Standard by a popular celebrity
(B)   The publication of a report indicating that all previous sneaker lines launched by Brand X have been profitable
(C)   A significant increase in the cost of the canvas used to construct The Gold Standard
(D)   The introduction of another new sneaker line by a rival manufacturer
(E)   An announcement by Brand X that The Gold Standard will be marketed as an exclusive offering, available only in limited quantities

7. *Machu Picchu*

In 2001 the Peruvian government began requiring tourists to buy permits to hike the Inca Trail to the ancient city of Machu Picchu. Only 500 people per day are now allowed to hike the Inca Trail, whereas before 2001 daily visitors numbered in the thousands. The Peruvian government claims that this permit program has successfully prevented deterioration of archaeological treasures along the Inca Trail.

Which of the following, if true, most strengthens the argument above?

(A) Since 2001, Incan ruins similar to Machu Picchu but without a visitor limit have disintegrated at a significantly greater rate than those on the Inca Trail.

(B) Villages near Machu Picchu have experienced declines in income, as fewer tourists buy fewer craft goods and refreshments.

(C) Many of the funds from the sale of Inca Trail permits are used to hire guards for archaeological sites without permit programs.

(D) Since 2001, tourist guides along the Inca Trail have received 50% to 100% increases in take-home pay.

(E) The total number of tourists in Peru has risen substantially since 2001, even as the number of tourists hiking the Inca Trail has remained constant.

8. *Ethanol*

Ethanol, a fuel derived from corn, can be used alone to power cars or along with gasoline to reduce the reduce the amount of gas consumed. Unlike gasoline, ethanol is easily renewable since it is primarily converted from the sun's energy. Moreover, compared with conventional gasoline, pure ethanol is a cleaner-burning fuel. To save energy and reduce pollution, many individuals advocate the increased usage of ethanol as a primary fuel source in conjunction with or in place of gasoline.

In evaluating the recommendation to increase the use of ethanol, it would be important to research all of the following EXCEPT:

(A) Whether the energy required to grow and process corn used as fuel is greater than the amount of energy ultimately produced

(B) Whether more energy is saved when using ethanol in conjunction with or in place of gasoline

(C) Whether ethanol is as efficient a fuel as gasoline

(D) Whether it is possible to produce more ethanol than is currently produced

(E) Whether the process of growing corn for fuel would result in as much pollution as does the production of conventional gasoline

9. *APR*

CEO: Over the past several years, we have more than doubled our revenues but profits have steadily declined because an increasing number of customers have failed to pay their balances. In order to compensate for these higher default rates, we will increase the interest charged on outstanding balances from an annual percentage rate (APR) of 9.5% to an APR of 12%. This increase will be sufficient to compensate for the current rate of defaults and allow us to increase our profits.

Which of the following statements, if true, would most seriously undermine a plan to increase interest rates in order to spur profitable growth?

(A)   Many other companies have experienced a similar trend in their default rates.

(B)   The company's operating expenses are above the industry average and can be substantially reduced, thus increasing margins.

(C)   The increase in default rates was due to a rise in unemployment, but unemployment rates are expected to drop in the coming months.

(D)   The proposed increase in the APR will, alone, more than double the company's profit margins.

(E)   An increase in the APR charged on credit card balances often results in higher rates of default.

P

10. *Jupiter vs. Mars*

Scientists suspect that Europa, a moon orbiting Jupiter, may contain living organisms. However, the government recently scrapped an unmanned science mission to Europa and replaced it with a project aimed at landing an astronaut on Mars. Polls show that the public is far more fascinated by space travel than by discovering life elsewhere in the universe. Critics argue that the government's decision-making process places a greater emphasis on popularity than it does on the importance of scientific research.

Which of the following, if true, would most strengthen a contention by the government that the new project is a better use of its funds?

(A) In the first year of the project, the government will spend 30% of its total budget on developing a space shuttle that can travel to Mars; that figure is expected to drop to 0% after five years.

(B) The government cannot be absolutely certain of the chances for success of either project.

(C) Some scientists are convinced that a mission to Europa would add immeasurably to our understanding of the universe.

(D) A new telescope that has just become available to scientists promises to yield more information than the planned mission to Europa was designed to provide.

(E) Most people feel that a shuttle to Mars is the next logical step in the development of a system that will allow humans to travel even further in the solar system.

Solutions

1. Digital Video Recorders: The correct answer is **C**.

Step 1: Identify the question.

Which of the following, if true, strengthens the claim that television commercials are less cost-effective than they used to be ?	S A B C D E Ⓒ TV comm < cost eff now	*The phrase "strengthens the claim" tells me that this is a Strengthen question. The question stem also tells me the conclusion: TV commercials are less cost-effective than they used to be. I'll write that down.*

Step 2: Deconstruct the argument.

Advertising Executive: More than 10 million households now own digital video recorders that can fast-forward over television commercials;	S A B C D E Ⓒ TV comm < cost eff now AE: 10m hh = DVR	*This is just a fact.*
approximately 75% of these households fast-forward over at least one commercial per 30-minute program.	S A B C D E Ⓒ TV comm < cost eff now AE: 10m hh = DVR 75% FF comms (#)	*Another fact. I don't think I need to write down the exact numerical details right now, but I'll note that there are more numerical details just to remind myself.*
Because television commercials are not as widely watched as they used to be, they are much less cost-effective today.	S A B C D E Ⓒ TV comm < cost eff now b/c ppl watch < AE: 10m hh = DVR 75% FF comms (#)	*This repeats the conclusion I already know from the Q stem, with a little more info.*

Step 3: State the Goal.

Okay, the AE claims that TV comms are not as cost-effective specifically because people aren't watching them as much, and that is specifically because most people fast-forward over at least some commercials. What assumptions are being made?

Let's see. They're assuming that people really did watch TV commercials more, but they don't provide any evidence of that. Maybe people used to tape programs on VCRs and then still fast-forward. They haven't actually told us what people used to do before these DVRs came along.

I want an answer that will make the claim a little more likely to be valid.

<u>Step 4: Work from wrong to right.</u>

(A) Product placement within television programs is a viable alternative to traditional television commercials.	S A̶ B C D E ©TV comm < cost eff now b/c ppl watch < AE: 10m hh = DVR 75% FF comms (#)	*That's nice for the advertisers who want to make money, but it's not talking about how to do so by NOT using commercials, so that can't affect the conclusion about whether TV commercials are less cost-effective now.*
(B) The television programs preferred by consumers without digital video recorders are similar to those preferred by consumers with the devices.	S A̶ B̶ C D E ©TV comm < cost eff now b/c ppl watch < AE: 10m hh = DVR 75% FF comms (#)	*Hmm. The DVR thing was used as evidence to show how some people are skipping commercials. I don't think making a distinction about people with or without the DVRs watch really tells us anything. The conclusion is about commercials, not what programs people watch.*
(C) Prior to the advent of digital video recorders, very few television viewers switched channels or left the room when commercials began.	S A̶ B̶ C D E S ©TV comm < cost eff now b/c ppl watch < AE: 10m hh = DVR 75% FF comms (#)	*That's interesting. This is about what people used to do before DVRs. Oh, look—I didn't think of that, but they mention two other ways that people could skip commercials: changing the channel or leaving the room. And this answer says that people really didn't used to do that, so maybe they really were watching more TV commercials!*
(D) The cost-effectiveness of television advertising is based less upon how many people watch a particular commercial and more upon the appropriateness of the demographic.	S A̶ B̶ C D̶ E S W ©TV comm < cost eff now b/c ppl watch < AE: 10m hh = DVR 75% FF comms (#)	*Hmm. They're saying that we should be using a different metric to evaluate cost-effectiveness, not how many people watch. Yeah, that sounds convincing. Wait! My goal is to find something that makes the argument MORE likely to be valid. If anything, this would weaken the argument; this is a Reverse Logic trap!*
(E) Many companies find it difficult to determine the exact return on investment for television commercials.	S A̶ B̶ ©D̶ E̶ S W W ©TV comm < cost eff now b/c ppl watch < AE: 10m hh = DVR 75% FF comms (#)	*A lot of companies can't tell how much money they earn from people watching TV commercials. But maybe they can still tell something about the relative differences between a few years ago and now. Also, if this were actually true, if anything, the conclusion would be a little less valid, because that would mean we couldn't tell that the TV commercials are less cost-effective today.*

2. Smithtown Theatre: The correct answer is **D**.

Step 1: Identify the question.

Which of the following, if true, would most seriously weaken the argument?	W A B C D E	The words "if true" and "weaken" tell me that this is a Weaken question.

Step 2: Deconstruct the argument.

The Smithtown Theatre, which stages old plays, has announced an expansion that will double its capacity along with its operating costs.	W A B C D E ST: exp to ↑↑ cap & cost	They have a plan. It's future, so it could be the conclusion, but I'm guessing there'll be more of a claim like "The ST will (or will not) be successful with its plan" or something like that.
The theatre is only slightly profitable at present.	W A B C D E ST: exp to ↑↑ cap & cost Now: barely prof	This is a fact. I wonder: if ST expands, will it get enough new business to continue covering costs?
In addition, all of the current customers live in Smithtown, and the population of the town is not expected to increase in the next several years.	W A B C D E ST: exp to ↑↑ cap & cost Now: barely prof, cust live in S, prob won't be more from S	The first half is a fact; the second half is a future predication. So far, the case for ST's new plan doesn't sound very good.
Thus, the expansion of the Smithtown Theatre will prove unprofitable.	W A B C D E ST: exp to ↑↑ cap & cost Now: barely prof, cust live in S, prob won't be more from S ⓒST exp unprof	Okay, here's the conclusion. The author thinks the plan will fail and provides some pieces of evidence to support that claim.

Step 3: State the Goal.

The ST has a plan to expand but the author claims that the plan will fail because the ST is only barely profitable right now and it doesn't seem like there are a lot more opportunities to get new customers.

I want something that will weaken the author's claim. I have to be careful here: weaken the idea that the plan will fail. I'm not weakening the plan itself—in fact, weakening the author's claim might mean strengthening the idea that the plan will work!

Step 4: Work from wrong to right.

(A) A large movie chain plans to open a new multiplex location in Smithtown later this year.	W $\underset{S}{\cancel{A}}$ B C D E ST: exp to ↑↑ cap & cost Now: barely prof, cust live in S, prob won't be more from S ©ST exp unprof	*I don't think what another business does will matter. If anything, you'd have to say that the new movie theatre would take business from ST, which would strengthen the author's claim that ST will fail.*
(B) Concession sales in the Smithtown Theatre comprise a substantial proportion of the theatre's revenues.	W $\underset{S}{\cancel{A}}$ $\underset{n}{\cancel{B}}$ C D E ST: exp to ↑↑ cap & cost Now: barely prof, cust live in S, prob won't be more from S ©ST exp unprof	*How would this change if ST expanded? That still depends upon whether they can get more people to come to the theatre, so this doesn't really tell me anything new.*
(C) Many recent arrivals to Smithtown are students that are less likely to attend the Smithtown Theatre than are older residents.	W $\underset{S}{\cancel{A}}$ $\underset{n}{\cancel{B}}$ $\underset{S}{\cancel{C}}$ D E ST: exp to ↑↑ cap & cost Now: barely prof, cust live in S, prob won't be more from S ©ST exp unprof	*So the new people moving to town are people who aren't likely to start going to ST. That strengthens the author's claim that ST's expansion is going to fail. Reverse Logic trap!*
(D) The expansion would allow the Smithtown Theatre to stage larger, more popular shows that will attract patrons from neighboring towns.	W $\underset{S}{\cancel{A}}$ $\underset{n}{\cancel{B}}$ $\underset{S}{\cancel{C}}$ $\underset{W}{\cancel{D}}$ E ST: exp to ↑↑ cap & cost Now: barely prof, cust live in S, prob won't be more from S ©ST exp unprof	*Hmm. This basically means that the expansion would attract a greater audience—that helps! If they have more people, they can fill the larger theatre and make more money. This one is looking good.*
(E) The Board of the Smithtown Theatre often solicits input from residents of the town when choosing which shows to stage.	W $\underset{S}{\cancel{A}}$ $\underset{n}{\cancel{B}}$ $\underset{S}{\cancel{C}}$ $\underset{W}{\cancel{D}}$ $\underset{\approx}{\cancel{E}}$ ST: exp to ↑↑ cap & cost Now: barely prof, cust live in S, prob won't be more from S ©ST exp unprof	*This is how they do things now. Would it stay the same, or change when they expand? I have no idea. This doesn't tell me that some new thing will happen that might make it more likely for the plan to succeed; it just talks about how things are already done.*

3. Books and Coffee: The correct answer is **D**.

Step 1: Identify the question.

Which of the following, if true, most weakens the owners' conclusion that a merger will increase revenue?	W A B C D E ©merger → ↑ rev	*The words "if true" and "weakens" tell me that this is a Weaken question. Further, I now know the conclusion: some merger will result in increased revenue.*

Step 2: Deconstruct the argument.

The owners of a book store and a nearby coffee shop have decided to combine their businesses.	W A B C D E ©merger → ↑ rev (B+C)	*This is a fact; they have already made this decision, although it sounds like they haven't actually merged yet.*
Both owners believe that this merger will increase the number of customers and therefore the gross revenue,	W A B C D E ©merger → ↑ rev (B+C)	*Here's the conclusion. This is the same thing the Q stem said: the merger will increase revenue.*
because customers who come for one reason may also decide to purchase something else.	W A B C D E ©B+C merger → ↑ cust → ↑ rev Cust of each will buy >	*Okay, so I need to rewrite because they just inserted another step in the middle. The individual customers of each store will end up buying both books and coffee, so there'll be more customers for both, which means more revenue for both. That's assuming, of course, that these customers weren't already going to both stores to buy stuff.*

Step 3: State the Goal.

The owners think that merging will lead to increased revenue because it'll increase the number of customers and the customers will buy more stuff. This assumes that the same customers weren't already going to both stores and buying stuff.

This is a Weaken question so I need to find something that will make the conclusion less likely to be valid.

Step 4: Work from wrong to right.

(A) Books and drinks can both be considered impulse purchases; often, they are purchased by customers without forethought.	W $\quad$ A B C D E $\quad\quad$ S $\quad$ ©B+C merger → ↑ cust → ↑ rev $\quad$ Cust of each will buy >	This could be a reason why people would buy more. If they normally just buy coffee but see a book they like, maybe they'll be more likely to buy. That would strengthen the plan to merge, but I want to weaken the plan. Reverse Logic trap!
(B) B Profit margins at a coffee shop are generally significantly higher than profit margins at a book store.	W $\quad$ A B C D E $\quad\quad$ S $\quad$ n $\quad$ ©B+C merger → ↑ cust → ↑ rev $\quad$ Cust of each will buy >	That might make the coffee shop owner not want to merge, but it doesn't address the revenue side of the equation at all—and the conclusion has to do with revenues, not profits.
(C) People who are able to read the first chapter of a book before buying are more likely to decide to buy the book.	W $\quad$ A B C D E $\quad\quad$ S $\quad$ n $\quad$ S $\quad$ ©B+C merger → ↑ cust → ↑ rev $\quad$ Cust of each will buy >	This helps the owners' argument again! If I can sit there and read while having my coffee, then I'm more likely to buy the book, which would increase revenues.
(D) A large majority of the book store's current customer base already frequents the coffee shop.	W $\quad$ A B C D E $\quad\quad$ S $\quad$ n $\quad$ S $\quad$ W $\quad$ ©B+C merger → ↑ cust → ↑ rev $\quad$ Cust of each will buy >	Let's see. Most of the people who shop at the book store also already go to the coffee shop. That's not so good for the owner's plan—it means that they're not going to pick up as many new customers as we might have thought before.
(E) A combination book store and coffee shop that opened in a neighboring city last year has already earned higher than expected profits.	W $\quad$ A B C D E $\quad\quad$ S $\quad$ n $\quad$ S $\quad$ W $\quad$ n $\quad$ ©B+C merger → ↑ cust → ↑ rev $\quad$ Cust of each will buy >	Two problems here. One, we're not talking about the same book store and coffee shop. Two, this choice talks about profits, not revenues.

4. Digital Coupons: The correct answer is **B**.

Step 1: Identify the question.

Which of the following, if true, does the most to support the claim that the digital divide is responsible for the lower usage of electronic coupons?	S $\quad$ A B C D E $\quad\quad$ ©DD → ↓ use e-coup	The language "if true" and "support the claim" tell me that this is a Strengthen question. The question also indicates the conclusion: something called the "digital divide" causes electronic coupons not to be used as much.

MANHATTAN
GMAT

Step 2: Deconstruct the argument.

The redemption rate for e-mailed coupons is far lower than that for traditionally distributed paper coupons.	S A B C D E ©DD → ↓ use e-coup e-C ↓↓ use than PC	*This is a fact. For some reason, e-mailed coupons don't get used as much as paper coupons.*
One factor is the "digital divide"—those who might benefit the most from using coupons, such as homemakers, the elderly, and those in low-income households, often do not have the knowledge or equipment necessary to go online and receive coupons.	S A B C D E ©DD → ↓ use e-coup e-C ↓↓ use than PC DD: ppl who use Cs can't get them online	*Okay, so the people who would typically use Cs are less likely to be able to get them electronically—they have to use the paper Cs instead. This doesn't really articulate the conclusion that well—the question stem did, so I'm going to add something here*

Step 3: State the Goal.

The author claims that the "digital divide" (DD) causes lower use of the e-coupons because people who use coupons aren't as likely to have access to e-coupons.

I need to find something that makes this a little more likely to be true.

Step 4: Work from wrong to right.

(A) Computers are available for free in libraries, schools, and community centers.	S A̶ B C D E W ©DD → ↓ use e-coup e-C ↓↓ use than PC DD: ppl who use Cs can't get them online	*If this is true, then people who don't have computers can still use them. Maybe they could even take classes to learn how to use them! If anything, this weakens the author's claim.*
(B) The redemption rate of ordinary coupons is particularly high among elderly and low income people that do not know how to use computers.	S A̶ B C D E W S ©DD → ↓ use e-coup e-C ↓↓ use than PC DD: ppl who use Cs can't get them online	*At first glance, I thought, "This is just saying what the argument already said, which is weird because usually they don't do that." Then I realized that there was a gap in the argument! The argument only says that these people without computers are the ones who would "benefit the most" from coupons, but it doesn't say that these people actually do use coupons more. This choice tells me that; this strengthens the conclusion.*

(C) Many homes, including those of elderly and low income people, do not have high-speed internet connections.	S　　A̶ B Ȩ D E 　　　　W S n ©DD → ↓ use e-coup e-C ↓↓ use than PC DD: ppl who use Cs can't get them online	The argument doesn't say that people have to have high-speed connections in order to get coupons. The issue was whether these groups had internet access at all, not how fast the internet access is.
(D) More homemakers than elderly people would use computers if they had access to them.	S　　A̶ B Ȩ D̶ E 　　　　W S n n ©DD → ↓ use e-coup e-C ↓↓ use than PC DD: ppl who use Cs can't get them online	The argument doesn't make any distinction between homemakers and the elderly; rather, they're both equally part of the group of people without easy access to the internet. This is irrelevant.
(E) The redemption rate for coupons found on the internet has risen in the last five years.	S　　A̶Ⓑ Ȩ D̶ E̶ 　　　W S n n n ©DD → ↓ use e-coup e-C ↓↓ use than PC DD: ppl who use Cs can't get them online	This means that more people are using electronic coupons today, but the argument doesn't claim that people aren't. Instead, it talks about the fact that paper coupons are still in wider use because some people find it harder to access the electronic coupons. This answer does nothing to affect the conclusion.

5. Teacher Compensation: The correct answer is **E**.

Step 1: Identify the question.

Which of the following, if true, most weakens the argument of the educational experts?	W　　A B C D E	The language "if true" and "weakens" tells me this is a Weaken question. In addition, the question tells me that I need to look for a reference to "educational experts" because whatever they claim is the conclusion.

Step 2: Deconstruct the argument.

Traditionally, public school instructors have been compensated according to seniority.	W　　A B C D E Old: PST comp by sen.	Fact. Teachers were getting paid based upon how long they've worked.
Recently, educational experts have criticized the system as one that rewards lackadaisical teaching and reduces motivation to excel.	W　　A B C D E Old: PST comp by sen. EE: ↓ motiv	I guess the EEs are implying that teachers don't have to feel motivated to work hard because they know they'll make more money regardless.

| Instead, these experts argue that, to retain exceptional teachers and maintain quality instruction, teachers should receive salaries or bonuses based on performance rather than seniority. | W   A B C D E

Old: PST comp by sen.

EE: ↓ motiv

ⒸEE: base comp on perf →
keep good Ts, good instr. | So the EEs want to base compensation on performance, and they claim this will lead to better teachers and instruction. |

Step 3: State the Goal.

Teachers normally get paid based on seniority, but the EEs want them to be paid based on performance because they say that the teachers will then be better.

I need to find something that weakens this plan at least a little bit.

Step 4: Work from wrong to right.

(A) Some teachers express that financial compensation is not the only factor contributing to job satisfaction and teaching performance.	W A̶ B C D E n Old: PST comp by sen. EE: ↓ motiv ⒸEE: base comp on perf → keep good Ts, good instr.	So maybe we should also consider other ways to reward good teachers too, but as long as financial compensation is a factor, then tying compensation to performance might be a good plan. According to this answer, financial compensation is a factor (though not the only one).
(B) School districts will develop their own unique compensation structures that may differ greatly from those of other school districts.	W A̶ B̶ C D E n n Old: PST comp by sen. EE: ↓ motiv ⒸEE: base comp on perf → keep good Ts, good instr.	The argument isn't claiming that every school district has to be identical. It just makes a recommendation that compensation be tied to performance in general.
(C) Upon leaving the teaching profession, many young, effective teachers cite a lack of opportunity for more rapid financial advancement as a primary factor in the decision to change careers.	W A̶ B̶ C̶ D E n n S Old: PST comp by sen. EE: ↓ motiv ⒸEE: base comp on perf → keep good Ts, good instr.	If anything, I think this would strengthen the EEs claim! It shows that teachers do care about the financial side of things and causes some good teachers to leave the profession at a young age.

| (D) In school districts that have implemented pay for performance compensation structures, standardized test scores have dramatically increased. | W   A̶ B C̶ D̶ E
      n   n   S   S
Old: PST comp by sen.

EE: ↓ motiv

Ⓒ EE: base comp on perf → keep good Ts, good instr. | *Again, if anything, this makes the EEs' plan sound better. Students in the school districts that have already followed the EEs' recommendation are doing better on tests!* |
| (E) A merit-based system that bases compensation on teacher performance reduces collaboration, which is an integral component of quality instruction. | W   A̶ B C̶ D̶ Ⓔ
      n   n   S   S   W
Old: PST comp by sen.

EE: ↓ motiv

Ⓒ EE: base comp on perf → kccp good Ts, good instr. | *The EE plan has a drawback: it reduces something that is considered an "integral component" of good teaching. If that's true, it could hurt the idea that basing compensation on performance will result in maintaining good instruction.* |

6. The Gold Standard: The correct answer is **C**.

Step 1: Identify the question.

| Which of the following, if it occurred, would cast the most serious doubt on the claim that The Gold Standard sneaker will be profitable ? | W   A B C D E
Ⓒ TGS will be prof | *This one is a little unusual. Instead of "if true," it says "if it occurred"—but that's a synonym of "if true." This language, in addition to "serious doubt," indicates that this is a Weaken question. Further, the claim is that TGS will be profitable.* |

Step 2: Deconstruct the argument.

| Brand X designs and builds custom sneakers, one sneaker at a time. | W   A B C D E
Ⓒ TGS will be prof | *This is just a fact. I'm not even sure I need to write it down—it's just telling me what kind of company Brand X is.* |
| It recently announced plans to sell "The Gold Standard," a sneaker that will cost five times more to manufacture than any other sneaker that has ever been created. | W   A B C D E
Ⓒ TGS will be prof

will sell TGS, 5x more to make | *It costs five times as much to make? Wow. And yet the claim is that they'll be profitable. There are a LOT of assumptions going on here.* |

Step 3: State the Goal.

The claim is that TGS will be profitable and the only piece of "evidence" says that the sneakers are ridiculously expensive to make. So there's no real evidence to support the idea that these will be profitable! Profitability is based on revenues minus costs, so the author is assuming that they can sell the sneakers for even more than it costs to make them.

I'm looking for an answer that makes the conclusion less likely to be true.

Step 4: Work from wrong to right.

(A) The endorsement of The Gold Standard by a popular celebrity	W A B C D E S ⓒTGS will be prof will sell TGS, 5x more to make	*Endorsements usually help companies sell more of a product, so this would help the claim that TGS will be profitable. Reverse logic!*
(B) The publication of a report indicating that all previous sneaker lines launched by Brand X have been profitable	W A B C D E S S ⓒTGS will be prof will sell TGS, 5x more to make	*Really, I think this has nothing to do with the given conclusion; there's no reason why TGS must be profitable just because other Brand X sneakers were profitable—especially because TGS sneakers cost so much to make. If anything, this answer makes it more likely that TGS will be profitable, too.*
(C) A significant increase in the cost of the canvas used to construct The Gold Standard	W A B C D E S S W ⓒTGS will be prof will sell TGS, 5x more to make	*Let's imagine that TGS is profitable when the costs are five times higher. This choice is saying that the costs are going to go up <u>even more</u>. Profits equal revenues minus costs, so increasing the per-product cost makes it less likely that the product can be profitable.*
(D) The introduction of another new sneaker line by a rival manufacturer	W A B C D E S S W n ⓒTGS will be prof will sell TGS, 5x more to make	*This one is so tempting! If another sneaker becomes popular, perhaps the sales of TGS will drop. That doesn't necessarily affect whether TGS will be profitable, though. Again, profits equal revenues minus costs. But if you make fewer sneakers, then costs will go down as well—so it's not necessarily the case that reducing revenues will also impact the level of profitability.*

| (E) An announcement by Brand X that The Gold Standard will be marketed as an exclusive offering, available only in limited quantities | W   A B Ⓒ D E
       S S W n n
Ⓒ TGS will be prof

will sell TGS, 5x more to make | *This doesn't seem to tell me much one way or the other. If anything, I think you could speculate that an "exclusive" product could sell for a premium price, so maybe that would make it more likely that TGS will be profitable.* |

7. Machu Picchu: The correct answer is **A**.

Step 1: Identify the question.

| Which of the following, if true, most strengthens the argument above ? | S   A B C D E | *The words "if true" and "strengthens the argument" indicate that this is a Strengthen question.* |

Step 2: Deconstruct the argument.

In 2001 the Peruvian government began requiring tourists to buy permits to hike the Inca Trail to the ancient city of Machu Picchu.	S A B C D E 01 PG: perm to hike IT	*This is a fact. People now have to pay to hike the Inca Trail.*
Only 500 people per day are now allowed to hike the Inca Trail, whereas before 2001 daily visitors numbered in the thousands.	S A B C D E 01 PG: perm to hike IT now: 500 ppl / d (old = 000's)	*More facts. Now, only 500 people a day can go; before, there were thousands a day.*
The Peruvian government claims that this permit program has successfully prevented deterioration of archaeological treasures along the Inca Trail.	S A B C D E 01 PG: perm to hike IT now: 500 ppl / d (old = 000's) Ⓒ PG: perm → ↓ deter of IT	*Here's the claim: the PG specifically says that the permit program is responsible for preventing deterioration.*

Step 3: State the Goal.

The PG claims that its permit program has been responsible for preventing deterioration along the IT. The only thing we know about the permit program is that it has reduced the number of people who can visit the IT. So the government is assuming that reducing the number of visitors was the cause, and that if the permit program hadn't been in place, then there would have been deterioration.

I need to find something that makes this a little more likely to be valid.

Step 4: Work from wrong to right.

(A) Since 2001, Incan ruins similar to Machu Picchu but without a visitor limit have disintegrated at a significantly greater rate than those on the Inca Trail.	S ~~A~~ B C D E S 01 PG: perm to hike IT now: 500 ppl / d (old = 000's) Ⓒ PG: perm → ↓ deter of IT	This sounds promising. The government's assumption was that the visitor limit helped prevent deterioration, so showing that other sites without limits did experience deterioration would make it more likely that the government's reasoning is valid. I'll definitely keep this one in.
(B) Villages near Machu Picchu have experienced declines in income, as fewer tourists buy fewer craft goods and refreshments.	S ~~A~~ ~~B~~ C D E S n 01 PG: perm to hike IT now: 500 ppl / d (old = 000's) Ⓒ PG: perm → ↓ deter of IT	This sounds bad for the villages, but it doesn't impact the specific claim about preventing deterioration along the IT.
(C) Many of the funds from the sale of Inca Trail permits are used to hire guards for archaeological sites without permit programs.	S ~~A~~ ~~B~~ ~~C~~ D E S n n 01 PG: perm to hike IT now: 500 ppl / d (old = 000's) Ⓒ PG: perm → ↓ deter of IT	This sounds like a good use of funds, but it has nothing to do with whether the permit program really did help prevent deterioration. All this tells us is that maybe _other_ sites are also better protected due to the guards.
(D) Since 2001, tourist guides along the Inca Trail have received 50% to 100% increases in take-home pay.	S ~~A~~ ~~B~~ ~~C~~ ~~D~~ E S n n n 01 PG: perm to hike IT now: 500 ppl / d (old = 000's) Ⓒ PG: perm → ↓ deter of IT	That's great for the guides. It doesn't impact the actual conclusion at all, though.
(E) The total number of tourists in Peru has risen substantially since 2001, even as the number of tourists hiking the Inca Trail has remained constant.	S Ⓐ ~~B~~ ~~C~~ ~~D~~ ~~E~~ S n n n 01 PG: perm to hike IT now: 500 ppl / d (old = 000's) Ⓒ PG: perm → ↓ deter of IT	This one's about the number of visitors again, so maybe it strengthens. Let's see. A lot more people are visiting Peru... oh, but the second part is what we were already told: visitors to the IT are limited. This doesn't add anything new that specifically affects the claim about deterioration along the IT.

8. Ethanol: The correct answer is **B**.

Did this one seem a little different from all of the others? We set a trap for you! This is an Evaluate question, not a Strengthen or a Weaken. We discussed Evaluate questions in the previous chapter. (And we did warn you at the beginning of this chapter to read the last chapter first!)

On the real test, you'll never have the luxury of knowing that the next question will be a certain type—so be prepared for _anything._

Step 1: Identify the question.

In evaluating the recommen-dation to increase the use of ethanol, it would be important to research all of the following EXCEPT :	Ev Ex A B C D E	The word "evaluating" (the conclusion) tells me that this is an Evaluate question. It's also an Except question. The four wrong ones WILL be important to evaluate; the correct answer will NOT be important to evaluate. The conclusion will have something to do with using ethanol.

Step 2: Deconstruct the argument.

Ethanol, a fuel derived from corn, can be used alone to pow-er cars or along with gasoline to reduce the reduce the amount of gas consumed.	Ev Ex A B C D E E: fuel, use alone or w/gas ↓ use of FF	All facts. This E stuff is a kind of fuel, and it can be used in cars, either alone or with gas.
Unlike gasoline, ethanol is easily renewable since it is primarily converted from the sun's energy.	Ev Ex A B C D E E: fuel, use alone or w/gas ↓ use of FF easy to get > E	Interesting. It's easier to get more ethanol than more gasoline.
Moreover, compared with con-ventional gasoline, pure ethanol is a cleaner-burning fuel.	Ev Ex A B C D E E: fuel, use alone or w/gas ↓ use of FF easy to get > E, clean burn	And ethanol is "cleaner-burning." This E stuff sounds pretty good so far.
To save energy and reduce pollu-tion, many individuals advocate the increased usage of ethanol as a primary fuel source in conjunction with or in place of gasoline.	Ev Ex A B C D E E: fuel, use alone or w/gas ↓ use of FF easy to get > E, clean burn ⓒ use E → save NRG, ↓ poll	Conclusion! People think that us-ing E will save NRG and reduce pollution. (Note: NRG is an ab-breviation for energy.)

Step 3: State the Goal.

The E fuel has various good qualities, so people say we should use it and we'll save energy and reduce pollu-tion.

On regular Evaluate questions, we try to find an answer that will tell us _whether_ the conclusion is more or less valid. The answer can take us down two "paths," one of which will make the conclusion a bit better and *the other of which will make it a bit worse. On this EXCEPT question, all four wrong answers will do this. I'm looking for the "odd one out" that does NOT do this.*

Step 4: Work from wrong to right.

(A) Whether the energy required to grow and process corn used as fuel is greater than the amount of energy ultimately produced	Ev Ex ~~A~~ B C D E E: fuel, use alone or w/gas ↓ use of FF easy to get > E, clean burn ⓒuse E → save NRG, ↓ poll	*The conclusion specifically claims that we'll <u>save</u> energy. If the amount of energy to produce ethanol is MORE than the amount of energy produced, then we aren't saving energy. If the amount of energy to produce ethanol is LESS than the amount of energy produced, then we are saving energy. This answer gives me "two paths" so it's wrong (since I want the EXCEPT answer).*
(B) Whether more energy is saved when using ethanol in conjunction with or in place of gasoline	Ev Ex ~~A~~ B C D E E: fuel, use alone or w/gas ↓ usc of FF easy to get > E, clean burn ⓒuse E → save NRG, ↓ poll	*This answer choice uses many of the same words as the conclusion. But that's a trap! The conclusion makes no distinction between these two methods of using ethanol; it just recommends in general that we do use ethanol. If more energy is saved using ethanol in conjunction with gasoline, then the conclusion holds. If more energy is saved using ethanol in place of gasoline, then the conclusion holds. Either way, it's the same thing! There aren't "two paths" here.*
(C) Whether ethanol is as efficient a fuel as gasoline	Ev Ex ~~A~~ B ~~C~~ D E E: fuel, use alone or w/gas ↓ use of FF easy to get > E, clean burn ⓒuse E → save NRG, ↓ poll	*If ethanol is as efficient as or more efficient than gasoline, then we could use less ethanol to get the same amount of power. That would save energy, making the conclusion a bit stronger. If ethanol is less efficient than gas, then we would have to use more ethanol to get the same amount of power. That might mean it takes more energy for the car to go the same distance, making the conclusion weaker. We have "two paths" here.*
(D) Whether it is possible to produce more ethanol than is currently produced	Ev Ex ~~A~~ B ~~C~~ ~~D~~ E E: fuel, use alone or w/gas ↓ use of FF easy to get > E, clean burn ⓒuse E → save NRG, ↓ poll	*The conclusion says we should "increase" the usage of ethanol. But is more ethanol available to use? If we can produce more ethanol, then that makes the argument a bit stronger. If we cannot produce any more ethanol, then how can we increase the usage? That would make the argument weaker.*

P

| (E) Whether the process of growing corn for fuel would result in as much pollution as does the production of conventional gasoline | Ev Ex   A ⓑ C̶ D̶ E̶

E: fuel, use alone or w/gas

↓ use of FF

easy to get > E, clean burn

ⓒ use E → save NRG, ↓ poll | *The conclusion claims that using ethanol will reduce pollution, but the argument tells us only that ethanol burns more cleanly than gas. If the process of making ethanol results in less pollution, this would be another point in favor of the conclusion. If the process of making ethanol results in <u>more</u> pollution than does the production of gasoline, however, then this would weaken the conclusion.* |

9. APR: The correct answer is E.

Step 1: Identify the question.

| Which of the following statements, if true, would most seriously undermine a plan to increase interest rates in order to spur profitable growth? | W   A B C D E

ⓒ ↑ int rate → ↑ prof growth | *The "if true" and "undermine" language indicate that this is a Weaken question. Further, the question stem tells me the conclusion: there's a plan to increase interest rates and that is then supposed to cause profits to grow.* |

Step 2: Deconstruct the argument.

| CEO: Over the past several years, we have more than doubled our revenues but profits have steadily declined because an increasing number of customers have failed to pay their balances. | W   A B C D E

ⓒ ↑ int rate → ↑ prof growth

C: 2x rev but ↓ prof b/c cust not pay bills | *Several facts here. Revenues have gone up but profits have gone down because the customers aren't paying what they owe.* |
| In order to compensate for these higher default rates, we will increase the interest charged on outstanding balances from an annual percentage rate (APR) of 9.5% to an APR of 12%. | W   A B C D E

ⓒ ↑ int rate → ↑ prof growth

C: 2x rev but ↓ prof b/c cust not pay bills

↑ % to comp | *Okay, here's the plan. They'll charge more interest to everyone to compensate for the people who aren't paying their bills.* |

| This increase will be sufficient to compensate for the current rate of defaults and allow us to increase our profits. | W   A B C D E
ⓒ ↑ int rate → ↑ prof growth

C: 2x rev but ↓ prof b/c cust not pay bills

↑ % to comp; 12% is suff for <u>now</u> default | *Hmm. They're claiming that 12% will be enough to compensate for the <u>current</u> rate of people who don't pay so that they can increase profits (which is the conclusion I already wrote down). They're assuming that the current rate isn't going to get worse in future.* |

Step 3: State the Goal.

The company plans to charge higher interest rates in order to become profitable again. The evidence shows only that the higher interest rate will be sufficient for today's default rate; that could change over time.

This is a Weaken question so I need to find something that makes the CEO's conclusion a bit less likely to be valid.

Step 4: Work from wrong to right.

| (A) Many other companies have experienced a similar trend in their default rates. | W   A̶ B C D E
_n
ⓒ ↑ int rate → ↑ prof growth

C: 2x rev but ↓ prof b/c cust not pay bills

↑ % to comp; 12% is suff for <u>now</u> default | *This doesn't address the company's plan to <u>fix</u> the problem: increasing the interest rate. This doesn't impact the conclusion at all.* |
| (B) The company's operating expenses are above the industry average and can be substantially reduced, thus increasing profits. | W   A̶ B̶ C D E
_{n   n}
ⓒ ↑ int rate → ↑ prof growth

C: 2x rev but ↓ prof b/c cust not pay bills

↑ % to comp; 12% is suff for <u>now</u> default | *Hmm. If the company does this, it could increase profits, which is the company's goal… but the conclusion is that the plan to increase interest rates will improve profits, and this choice doesn't address that plan. Plus, if anything, this choice makes it more likely that the company will increase profits, but we want to weaken the conclusion.* |

(C) The increase in default rates was due to a rise in unemployment, but unemployment rates are expected to drop in the coming months.	W A̶ B̶ E̶ D E n n n Ⓒ ↑ int rate → ↑ prof growth C: 2x rev but ↓ prof b/c cust not pay bills ↑ % to comp; 12% is suff for <u>now</u> default	*If unemployment caused people not to pay their bills, and fewer people are going to be unemployed, then maybe more will pay their bills? That would help the company, but we want something that will weaken the conclusion. And the conclusion is specifically about the plan. This choice doesn't address the specific plan about interest rates.*
(D) The proposed increase in the APR will, alone, more than double the company's profit margins.	W A̶ B̶ E̶ D̶ E n n n S Ⓒ ↑ int rate → ↑ prof growth C: 2x rev but ↓ prof b/c cust not pay bills ↑ % to comp; 12% is suff for <u>now</u> default	*This supports the company's claim that increasing the interest rate will help raise profits. I want something that weakens that claim.*
(E) An increase in the APR charged on credit card balances often results in higher rates of default.	W A̶ B̶ E̶ D̶ Ⓔ n n n S W Ⓒ ↑ int rate → ↑ prof growth C: 2x rev but ↓ prof b/c cust not pay bills ↑ % to comp; 12% is suff for <u>now</u> default	*Okay, if they do increase the APR, then more people may stop paying their bills as a result! The conclusion specifically said that raising the APR would compensate for the "current rate of defaults," so if the rate goes up, then the company is less likely to increase its profits. This does weaken the conclusion.*

10. Jupiter vs. Mars: The correct answer is **D**.

<u>Step 1: Identify the question.</u>

Which of the following, if true, would most strengthen a contention by the government that the new project is a better use of its funds?	S A B C D E Ⓒ G: new proj = better	*The words "if true" and "strengthen a contention" indicate that this is a Strengthen question. Further, the question stem tells me the conclusion: the government claims that the new project is a better use of funds.*

Step 2: Deconstruct the argument.

Scientists suspect that Europa, a moon orbiting Jupiter, may contain living organisms.	S A B C D E ⓒG: new proj = better S: E may have life	*There is a fact: scientists suspect something is true. We don't actually know whether it's true, though.*
However, the government recently scrapped an unmanned science mission to Europa and replaced it with a project aimed at landing an astronaut on Mars.	S A B C D E ⓒG: new proj = better S: E may have life cncl E project, rplc w/M project	*There was a project to send an unmanned mission to E, but that was replaced by another project to send a person to Mars. More facts.*
Polls show that the public is far more fascinated by space travel than by discovering life elsewhere in the universe.	S A B C D E ⓒG: new proj = better S: E may have life cncl E project, rplc w/M project ppl like spc trvl >	*More facts—a survey showed that people like space travel more.*
Critics argue that the government's decision-making process places a greater emphasis on popularity than it does on the importance of scientific research.	S A B C D E ⓒG: new proj = better S: E may have life cncl E project, rplc w/M project ppl like spc trvl C: govt cares popul > rsrch	*This is a counter-conclusion. The critics say that the government is just paying attention to popularity of projects, but the question stem told me that the government claims that the new project is a better use of funds.*

Step 3: State the Goal.

There are two opposing points of view, the government and the critics. The government claims that the new project is a better use of funds. The critics claim that the government is paying more attention to popularity than to scientific research. The critics are assuming that, just because the public finds the Mars project more interesting, there aren't also good scientific reasons for replacing the Europa project with the Mars project.

I need to strengthen the government's claim. I need to be really careful that I don't mistakenly strengthen the critics' claim.

Step 4: Work from wrong to right.

(A) In the first year of the project, the government will spend 30% of its total budget on developing a space shuttle that can travel to Mars; that figure is expected to drop to 0% after five years.	S Ⱥ B C D E 　　n Ⓒ G: new proj = better S: E may have life cncl E project, rplc w/M project ppl like spc trvl C: govt cares popul > rsrch	*This doesn't give us any additional information as to why the Mars project is better than the Europa project. We don't know whether they'd be spending more or less on the E project, nor do we know what kind of good research they'll expect to get in return.*
(B) The government cannot be absolutely certain of the chances for success of either project.	S Ⱥ Ƀ C D E 　　n n Ⓒ G: new proj = better S: E may have life cncl E project, rplc w/M project ppl like spc trvl C: govt cares popul > rsrch	*Was there anything in the argument that hinged on being absolutely certain of success? No. If they told us that the Mars project has a greater chance for success, that would be good—but knowing that we <u>don't</u> know the chances for either project… that doesn't add anything.*
(C) Some scientists are convinced that a mission to Europa would add immeasurably to our understanding of the universe.	S Ⱥ Ƀ Ҽ D E 　　n n W Ⓒ G: new proj = better S: E may have life cncl E project, rplc w/M project ppl like spc trvl C: govt cares popul > rsrch	*This is a good reason to continue funding the mission to E. But that would support the critics, not the government. This is a trap.*
(D) A new telescope that has just become available to scientists promises to yield more information than the planned mission to Europa was designed to provide.	S Ⱥ Ƀ Ҽ D E 　　n n W S Ⓒ G: new proj = better S: E may have life cncl E project, rplc w/M project ppl like spc trvl C: govt cares popul > rsrch	*Now they have a new telescope that they can use to get even more research than they would have if they sent an unmanned mission? That's a good reason to cancel the unmanned mission. If that's true, then pretty much any other decent project would be a better use of funds!*

P

| (E) Most people feel that a shuttle to Mars is the next logical step in the development of a system that will allow humans to travel even further in the solar system. | S $\overset{A}{\underset{n}{}}$ $\overset{B}{\underset{n}{}}$ $\overset{\cancel{C}}{\underset{W}{}}$ $\overset{\boxed{D}}{\underset{S}{}}$ $\overset{E}{\underset{n}{}}$

 Ⓒ G: new proj = better

 S: E may have life

 cncl E project, rplc w/M project

 ppl like spc trvl

 C: govt cares popul > rsrch | *That's interesting, but it doesn't tell us anything <u>new</u> about why spending the money on the Mars project is better than spending money on the Europa project. We already know that people are more interested in space travel. This answer is a tangent that's trying to get us to think more about that and make us forget about the conclusion, which centered on a comparison of the two projects.* |

P

Chapter 6
of
Critical Reasoning

Evidence Family

In This Chapter...

Chapter 6:
Evidence Family

The Evidence Family of questions is our third main family. Here's a recap of what we discussed in Chapter 2:

- No Conclusions! These are made up entirely of premises
- No Assumptions either!
- Two main question types: Inference and Explain a Discrepancy

Inference questions require us to find an answer that *must be true* according to the premises given in the argument.

Explain a Discrepancy questions require us to identify some kind of paradox or puzzling result in an argument and find an answer that explains, or resolves, the puzzling part of the argument. Before we delve further into each type, let's talk about what inferences are in general.

What Are Inferences?

In order to answer inference questions accurately, we first need to understand what the GMAT test writers mean when they ask us to infer something. In the GMAT World, an inference is something that must be true according to the evidence given in the argument. In the Real World, by contrast, we don't think of inferences in this way; rather, in the Real World, inferences are *likely* to be true based on the available evidence, but they don't absolutely have to be true.

For example, if a friend tells you that chocolate is her favorite flavor of ice cream, what kind of real-world inferences might you make?

You might infer that she likes chocolate in general and that she likes ice cream in general. Maybe she likes all desserts in general—perhaps she has a sweet tooth. All of these things are perfectly reasonable to infer in a "likely to be true" situation, but not a single one has to be true. It's possible that she really likes chocolate only when it's in the form of ice cream, and she really likes ice cream only when it's chocolate. The kinds of answers discussed in this paragraph would be tempting *incorrect* answers on the GMAT.

What does have to be true? She can't like vanilla ice cream better than she likes chocolate ice cream—if chocolate is her *favorite* flavor of ice cream, then by definition she doesn't like any other flavor better. She has to have tried at least one other flavor of ice cream at some point in her life—she has to have had the ability to compare with at least one other flavor in order to decide that chocolate is her *favorite* flavor. These kinds of answers would be correct answers on the GMAT.

From now on, when we discuss how to infer something, we'll be referring to the GMAT's definition: something that must be true based on the available evidence.

Percentages vs. Real Numbers

Let's say that we're discussing a company that sells only vanilla and chocolate ice cream. We're told that 55% of the company's profits last year were derived from chocolate ice cream sales and 40% of the revenues last year were derived from vanilla ice cream sales. What can we infer?

Because we know that the company sells only these two products, we can figure out two additional numbers. If 55% of profits came from chocolate, then 45% of profits came from vanilla. If 40% of revenues came from vanilla, then 60% of revenues came from chocolate. These things must be true, but these inferences are probably too easy for any GMAT question. What else can we infer?

The company earned 60% of its revenues, but only 55% of its profits, from chocolate. By contrast, the company earned 40% of its revenues and a *higher* percentage of its profits, 45%, from vanilla. That's interesting. We made more money on vanilla than we would have expected based on the percentage of revenues, and we made less money on chocolate than we would have expected based on the revenues. *Profitability* is a measure of profits versus revenues. The vanilla ice cream product is more *profitable* than the chocolate ice cream product. That must be true.

What doesn't have to be true? It doesn't have to be true that vanilla will continue to be more profitable in the future. The trend might not continue in the future.

Let's say there are two ice cream companies, X and Y. Chocolate ice cream represents 60% of Company X's sales and 50% of Company Y's sales. Clearly, then, Company Y sells more chocolate ice cream, right?

Not necessarily. We have no information about real numbers here, only percentages, and we don't even know how those percentages relate to each other. What if company Y has $1 million in annual revenues and company X has only $10,000 in annual revenues? We can't conclude anything about actual dollar amounts from this information about percentages.

Inference Questions

Inference questions require us to find an answer that must be true according to the information in the argument. Most of the time, we will need to use only some of the information in the argument, though we may use all of it.

Most Inference question stems contain some form of the word "conclude" or some form of the word "infer," though there are some variations that don't include those specific words. Examples of words or phrases contained in Inference questions include:

- which answer can be " logically concluded" or the "statements above most strongly support which of the following conclusions"?
- which answer can be "properly inferred"?
- the statements above "best support" which of the following "assertions"?
- which answer "must be true" based upon the above statements?

Note that Inference question stems can contain the language "most strongly support." We also saw this language on Strengthen questions, so it is critical to ensure that we don't mix up the two question types.

The below diagram shows the "direction" of the support. On Inference questions, the argument (above) is used to support the correct answer (below). On Strengthen questions, the correct answer (below) is used to support the conclusion of the argument (above):

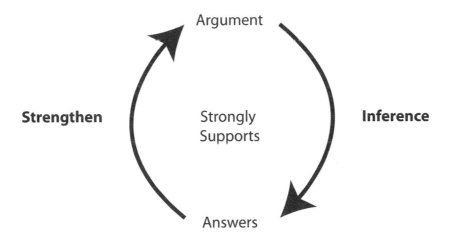

Inference questions ask us to **use the argument to support an answer** (the answer concludes something from the argument). By contrast, Strengthen questions ask us to **use an answer to support the argument** (strengthen the argument / conclusion). Strengthen questions will contain a conclusion in the argument or question stem; Inference arguments will <u>not</u> contain a conclusion in the argument or question stem.

Let's take a look at a short example.

> Both enrollment and total tuition revenue at Brownsville University have increased during each of the last four years. During the same period, enrollment at Canterbury University has steadily decreased, while total tuition revenue has remained constant.
>
> Which of the following hypotheses is best supported by the statement given?
>
> (A)   Brownsville University now collects more total tuition revenue than does Canterbury University.
> (B)   The per-student tuition at Canterbury University has risen over the last four years.
> (C)   Brownsville University will continue to increase its revenues as long as it continues to increase enrollment.

The question stem is one of the slightly different variations. It uses the word "hypotheses" instead of "conclusions," but it means the same thing: an inference question. Our core might look like this:

therefore

4 yrs:
BU: enrol, tuit ↑
CU: enrol ↓, tuit =

⟹

[what must be true?]

(premise)   (inference)

Note that, on all inference questions, the right-hand side of the core will always look like the above. We'll only be given premises.

Hmm. There are two schools but different trends are happening. BU's enrollment and tuition revenues are both going up. CU's enrollment is going down, but tuition revenues are the same.

This is an Inference question, so I have to find an answer that must be true according to my premises.

(A) Brownsville University now collects more total tuition revenue than does Canterbury University.	In A̶ B C 4 yrs: BU: enrol, tuit ↑ CU: enrol ↓, tuit =	*Things have certainly been looking up for BU lately, but I know absolutely nothing about the actual dollar values that the schools are collecting. It's entirely possible that CU still collects more money than BU.*

(B) The per-student tuition at Canterbury University has risen over the last four years.	In A̶ B C 4 yrs: BU: enrol, tuit ↑ CU: enrol ↓, tuit =	*Let's see. "Per-student tuition" = revenues / # of students. CU has the same revenues today, so the numerator stays the same, but fewer students, so the denominator gets smaller. Dividing by a smaller number = a larger number. This must be true! I'll check C, but I'm feeling good about this one.*
(C) Brownsville University will continue to increase its revenues as long as it continues to increase enrollment.	In A̶ Ⓑ E̶ 4 yrs: BU: enrol, tuit ↑ CU: enrol ↓, tuit =	*This might be reasonable to believe in the real world, but it doesn't have to be true. A trend never absolutely has to continue in the future.*

The argument provides us with several fact-based premises. (It is also possible to have premises that are somewhat more claim-based.) The correct answer is something that must be true based on those premises, though note that, in this case, we only needed to use the information about Canterbury in order to draw the correct conclusion. Answer B didn't use the Brownsville data at all.

Answer A tried to trap us by getting us to make a conclusion based on information we don't have (actual dollar values). Answer C is a classic "real-world inference" trap — it might be reasonable to believe that the trend will continue, but nothing says that a trend must continue in the future.

Let's try a full example; set your timer for 2 minutes:

> Curbing government spending has been demonstrated to raise the value of a country's currency over time. However, many economists no longer recommend this policy. A currency of lesser value causes a country's exports to be more competitive in the international market, encouraging domestic industries and making the economy more attractive to foreign investment.
>
> The statements above most strongly support which of the following inferences?
>
> (A) Limited government spending can also lead to a reduction in the national deficit.
> (B) Curbing government spending can make a country's exports less competitive.
> (C) Many economists now recommend higher levels of government spending.
> (D) An increase in the value of a currency will result in reduced government spending.
> (E) Competitive exports indicate a weak currency.

Step 1: Identify the question.

The statements above most strongly support which of the following inferences?	In A B C D E	*They're asking me to support something below (in the answers), and they use the word "inference." This is an Inference question.*

Step 2: Deconstruct the argument.

Curbing government spending has been demonstrated to raise the value of a country's currency over time.	In A B C D E ↓ gov sp → ↑ val curr	*This is a fact. Fairly straight-forward—one thing leads to another.*
However, many economists no longer recommend this policy.	In A B C D E ↓ gov sp → ↑ val curr BUT E don't rec	*Hmm. According to the first sentence, raising the value of currency sounds like a good thing, so why wouldn't the Es want us to do that?*
A currency of lesser value causes a country's exports to be more competitive in the international market, encouraging domestic industries and making the economy more attractive to foreign investment.	In A B C D E ↓ gov sp → ↑ val curr BUT E don't rec ↓ val curr → exp > comp → benefits	*Oh, okay, so there are some good reasons to have a lower currency value. I guess those economists think these benefits outweigh the lower value.*

Step 3: State the Goal.

Reducing government spending will increase currency value. It seems like it would be good to have a high currency value, but some Es say that we shouldn't do that, because there are other benefits involved in having a lower currency value.

I need to find an answer that must be true given the information in the argument. I don't need to use all of the info in the argument, though I may.

Step 4: Work from wrong to right.

(A) Limited government spending can also lead to a reduction in the national deficit.	In A̶ B C D E ↓ gov sp → ↑ val curr BUT E don't rec ↓ val curr → exp > comp → benefits	*Deficit? This might be reasonable to believe in the real world, but there was nothing about the deficit in the argument—I don't have any evidence to support this statement.*

MANHATTAN
GMAT

(B) Curbing government spending can make a country's exports less competitive.	In A B̲ C D E ↓ gov sp → ↑ val curr BUT E don't rec ↓ val curr → exp > comp → benefits	*Let's see. The author said that curbing spending leads to a higher currency value. And then the Es said that a lower currency value makes exports more competitive. If that's true, then a higher currency value could make exports less competitive… so, hey, it is actually the case that curbing spending might lead to less-competitive exports! Keep this one in.*
(C) Many economists now recommend higher levels of government spending.	In A B̲ C̶ D E ↓ gov sp → ↑ val curr BUT E don't rec ↓ val curr → exp > comp → benefits	*The argument says "many economists," and the answer says "many economists," so that part is okay. If you tell someone not to lower their spending, is that the same thing as telling them to increase their spending? No. You could also recommend spending the same amount. Tricky! This one isn't a "must be true" statement.*
(D) An increase in the value of a currency will result in reduced government spending.	In A B̲ C D E ↓ gov sp → ↑ val curr BUT E don't rec ↓ val curr → exp > comp → benefits	*This one feels similar to B—language pretty similar to the argument, and I have to figure out what leads to what. The author said that X (curbing spending) will lead to Y (a higher currency value). This answer reverses the direction: Y will lead to X. That's not what the author said!*
(E) Competitive exports indicate a weak currency.	In A B̲ C̶ D̶ E̲ ↓ gov sp → ↑ val curr BUT E don't rec ↓ val curr → exp > comp → benefits	*The Es said that M (a lower currency value) leads to N (more competitive exports). The answer reverses the direction but changes the description a bit: N indicates that M is true or has happened. If M leads to N, then isn't it the case that having N could indicate that M happened? Yes. Leave this one in.*

Now I need to compare B and E. I checked the logic on B and E, and they both seem good—in both cases, the causal direction could be true. Let me check the wording of the answers to make sure I'm reading them correctly. Oh, I see. B says that curbing spending "can make" exports less competitive, which is true, while E says that competitive exports "indicate" a weak currency. Answer E is missing the "can" or "could" part. It might be the case that competitive exports indicate a weak currency, but the argument never says that this is definitely the case.

The correct answer is B.

Common Trap Answers

The most tempting wrong answers on Inference questions tend to revolve around making Real World Inferences — things that we would reasonably assume to be true in the real world but don't absolutely have to be true. Some of these wrong answers may go way too far and be quite obviously out of scope, but the trickiest ones will seem very reasonable… until we ask ourselves whether that answer MUST be true.

Answer choice E in our last problem did this, and so did answer choice C. The argument said merely that economists "no longer recommend" a policy to reduce spending. The trap answer said that the economists recommend *higher* spending. Many people in the real world might assume or infer this, but it doesn't have to be true! There's also a third option: maintaining the same level of spending.

Other wrong answers will use language very similar to the language in the argument but will Reverse Direction or Switch Terms somehow. If we're told that eating honey causes people to hiccup, then a wrong answer might say that hiccupping causes people to eat honey! Alternatively, if we're told that the flu causes higher temperatures, then a wrong answer might say that the flu causes a fever. Higher temperatures and fevers are not interchangeable, but may seem to be if you're not reading carefully. Term switching is only acceptable if both terms are synonyms.

Takeaways for Inference Questions

Most of the time, inference questions will contain some form of the word "conclude" or "infer," though other variations are possible. Common synonyms include "assertion" or "hypothesis" in place of "conclusion" or "must be true" in place of "infer."

We have to be careful not to mix up Inference and Strengthen questions. Inference questions ask us to use the argument to support an answer. Strengthen questions ask us to use an answer to support the argument.

Inference arguments will not contain conclusions or assumptions, so don't waste time trying to find conclusions or brainstorm assumptions! (And that lack of a conclusion is another way by which we can distinguish between Inference and Strengthen questions — Inference arguments never have conclusions, and Strengthen arguments always do.)

The correct answer to an inference question *must be true* according to the information given in the argument. The correct answer does not have to use all of the information given in the argument.

Trap answers will include Real World inferences — they're reasonable and *could* be true, but they don't have to be true. Inference questions also often include Reverse Direction or Switch Terms traps. These traps will often contain language that is very similar to the language in the argument, but the trap will mix up the order of what the argument actually said.

6

Explain a Discrepancy

As was the case with Inference questions, Discrepancy questions consist only of premises, mostly on the fact-based side (though it is possibly to have more claim-like premises). There are no conclusions. Most of the time, two sets of premises will be presented, and those premises will be contradictory in some way. They won't "make sense" together. Sometimes, the argument will include indicator words such as "surprisingly" or "yet."

Most discrepancy question stems will include some form of the words "explain" or "resolve" and the vast majority will also contain the words "if true." Here are two typical examples:

> Which of the following, if true, most helps to resolve the paradox described above?

> Which of the following, if true, best explains the fact that many economists no longer recommend curbing spending in order to increase currency values?

Our task on Discrepancy questions is to find an answer that *resolves* or *fixes* the discrepancy—that makes all of the information make sense together. If we leave the argument as is, people should say, "Wait. That doesn't make sense." If we insert the correct answer into the argument, people should say, "Oh, I see. That makes sense now."

Take a look at this short example.

> According to researchers, low dosages of aspirin taken daily can significantly reduce the risk of heart attack or stroke. Yet doctors have stopped recommending daily aspirin for most patients.

> Which of the following, if true, most helps to explain why doctors no longer recommend daily low dosages of aspirin?

> (A) Only a small percentage of patients have already experienced a heart attack or stroke.
> (B) Patients who are at low risk for heart attack or stroke are less likely to comply with a doctor's recommendation to take aspirin daily.
> (C) Aspirin acts as a blood thinner, which can lead to internal bleeding, particularly in the stomach or brain.

The question stem asks us to "explain" something that doesn't make sense: the aspirin is apparently beneficial but "doctors have *stopped* recommending" its use for most people (implying that they did used to recommend it more). Why would they do that? We might sketch or think of our info visually in this way:

daily asp ↓   *BUT*   Drs <u>stop</u> for most
hrt att / strk

WHY?

Note that, for Discrepancy questions, we didn't set up a core. Not only don't we have a conclusion, but we're not even trying to find a conclusion (as we were on Inference questions). We're trying to find a third premise that will help these two facts to make sense together. In this case, what we want to do is highlight the apparent discrepancy between the two facts: on the one hand, daily aspirin is beneficial, and, on the other, doctors have stopped recommending it.

Back to step 3: what's our goal?

So far, they've told me something really good about taking aspirin daily: it significantly reduces the risk of some pretty bad things. The fact that the doctors have <u>stopped</u> recommending it means that they used to recommend it, so why would they stop doing so? Maybe there's something else that's bad about taking aspirin daily.

(A) Only a small percentage of patients have already experienced a heart attack or stroke.	ED A̶ B C daily asp ↓ hrt att, strk BUT drs <u>stop</u> rec for most	*So maybe this means the doctors think it won't help that many people? Wait. The purpose of taking the aspirin is to try to <u>prevent</u> a heart attack or stroke. If most people haven't had a heart attack or stroke, you'd want them to do something that would help lower the risk.*
(B) Patients who are at low risk for heart attack or stroke are less likely to comply with a doctor's recommendation to take aspirin daily.	ED A̶ B C daily asp ↓ hrt att, strk BUT drs <u>stop</u> rec for most	*I can believe this is true in the real world, but that doesn't affect a doctor's behavior. They don't say, "Oh, I know a lot of people won't take the life-saving medication properly, so I just won't bother to prescribe it." Plus, why would they recommend aspirin to people who are at low risk?*
(C) Aspirin acts as a blood thinner, which can lead to internal bleeding, particularly in the stomach or brain.	ED A̶ B̶ Ⓒ daily asp ↓ hrt att, strk BUT drs <u>stop</u> rec for most	*Oh, this is a bad thing about aspirin—it can cause you to bleed internally. The brain? Yeah, if it could make your brain start bleeding, I can imagine that doctors would want to avoid prescribing it unless there were a really good reason to do so.*

The fact that doctors once prescribed daily aspirin but mostly stopped is perplexing when all we're told is that daily aspirin does something good. Possibly that benefit doesn't apply to most people so the doctors don't waste time recommending the daily treatment. Alternatively, maybe there's some other bad thing going on to make the doctors stop prescribing daily aspirin. In this case, answer C gives us that bad thing.

Answer A tries to get us to think about the first possibility: maybe it doesn't really help very many people, so the doctors don't bother. However, answer A limits the group to those who have already had a heart attack or stroke—but the argument is not limited to that group. Answer A does nothing to explain why the doctors stopped prescribing the treatment to most people.

Answer B again tries to distract us: patients wouldn't benefit if they didn't actually take the medication. That's true, but this doesn't explain why doctors would stop recommending aspirin. In addition, this choice limits itself to those who are at low risk for heart attack or stroke—why would doctors need to recommend daily aspirin for a group that doesn't have the risk factors?

Let's try this again, this time with a full example:

> In a recent poll, 71% of respondents reported that they cast votes in the most recent national election. Voting records show, however, that only 60% of eligible voters actually voted in that election.
>
> Which of the following pieces of evidence, if true, would provide the best explanation for the discrepancy?
>
> (A) The margin of error for the survey was plus or minus five percentage points.
> (B) Fifteen percent of the survey's respondents were living overseas at the time of the election.
> (C) Prior research has shown that people who actually do vote are also more likely to respond to polls than those who do not vote.
> (D) Some people who intend to vote are prevented from doing so by last-minute conflicts on election day or other complications.
> (E) People are less likely to respond to a voting poll on the same day that they voted.

Step 1: Identify the question.

Which of the following pieces of evidence, if true, would provide the best explanation for the discrepancy ?	ED A B C D E	*The question stem uses the word "explanation" and explicitly mentions a "discrepancy," so this is an Explain the Discrepancy question.*

Step 2: Deconstruct the argument.

In a recent poll, 71% of respondents reported that they cast votes in the most recent national election.	ED A B C D E poll: 71% voted in elec	*Pure fact. There was a poll, and 71% of the people who responded said they voted in the last election.*
Voting records show, however, that only 60% of eligible voters actually voted in that election.	ED A B C D E poll: 71% voted in elec records: 60% of elig voters voted	*Okay, that's strange. Records show that only 60% of people who were allowed to vote actually voted.*

Step 3: State the Goal.

How can it be the case that, when asked, 71% of the people said they voted, but records show only 60% of those who were allowed to vote actually voted? I don't think it would be because some people voted who weren't allowed to—I guess that would technically resolve the discrepancy, but I doubt the GMAT is going to say that! So what could it have been? Maybe some people are remembering incorrectly or mixed up the election in question. Oh, I know! Polls always have a margin of error, so maybe the margin of error accounts for the discrepancy.

Okay, I need to find something that will make the whole thing make sense—it'll explain why 71% said they voted but records showed that only 60% actually voted.

Step 4: Work from wrong to right.

(A) The margin of error for the survey was plus or minus five percentage points.	ED A B C D E ? poll: 71% voted in elec records: 60% of elig voters voted	*Margin of error, bingo! Excellent. So the real percentage could've been anywhere from… 71% + 5% to 71% − 5%… which is still 66%. This doesn't go far enough. Still, it's about margin of error. I'm going to mark this one and come back to it later.*
(B) Fifteen percent of the survey's respondents were living overseas at the time of the election.	ED A B C D E ? poll: 71% voted in elec records: 60% of elig voters voted	*This percentage is larger than the 11% discrepancy mentioned in the argument. But what group are they talking about? Are these the people who did vote, or didn't vote, or some mix of the two? And what does "living overseas" imply? This country might allow people to vote by absentee ballot. This doesn't resolve anything.*

(C) Prior research has shown that people who actually do vote are also more likely to respond to polls than those who do not vote.	ED A B C̲ D E ? poll: 71% voted in elec records: 60% of elig voters voted	*People who vote are also more likely to respond to a survey. What does that mean? Of the people who responded, more were likely to have been voters than is represented in the overall population. Oh, I see—the survey group was skewed towards those who voted. That's why 71% of that sub-group could have voted while only 60% of the overall population of eligible voters voted. That's better than A—I'll get rid of A.*
(D) Some people who intend to vote are prevented from doing so by last-minute conflicts on election day or other complications.	ED A̲ B C̲ D̶ E ? poll: 71% voted in elec records: 60% of elig voters voted	*I'm sure this is true in the real world. How does it affect this argument? The survey took place after the election; it asked people whether they had voted in the past. It doesn't address what people intended to do before the election.*
(E) People are less likely to respond to a voting poll on the same day that they voted.	ED A̲ B Ⓒ D̶ E ? poll: 71% voted in elec records: 60% of elig voters voted	*We have no idea when the poll was taken, so I can't do much with this. Even if the poll were done the same day as the election, this just highlights the discrepancy—it's even more puzzling now. I would expect the percentage of people who said they voted to be lower than the real percentage because those who didn't vote that day would be more likely to agree to participate in the poll.*

Common Trap Answers

One common wrong answer trap will seem to be on topic because it will address one of the premises, but it won't actually resolve the discrepancy between the two premises. This trap answer is actually Out Of Scope because it doesn't address the discrepancy between the premises. Some of these will be more obviously out of scope, such as answer D, while others will be trickier because they just don't go quite far enough, such as answer A. If answer A had said that the margin of error was plus or minus 15 percentage points, that could have been the correct answer.

We can also see Reverse Logic traps, where the answer choice actually highlights or points out the discrepancy—that is, the answer tells us that there is a discrepancy rather than providing new information to show that there really isn't a discrepancy.

Takeaways for Explain a Discrepancy Questions

Discrepancy question stems will usually contain the words "explain" or "resolve" as well as the words "if true" (or synonyms).

The argument will consist of premises only; it will not contain a conclusion. The premises will not make sense together. Upon reading the argument, we should think, "Hmm, why would those two things both happen? That doesn't make sense!"

The correct answer will resolve the discrepancy—that is, the correct answer will show that there really isn't any discrepancy at all. If we insert the correct answer into the argument, we should be able to say, "Oh, okay, that makes sense now."

The most common trap answers will try to address something in the argument but will be Out Of Scope in some way. Perhaps the answer will address only one premise and not the other. Perhaps the answer will discuss a group that isn't at issue or a circumstance that occurred at the wrong time. The trickiest wrong answers of this type will address both premises but won't go far enough to resolve the discrepancy.

We may also see Reverse Logic trap answers, which will highlight or point out the discrepancy rather than fix it. These can be tricky if we forget that our task is to fix the discrepancy, not point out what the discrepancy is.

EXCEPT Questions

As we saw with Assumption Family questions, Evidence Family questions can also be presented in the negative "Except" format. These are more likely to occur on Discrepancy questions than on Inference questions.

A regular Discrepancy question might read:

> Which of the following, if true, would best help to explain the surprising finding?

An EXCEPT Discrepancy question might read:

> Each of the following, if true, could help to explain the surprising finding EXCEPT:

What is the difference in wording between those two questions?

The first one tells us that one answer choice, and only one, explains the discrepancy. That is the answer choice that we want to pick.

The second one tells us that four answer choices explain the discrepancy. These four are all wrong answers. The fifth answer will NOT explain or resolve the discrepancy. This is the "odd one out" and, as we saw in the Strengthen and Weaken chapter, it's the answer that we want to pick.

Similarly, on an Inference EXCEPT question, four answer choices would represent things that must be true according to the argument, and we will eliminate these four. One answer will represent something that does not have to be true; this is our "odd one out" and the correct answer.

6

Problem Set

1. *Nitrogen Triiodide*

Nitrogen triiodide is a highly explosive chemical that is easy to make from only two ingredients: ammonia and concentrated iodine. However, nitrogen triiodide has never been known to be used in a terrorist or criminal attack.

Which of the following, if true, is the most likely explanation for the discrepancy described above?

(A) Ammonia can be bought in a grocery store, but concentrated iodine must be obtained from somewhat more restricted sources, such as chemical supply houses.
(B) Nitrogen triiodide is only one of several powerful explosives that can be made from ammonia.
(C) Many terrorists and criminals have used other chemical explosives such as TNT or PETN.
(D) Airport security devices are typically calibrated to detect nitrogen compounds, such as ammonia and ammonium compounds.
(E) Nitrogen triiodide is extremely shock sensitive and can detonate as a result of even slight movement.

2. *Mycenaean Vase*

Museum A will display only undamaged objects of proven authenticity. Doubts have been raised about the origins of a supposedly Mycenaean vase currently on display in the museum's antiquities wing. The only way to establish this vase's authenticity would be to pulverize it, then subject the dust to spectroscopic analysis.

The claims above, if true, most strongly support which of the following conclusions?

(A) Authentic Mycenaean vases are valuable and rare.
(B) Museum A has been beset with questions about the provenance of many of the items in its antiquities wing.
(C) The vase in question will no longer be displayed in Museum A.
(D) Spectroscopic analysis has revolutionized the forensic investigation of art forgery.
(E) Knowingly or not, many of the world's museums display some forgeries.

3. *Gas Mileage*

The average fuel efficiency of vehicles sold nationwide during the period 2000–2004 was 25 miles per gallon; the corresponding figure during the period 1995–1999 was 20 miles per gallon. The national average price of gasoline during the period 2000–2004 was $2 per gallon; the corresponding figure during the period 1995–1999 was $1.60 per gallon.

The statements above, if true, best support which of the following conclusions?

(A)   The average fuel efficiency of vehicles sold nationwide should reach 30 miles per gallon for the period 2005–2009.

(B)   The national average price of gasoline during 1997 was lower than the corresponding price during 2003.

(C)   Rising gasoline prices led consumers to purchase more fuel-efficient cars.

(D)   Between the two described time periods, the national average fuel efficiency and the national average gasoline price both increased at roughly the same rate.

(E)   Consumers spent more money on gasoline during the period 2000–2004 than during the period 1995–1999.

4. *CarStore*

CarStore's sales personnel have an average of fifteen years' experience selling automobiles, and they regularly sell more cars than other local dealers. Despite this, CarStore has recently implemented a mandatory training program for all sales personnel.

Which of the following, if true, best explains the facts given above?

(A)   The sales personnel in CarStore have historically specialized in aggressively selling automobiles and add-on features.

(B)   Salespeople at other local dealers average 10 years' experience.

(C)   It is common for new or less experienced employees to participate in training programs.

(D)   Pricing information, which used to be confidential, has recently been released on the internet, and many customers try to negotiate lower prices using this data.

(E)   Several retailers that compete directly with CarStore use "customer-centered" sales approaches.

5. Stem Cell Research

Government restrictions have severely limited the amount of stem cell research United States companies can conduct. Because of these restrictions, many United States scientists who specialize in the field of stem cell research have signed long-term contracts to work for foreign companies. Recently, Congress has proposed lifting all restrictions on stem cell research.

Which of the following statements can most properly be inferred from the information above?

(A) Some foreign companies that conduct stem cell research work under fewer restrictions than some United States companies do.

(B) Because United States scientists are under long-term contracts to foreign companies, there will be a significant influx of foreign professionals into the United States.

(C) In all parts of the world, stem cell research is dependent on the financial backing of local government.

(D) In the near future, United States companies will no longer be at the forefront of stem cell research.

(E) If restrictions on stem cell research are lifted, many of the United States scientists will break their contracts to return to United States companies.

6. Hunting Season

In an effort to reduce the number of deer, and therefore decrease the number of automobile accidents caused by deer, the government lengthened the deer hunting season earlier this year. Surprisingly, the number of accidents caused by deer has increased substantially since the introduction of the longer hunting season.

All of the following, if true, help to explain the increase in traffic accidents caused by deer EXCEPT:

(A) The presence of humans in the woods causes the deer to move to new areas, which causes the deer to cross roads more frequently than normal.

(B) In the area where the deer live, traffic has increased substantially precisely because of the lengthened hunting season.

(C) Most automobile accidents involving deer result from cars swerving to avoid deer, and leave the deer in question unharmed.

(D) Deer tend to bolt when hearing gunshots or other loud sounds and are more likely to run across a road without warning.

(E) A new highway was recently built directly through the state's largest forest, which is the primary habitat of the state's deer population.

P

7. World Bank

In 2010, China comprised about 10 percent of the world's gross domestic product (GDP), and its voting share in the World Bank was increased from under 3 percent to 4.4 percent. During the same timeframe, France comprised about 4 percent of the world's GDP and saw its voting share in the World bank drop from 4.3 percent to 3.8 percent.

Which of the following can be logically concluded from the passage above?

(A) World Bank voting shares are allocated based upon each country's share of the world's GDP.

(B) The new ratio of voting share to percentage of world GDP is lower for China than it is for France.

(C) Gross domestic product is the most important factor in determining voting share at the World Bank.

(D) China should be upset that its voting share does not match its proportion of the world's GDP.

(E) France lost some of its voting share to China because China comprised a larger portion of the world's GDP.

8. Bar Codes

Two-dimensional bar codes are omni-directional; that is, unlike one-dimensional bar codes, they can be scanned from any direction. Additionally, two-dimensional bar codes are smaller and can store more data than their one-dimensional coun- terparts. Despite such advantages, two-dimensional bar codes account for a much smaller portion of total bar code usage than one-dimensional bar codes.

Which of the following, if true, most helps to resolve the apparent paradox?

(A) Many smaller stores do not use bar codes at all because of the expense.

(B) For some products, the amount of data necessary to be coded is small enough to fit fully on a one-dimensional bar code.

(C) Two-dimensional bar codes are, on average, less expensive than one-dimen- sional bar codes.

(D) Two-dimensional bar codes can also be scanned by consumer devices, such as cell phones.

(E) One-dimensional bar codes last longer and are less prone to error than two- dimensional bar codes.

Solutions

1. Nitrogen Triiodide: The correct answer is **E**.

Step 1: Identify the question.

Which of the following, if true, is the most likely explanation for the discrepancy described above?	ED A B C D E	*The word "discrepancy" indicates that this is a Discrepancy question.*

Step 2: Deconstruct the argument.

Nitrogen triiodide is a highly explosive chemical that is easy to make from only two ingredients: ammonia and concentrated iodine.	ED A B C D E NT expl, easy to make	*This is a fact. I think the main point is that it's easy to make, not that I need those two specific chemicals, so I'm not going to write them down.*
However, nitrogen triiodide has never been known to be used in a terrorist or criminal attack.	ED A B C D E NT expl, easy to make BUT never used by terr or crims	*That's weird. If it's so easy to make, why haven't criminals and terrorists used it? Maybe it's hard to get one of the ingredients, or they're really expensive?*

Step 3: State the Goal.

This is a Discrepancy question, so the argument will provide two seemingly contradictory pieces of information. I need to find something that will make everything make sense.

In this case, there's an explosive that's easy to make, and yet criminals have never used it. I need to find something that explains why.

Step 4: Work from wrong to right.

(A) Ammonia can be bought in a grocery store, but concentrated iodine must be obtained from somewhat more restricted sources, such as chemical supply houses.	ED A̲ B C D E NT expl, easy to make BUT never used by terr or crims	*This is kind of like what I said before—it's harder to get one of the chemicals. This might explain it… except it doesn't say that you can't get iodine. It just says you have to go to a special place, but you can still get it. So I'm not sure that really explains why no criminals have ever used it. I'll leave this in until I find something better.*

(B) Nitrogen triiodide is only one of several powerful explosives that can be made from ammonia.	ED A̰ B C D E NT expl, easy to make BUT never used by terr or crims	*So you can make even more explosives from this chemical? That doesn't explain why the criminals have never made it.*
(C) Many terrorists and criminals have used other chemical explosives such as TNT or PETN.	ED A̰ B C̶ D E NT expl, easy to make BUT never used by terr or crims	*Again, this doesn't explain why they haven't used the NT explosive. Maybe if TNT or PETN are a lot cheaper or easier to make—but this choice doesn't say that.*
(D) Airport security devices are typically calibrated to detect nitrogen compounds, such as ammonia and ammonium compounds.	ED A̰ B C̶ D̶ E NT expl, easy to make BUT never used by terr or crims	*This might explain why no one has tried to bring these explosives into airports, but it doesn't explain why these explosives have never been used in any type of attack anywhere.*
(E) Nitrogen triiodide is extremely shock sensitive and can detonate as a result of even slight movement.	ED A̰ B C̶ D̶ Ⓔ NT expl, easy to make BUT never used by terr or crims	*Here we go. If the bomb is so unstable that it could go off at any moment, including right after you make it, then it makes sense that criminals don't want to use these explosives. This is better than answer A.*

2. Mycenaean Vase: The correct answer is **C**.

Step 1: Identify the question.

The claims above, if true, most strongly support which of the following conclusions?	In A B C D E	*The language "strongly support" could indicate an Inference or a Strengthen question. The question stem indicates that the answer choice contains the conclusions, though (and the argument didn't have a conclusion), so this is an Inference question.*

Step 2: Deconstruct the argument.

Museum A will display only undamaged objects of proven authenticity.	In A B C D E MA: only perfect, auth objects	*This is a fact—all objects have to be perfect and authenticated for MA to display them.*

Doubts have been raised about the origins of a supposedly Mycenaean vase currently on display in the museum's antiquities wing.	In A B C D E MA: only perfect, auth objects MV: auth doubtful	*Another fact: they're not sure whether this vase is authentic.*
The only way to establish this vase's authenticity would be to pulverize it, then subject the dust to spectroscopic analysis.	In A B C D E MA: only perfect, auth objects MV: auth doubtful to auth MV, must destroy it	*That's interesting. In order to prove whether the vase is authentic, you've got to destroy it!*

Step 3: State the Goal.

This is an Inference question; I need to find something that must be true according to the info given in the argument. In this case, they're not sure whether this vase is authentic, and the only way to establish its authenticity is to destroy it. But then they can't display it anymore because they'll only display it if it's perfect!

Step 4: Work from wrong to right.

(A) Authentic Mycenaean vases are valuable and rare.	In A̶ B C D E MA: only perfect, auth objects MV: auth doubtful to auth MV, must destroy it	*This might be true, but it doesn't have to be true. The argument says nothing about value or rarity.*
(B) Museum A has been beset with questions about the provenance of many of the items in its antiquities wing.	In A̶ B̶ C D E MA: only perfect, auth objects MV: auth doubtful to auth MV, must destroy it	*The argument is only about one particular vase. Any other items are out of scope.*
(C) The vase in question will no longer be displayed in Museum A.	In A̶ B̶ C̲ D E MA: only perfect, auth objects MV: auth doubtful to auth MV, must destroy it	*This is exactly what I said before! If they try to authenticate it, they'll destroy the vase, in which case they can't display it. And if they don't try to authenticate it, then they won't know whether it's authentic, in which case Museum A still won't display it. This has to be true (though I'll check the other two answers to be sure).*

P

MANHATTAN
GMAT

(D) Spectroscopic analysis has revolutionized the forensic investigation of art forgery.	In A B C̲ D̶ E MA: only perfect, auth objects MV: auth doubtful to auth MV, must destroy it	*This might be true, but it doesn't have to be true that it "revolutionized" the field. It just has to work in general.*
(E) Knowingly or not, many of the world's museums display some forgeries.	In A B Ⓒ D̶ E MA: only perfect, auth objects MV: auth doubtful to auth MV, must destroy it	*I can believe that this is probably true, but it doesn't absolutely have to be true.*

3. Gas Mileage: The correct answer is **D**.

Step 1: Identify the question.

The statements above, if true, best support which of the following conclusions ?	In A B C D E	*The language "best support" could indicate an Inference or a Strengthen question. The question stem indicates that the answer choice contains the conclusions, though (and the argument didn't have a conclusion), so this is an Inference question.*

Step 2: Deconstruct the argument.

The average fuel efficiency of vehicles sold nationwide during the period 2000–2004 was 25 miles per gallon; the corresponding figure during the period 1995–1999 was 20 miles per gallon.	In A B C D E | 95–99	00–04 | |-------|-------| | AFE 20 | AFE 25 |	*These are all facts, which I'm expecting because this is an Inference question. They're talking about time periods and figures, so maybe a table is the best way to keep track.*

| The national average price of gasoline during the period 2000–2004 was $2 per gallon; the corresponding figure during the period 1995–1999 was $1.60 per gallon. | In   A B C D E

 95–99 \| 00–04
 AFE 20 \| AFE 25
 AG $1.60 \| AG $2 | *Yep, a table was a good idea! More facts and figures for the same timeframe.* |

Step 3: State the Goal.

This is an Inference question, so I'm looking for something that must be true based on all this data. I was given specific figures for average fuel efficiency and average gas price for two time periods. Both went up over time.

Step 4: Work from wrong to right.

(A) The average fuel efficiency of vehicles sold nationwide should reach 30 miles per gallon for the period 2005–2009.	In A̶ B C D E **95–99** | **00–04** AFE 20 | AFE 25 AG $1.60 | AG $2	*"Should reach?" That doesn't have to be true. Who knows what's going to happen in the future?*
(B) The national average price of gasoline during 1997 was lower than the corresponding price during 2003.	In A̶ B̶ C D E **95–99** | **00–04** AFE 20 | AFE 25 AG $1.60 | AG $2	*The data given is only for the 5-year periods 95 to 99 and 00 to 04. I have no idea what the numbers were for 1997 and 2003 specifically.*
(C) Rising gasoline prices lead consumers to purchase more fuel-efficient cars.	In A̶ B̶ C̶ D E **95–99** | **00–04** AFE 20 | AFE 25 AG $1.60 | AG $2	*That might be true, but it doesn't have to be true. The argument doesn't say anything about why consumers decide to purchase certain cars.*
(D) Between the two described time periods, the national average fuel efficiency and the national average gasoline price both increased at roughly the same rate.	In A̶ B̶ C̶ D̲ E **95–99** | **00–04** AFE 20 | AFE 25 AG $1.60 | AG $2	*Increased at the same rate? Hmm. I don't know, but I can calculate based on the figures I was already given. The AFE figure went from 20 to 25. The increase, then, was 5 over a base (or starting point) of 20. 5/20 = 1/4, or a rate of 25%. The AG figure went from 1.6 to 2, which is an increase of 0.4 over a starting point of 1.6. 0.4/1.6 = 1/4, or a rate of 25% again. Hey, this is true!*

(E) Consumers spent more money on gasoline during the period 2000–2004 than during the period 1995–1999.	In ~~A~~ ~~B~~ ~~C~~ Ⓓ ~~E~~ 	**95–99**	**00–04**
AFE 20	AFE 25
AG $1.60	AG $2		*Tricky! This one seems pretty good at first glance, but average price per gallon is not the same thing as total amount of money spent. It's true that the average price was higher, but maybe people bought fewer gallons of gasoline (especially because fuel efficiency was better!). This one might be true, but it doesn't have to be.*

4. CarStore: The correct answer is **D**.

Step 1: Identify the question.

| Which of the following, if true, best explains the facts given above? | ED   A B C D E | *The language "best explains the facts" is a slightly unusual form for a Discrepancy question.* |

Step 2: Deconstruct the argument.

| CarStore's sales personnel have an average of fifteen years' experience selling automobiles, and they regularly sell more cars than other local dealers. | ED   A B C D E

SP: avg 15y exp; sell more than comp | *CarStore's people have 15 years' experience on average, and they sell more cars than the competition. These are facts.* |
| Despite this, CarStore has recently implemented a mandatory training program for all sales personnel. | ED   A B C D E

SP: avg 15y exp; sell more than comp

BUT CS req trng for all | *Here's the contrast. Why are they going to make them all go through training? Maybe something has changed in the marketplace?* |

Step 3: State the Goal.

This is a Discrepancy question, so I need to find an answer that explains why these two facts are actually NOT contradictory after all. What would explain why CS is requiring its employees to go through new training? Maybe something has changed in the marketplace that would require new training.

Step 4: Work from wrong to right.

(A) The sales personnel in CarStore have historically specialized in aggressively selling automobiles and add-on features.	ED A̶ B C D E SP: avg 15y exp; sell more than comp BUT CS req trng for all	*If CS wants to change the way their people sell cars, then new training would make sense... but this choice just talks about what they've done in the past, not what they want to do in the future. This doesn't explain the discrepancy.*
(B) Salespeople at other local dealers average 10 years' experience.	ED A̶ B̶ C D E SP: avg 15y exp; sell more than comp BUT CS req trng for all	*So the CS people are more experienced, on average, than other salespeople in the area. If anything, this just accentuates the discrepancy: why do the more experienced people need training?*
(C) It is common for new or less experienced employees to participate in training programs.	ED A̶ B̶ C̶ D E SP: avg 15y exp; sell more than comp BUT CS req trng for all	*This makes sense, but again does not explain why the employees who average 15 years' experience need training. The argument said that all sales personnel have to undergo the training, not just the new ones.*
(D) Pricing information, which used to be confidential, has recently been released on the internet, and many customers try to negotiate lower prices using this data.	ED A̶ B̶ C̶ D̲ E SP: avg 15y exp; sell more than comp BUT CS req trng for all	*Ah, so the situation has changed. Customers now know some info that used to be confidential. That might change negotiations, so it makes sense that the salespeople might need new training.*
(E) Several retailers that compete directly with CarStore use "customer-centered" sales approaches.	ED A̶ B̶ C̶ Ⓓ E̶ SP: avg 15y exp; sell more than comp BUT CS req trng for all	*That's what they already use—the answer doesn't indicate that anything has changed. Nor does it indicate that CS doesn't use a customer-centered approach or that consumers prefer a customer-centered approach. This doesn't explain why the CS people need training.*

P

5. Stem Cell Research: The correct answer is **A**.

Step 1: Identify the question.

Which of the following statements can most properly be inferred from the information above?	In A B C D E	*The word "inferred" indicates that this is an Inference question.*

Step 2: Deconstruct the argument.

Government restrictions have severely limited the amount of stem cell research United States companies can conduct.	In A B C D E SCR restrict by US govt	*This is a fact. The US government restricts this stem cell research (SCR).*
Because of these restrictions, many United States scientists who specialize in the field of stem cell research have signed long-term contracts to work for foreign companies.	In A B C D E SCR restrict by US govt → US sci work foreign coms instead	*"Because of" that—so the first sentence leads to the second sentence.*
Recently, Congress has proposed lifting all restrictions on stem cell research.	In A B C D E SCR restrict by US govt → US sci work foreign coms instead US gov: maybe lift restrict?	*Still a fact: the government is considering lifting the restrictions. Maybe that'll bring the scientists back to work for US companies?*

Step 3: State the Goal.

This is an Inference question, so I need to find something that must be true based on the info given so far. The US government restricts a certain kind of research, so many US scientists who do this type of research are working for foreign companies instead. Congress might lift the restrictions.

MANHATTAN
GMAT

Step 4: Work from wrong to right.

(A) Some foreign companies that conduct stem cell research work under fewer restrictions than some United States companies do.	In $\underline{A}$ B C D E SCR restrict by US govt → US sci work foreign coms instead US gov: maybe lift restrict?	*If the researchers decided to work for foreign companies specifically <u>because</u> the U.S. companies had restrictions, then that would mean that at least some foreign companies did have fewer restrictions. Yes, this one must be true! I'll check the other answers just in case, though.*
(B) Because United States scientists are under long-term contracts to foreign companies, there will be a significant influx of foreign professionals into the United States.	In $\underline{A}$ B C D E SCR restrict by US govt → US sci work foreign coms instead US gov: maybe lift restrict?	*This might be true, but it certainly doesn't have to be true. The argument doesn't say anything about foreign professionals coming into the U.S.*
(C) In all parts of the world, stem cell research is dependent on the financial backing of local government.	In $\underline{A}$ B $\in$ D E SCR restrict by US govt → US sci work foreign coms instead US gov: maybe lift restrict?	*The argument doesn't say anything about how this type of research gets its financial backing. This doesn't have to be true.*
(D) In the near future, United States companies will no longer be at the forefront of stem cell research.	In $\underline{A}$ B $\in$ Đ E SCR restrict by US govt → US sci work foreign coms instead US gov: maybe lift restrict?	*Out of scope. The argument doesn't discuss who is or will be at the forefront of this kind of research.*
(E) If restrictions on stem cell research are lifted, many of the United States scientists will break their contracts to return to United States companies.	In $\textcircled{A}$ B $\in$ Đ Ɇ SCR restrict by US govt → US sci work foreign coms instead US gov: maybe lift restrict?	*Maybe this will happen, but it doesn't have to happen. It isn't easy to break a contract.*

P

6. Hunting Season: The correct answer is **C**.

Step 1: Identify the question.

Q stem All of the following, if true, help to explain the increase in traffic accidents caused by deer EXCEPT.	ED Ex A B C D E	*The language "help to explain" indicates that this is a Discrepancy question. This is also an Except question.*

Step 2: Deconstruct the argument.

In an effort to reduce the number of deer, and therefore decrease the number of automobile accidents caused by deer, the government lengthened the deer hunting season earlier this year.	ED Ex A B C D E G: ↑ HS → ↓ #D → ↓ #car acc from D	*Multiple levels here. First, the government lengthened hunting season, which is supposed to reduce the number of deer, which is then supposed to reduce the number of car accidents caused by deer.*
Surprisingly, the number of accidents caused by deer has increased substantially since the introduction of the longer hunting season.	ED Ex A B C D E G: ↑ HS → ↓ #D → ↓ #car acc from D BUT # car acc ↑	*That's weird. The exact opposite has happened: there have been more car accidents caused by deer!*

Step 3: State the Goal.

This is a Discrepancy Except question. Normally on discrepancy questions, I'm looking for the answer that makes the contradictory evidence make sense. On this one, though, all four wrong answers will fix the discrepancy. The "odd one out"—the one that doesn't fix the discrepancy—will be the right answer.

So I need to find (and cross off) four things that explain why there have been even more car accidents caused by deer.

Step 4: Work from wrong to right.

(A) The presence of humans in the woods causes the deer to move to new areas, which causes the deer to cross roads more frequently than normal.	ED Ex A̶ B C D E G: ↑ HS → ↓ #D → ↓ #car acc from D BUT # car acc ↑	*If hunting season is lengthened, then there will be people in the woods for a longer period of time. According to this choice, that means the deer are going to cross the roads more frequently than they otherwise would have. That could increase the likelihood of accidents due to deer, which explains the discrepancy. Cross this one off.*

(B) In the area where the deer live, traffic has increased substantially precisely because of the lengthened hunting season.	ED Ex A B̶ C D E G: ↑ HS → ↓ #D → ↓ #car acc from D BUT # car acc ↑	*Oh, this makes sense. The lengthened hunting season actually caused more traffic, so there are more chances for accidents between cars and deer where the deer live. This explains the discrepancy, too.*
(C) Most automobile accidents involving deer result from cars swerving to avoid deer, and leave the deer in question unharmed.	ED Ex A̶ B̶ C̲ D E G: ↑ HS → ↓ #D → ↓ #car acc from D BUT # car acc ↑	*This one is tricky! It sounded like it explained the discrepancy when I first read it, but then I realized something: it's just explaining how the accidents tend to happen, but it doesn't address why there are MORE accidents now than there used to be.*
(D) Deer tend to bolt when hearing gunshots or other loud sounds and are more likely to run across a road without warning.	ED Ex A B C̲ D̶ E G: ↑ HS → ↓ #D → ↓ #car acc from D BUT # car acc ↑	*Ah, so if there are gunshots for a longer length of time, then there are more chances for the deer to bolt and cross the road suddenly… increasing the chances of an accident.*
(E) A new highway was recently built directly through the state's largest forest, which is the primary habitat of the state's deer population.	ED Ex A̶ B Ⓒ D̶ E̶ G: ↑ HS → ↓ #D → ↓ #car acc from D BUT # car acc ↑	*The situation has changed from the year before: a new highway was built right through the area where the deer live. So it would make sense that there are now more accidents caused by deer.*

P

7. World Bank: The correct answer is **B**.

Step 1: Identify the question.

Which of the following can be logically concluded from the passage above?	In A B C D E	*The language "logically concluded" indicates that this is an Inference question.*

Step 2: Deconstruct the argument.

In 2010, China comprised about 10 percent of the world's gross domestic product (GDP), and its voting share in the World Bank was increased from under 3 percent to 4.4 percent.	In A B C D E 	2010	GDP	VS
C	10	<3 → 4.4		*A bunch of stats about China in 2010. I just need to keep this straight because, glancing down, I can see the next sentence has more numbers.*

| During the same timeframe, France comprised about 4 percent of the world's GDP and saw its voting share in the World bank drop from 4.3 percent to 3.8 percent. | In   A B C D E <table><tr><td>2010</td><td>GDP</td><td>VS</td></tr><tr><td>C</td><td>10</td><td><3 → 4.4</td></tr><tr><td>F</td><td>4</td><td>4.3 → 3.8</td></tr></table> | *Same type of stats, but about France this time. Same time-frame.* |

Step 3: State the Goal.

This is an Inference question, so I need to find something that must be true based upon the info given so far. There are a lot of numbers to keep straight, but generally, China has a larger share of the world GDP than France. China used to have a lower voting share than France, but now it has a higher share.

Step 4: Work from wrong to right.

(A) World Bank voting shares are allocated based upon each country's share of the world's GDP.	In ~~A~~ B C D E <table><tr><td>2010</td><td>GDP</td><td>VS</td></tr><tr><td>C</td><td>10</td><td><3 → 4.4</td></tr><tr><td>F</td><td>4</td><td>4.3 → 3.8</td></tr></table>	*Maybe. It is the case now that China has a larger GDP and a larger voting share. But it didn't used to be that way. And we only have two data points; I don't know the numbers with all of the other countries. This doesn't have to be true.*
(B) The new ratio of voting share to percentage of world GDP is lower for China than it is for France.	In ~~A~~ B̰ C D E <table><tr><td>2010</td><td>GDP</td><td>VS</td></tr><tr><td>C</td><td>10</td><td><3 → 4.4</td></tr><tr><td>F</td><td>4</td><td>4.3 → 3.8</td></tr></table>	*Let's see. China's ratio is 4.4 / 10. And the ratio for France is 3.8 / 4. The first number is a lot smaller than the second number: the first one is 0.44 and the second one is almost 1. So, yes, it's true that China's ratio is lower than France's.*
(C) Gross domestic product is the most important factor in determining voting share at the World Bank.	In ~~A~~ B̰ ~~C~~ D E <table><tr><td>2010</td><td>GDP</td><td>VS</td></tr><tr><td>C</td><td>10</td><td><3 → 4.4</td></tr><tr><td>F</td><td>4</td><td>4.3 → 3.8</td></tr></table>	*"Most important?" The argument didn't say anything about how voting share is determined or which factor is most important.*
(D) China should be upset that its voting share does not match its proportion of the world's GDP.	In ~~A~~ B̰ ~~C~~ ~~D~~ E <table><tr><td>2010</td><td>GDP</td><td>VS</td></tr><tr><td>C</td><td>10</td><td><3 → 4.4</td></tr><tr><td>F</td><td>4</td><td>4.3 → 3.8</td></tr></table>	*China might be upset but this doesn't have to be true—and it doesn't have to be true that China "should" be upset. That's a judgment call.*
(E) France lost some of its voting share to China because China comprised a larger portion of the world's GDP.	In ~~A~~ Ⓑ ~~C~~ ~~D~~ ~~E~~ <table><tr><td>2010</td><td>GDP</td><td>VS</td></tr><tr><td>C</td><td>10</td><td><3 → 4.4</td></tr><tr><td>F</td><td>4</td><td>4.3 → 3.8</td></tr></table>	*Maybe this is true, but they didn't actually say why the voting shares were changed. I could speculate, but this doesn't have to be true.*

P

8. Bar Codes: The correct answer is E.

Step 1: Identify the question.

Which of the following, if true, most helps to resolve the apparent paradox ?	ED A B C D E	*The word "paradox" indicates that this is a Discrepancy question.*

Step 2: Deconstruct the argument.

Two-dimensional bar codes are omni-directional; that is, unlike one-dimensional bar codes, they can be scanned from any direction.	ED A B C D E 2D BC scan any dir; 1D BC can't	*Okay, so 2D barcodes have a better feature than 1D barcodes.*
Additionally, two-dimensional bar codes are smaller and can store more data than their one-dimensional counterparts.	ED A B C D E 2D BC scan any dir; 1D BC can't 2D BC smaller, more data	*Even more advantages for the 2D barcodes.*
Despite such advantages, two-dimensional bar codes account for a much smaller portion of total bar code usage than one-dimensional bar codes.	ED A B C D E 2D BC scan any dir; 1D BC can't 2D BC smaller, more data BUT 1D is used >>	*But the 1D barcodes are used a lot more—why? There must be some advantages to the 1Ds or disadvantages for the 2Ds.*

Step 3: State the Goal.

I need to find something that fixes the discrepancy described in the argument: the 2D barcodes have a bunch of advantages, but people mostly still use the 1D barcodes. Why? Maybe the 2D ones are super-expensive or something like that.

Step 4: Work from wrong to right.

(A) Many smaller stores do not use bar codes at all because of the expense.	ED A̶ B C D E 2D BC scan any dir; 1D BC can't 2D BC smaller, more data BUT 1D is used >>	*Expense—does this explain why 1D barcodes are still being used? No, wait—this says the stores aren't using any type of barcode at all. So that doesn't explain why the ones who do use barcodes seem to prefer the 1D models.*

P

(B) For some products, the amount of data necessary to be coded is small enough to fit fully on a one-dimensional bar code.	ED A̶ B C D E 2D BC scan any dir; 1D BC can't 2D BC smaller, more data BUT 1D is used >>	*Okay, so some products might not need the 2D barcodes. Except, this only mentions "some" products, while the argument says that the 2D barcodes are a "much smaller" portion of total usage. This doesn't fully explain the discrepancy.*
(C) Two-dimensional bar codes are, on average, less expensive than one-dimensional bar codes.	ED A̶ B̶ C̶ D E 2D BC scan any dir; 1D BC can't 2D BC smaller, more data BUT 1D is used >>	*Less expensive, this is it! Wait a second. No, this says the 2D barcodes are less expensive—that gives them yet another advantage! If they're less expensive, you'd expect people to use them more. This isn't it.*
(D) Two-dimensional bar codes can also be scanned by consumer devices, such as cell phones.	ED A̶ B̶ C̶ D̶ E 2D BC scan any dir; 1D BC can't 2D BC smaller, more data BUT 1D is used >>	*This sounds like yet another advantage for the 2D barcodes. This isn't it either!*
(E) One-dimensional bar codes last longer and are less prone to error than two-dimensional bar codes.	ED A̶ B̶ C̶ D̶ Ⓔ 2D BC scan any dir; 1D BC can't 2D BC smaller, more data BUT 1D is used >>	*Ah, here we go. Here are two advantages for the 1D barcodes. If it's true that they last longer and are less prone to error, then that would explain why people would want to use them rather than the 2D barcodes.*

Chapter 7 of Critical Reasoning

Complete the Argument

In This Chapter...

Negatively-Worded Claims

Alternate Wording

Chapter 7:
Complete the Argument

Complete the Argument (CA) questions don't fall into any one Family of questions. Rather, "Complete the Argument" is a structure for writing the argument itself, and any of the question types we've already discussed could theoretically be written using this structure. In practice, however, most CA questions resemble Assumption or Strengthen questions; most will ask us to find an answer that makes a claim or conclusion true or much more likely to be true.

Let's look at an example:

> Which of the following most logically completes the argument below?
>
> XYZ Industries sells both a premium line of televisions and a basic line. The higher-end line sells at a 20% premium but also costs 30% more to produce and market. The company has announced that it will stop producing premium televisions and sell only the regular line in future. This plan will help to improve profitability since _____.

Right away, you'll notice that we have no question stem after the argument. Most of the time, the question will come before, as in the example above, and the question stem also won't help to tell us anything other than that we have a "Complete the Argument" structure.

In the vast majority of Complete the Argument (CA) problems, the last sentence will contain a conclusion or claim followed by the word "since" or "because" and a blank. In these cases, the arguments are asking us to find some kind of a premise that will support the claim given in the same sentence.

In our above example, the author claims that "this plan will help to improve profits." Our task is to find an answer that will make this claim true or much more likely to be true.

For the above example, for instance, a correct answer might read:

> basic televisions are more profitable for the company than are premium televisions

If it's the case that the basic televisions are more profitable, then getting rid of the less profitable product and selling only the more profitable product will likely improve overall profitability—this strengthens the author's case. The interesting thing is that the argument itself gave us enough information to determine that the basic televisions are more profitable. If the company charges 20% more on a premium television but has to pay 30% more to produce it, then we can conclude that the premium televisions are less profitable than the basic televisions. The answer choice, then, is almost repeating a premise that we were already told in the argument.

Contrast that answer with this alternative for a correct answer:

> cutting the production of premium televisions will allow XYZ Industries to increase production of its basic television line

In this case, the correct answer provides us with some new information, similar to a strengthen question. If it's the case that the company can produce even more of the more-profitable basic TVs, then that again makes it much more likely that this plan will improve overall profitability.

On CA questions, the correct answer might be a restatement of a premise we were already told. Alternatively, the correct answer may introduce a new premise. Either way, the result will be the same: the answer will strongly bolster the author's conclusion.

Negatively-Worded Claims

Many Complete the Argument questions introduce a negatively-worded twist. Take a look at this variation on our original argument:

> Which of the following most logically completes the argument below?
>
> XYZ Industries sells both a premium line of televisions and a basic line. The higher-end line sells at a 20% premium but also costs 30% more to produce and market. Producing more televisions from the basic line, however, will not necessarily help to improve profitability since _____.

These questions will *not* put the negative wording in capital letters, as we've seen on the "EXCEPT" question variations. Rather, the conclusion itself is that last sentence: this will *not* necessarily help to improve profitability. Why? Consider this possible correct answer:

> the market for basic televisions is shrinking

In other words, producing more TVs doesn't necessarily mean we can *sell* more TVs, and we have to sell them in order to make money. If the market for basic TVs is shrinking, then producing more of those TVs won't necessarily be beneficial for the company's profitability.

Alternate Wording

The first two variations we discussed represent the most common ways in which Complete the Argument questions can be presented. There are a few alternate examples, however, that might pop up. Students aiming for 90th percentile or higher on the verbal section may want to be prepared for these rare variations.

The rare variants will still typically include the conclusion or claim in the final sentence with the blank, but the "lead in" wording to the blank might be different, and what we need to do to find the answer might be different as well.

"lead in" wording	answer choice should	most resembles?
(something) is "illustrated by" _____	provide a concrete example of a premise from the argument	n/a
if (some claim is true), "it should be expected that"	represent something that must be true given the information in the argument	Inference questions
(in order for some claim to be true) "it must be shown that"	represent something that must be true given the information in the argument	Inference questions

Let's look at a full example of one of the more common forms of the Complete the Argument (CA) question type.

> Which of the following best completes the passage below?
>
> The Farmsley Film and Performing Arts Center was built three years ago in downtown Metropolis. A recent study shows that, on average, a person who attends a show at the Farmsley Center spends $96 at other downtown businesses on the day of the show. This fact, however, does not necessarily indicate that the Farmsley Center is a significant driver of the economic revitalization of downtown Metropolis, since _____.
>
> (A) people who do not attend a Farmsley Center show spend $63 on average when shopping in the downtown area
>
> (B) restaurants near the Farmsley Center tend to be more expensive than restaurants in outlying areas
>
> (C) the Farmsley center generally earns more from films than from plays or other performance art projects
>
> (D) the Farmsley Center is the only downtown theatre large enough to afford to show newly-released major Hollywood films
>
> (E) most of the people who attend films or performances at the Farmsley Center do so because they are already in the area to shop

7

Step 1: Identify the question.

Which of the following best completes the passage below?	CA:S A B C D E	*The blank and the fact that the question appears first both indicate that this is a "Complete the Argument" question. The word "since" right before the blank indicates that this is likely a classic "Strengthen the Conclusion" variation.*

Step 2: Deconstruct the argument.

The Farmsley Film and Performing Arts Center was built three years ago in downtown Metropolis.	CA:S A B C D E 3ya: F built	*Pure fact. I'm not even sure I need to write this down.*
A recent study shows that, on average, a person who attends a show at the Farmsley Center spends $96 at other downtown businesses on the day of the show.	CA:S A B C D E 3ya: F built RS: F ppl spend $96 avg other stuff	*It sounds like the other businesses in the downtown area should be happy that the F place is there.*
This fact, however, does not necessarily indicate that the Farmsley Center is a significant driver of the economic revitalization of downtown Metropolis, since _____.	CA:S A B C D E 3ya: F built RS: F ppl spend $96 avg other stuff ©F NOT nec → M econ +	*Oh, wait—but this is saying that the $96 thing is NOT necessarily evidence that F is one of the businesses driving the "economic revitalization" of the area. That's interesting.*

Step 3: State the Goal.

The conclusion said that F is <u>not necessarily</u> driving M's economic revitalization (so it could be contributing, but it also might not be). "Revitalization" implies that the economy was worse for a while but has been getting better lately, and F was just built 3 years ago, so that would be a (very small) point in favor of F helping drive the revitalization.

Plus, the other piece of evidence sounds pretty good: that people spend nearly a hundred bucks in other stores on the day of a performance. So why is that F isn't necessarily driving M's revitalization? Maybe people ordinarily spend $150 if they don't attend a show, so they spend <u>less</u> if they see a show at F? I was just assuming that the $96 figure was a good figure; maybe it's not.

I need to find a piece of evidence that makes the claim at least a little more likely to be true—that F isn't <u>necessarily</u> a major driver in revitalizing M's economy.

Step 4: Work from wrong to right.

(A) people who do not attend a Farmsley Center show spend $63 on average when shopping in the downtown area	CA:S ~~A~~ B C D E 3ya: F built RS: F ppl spend $96 avg other stuff ⒸF NOT nec → M econ +	*I did think of something like this… but wait, this says people who don't attend a show spend less than those who do. If anything, that would strengthen the idea that F DOES help drive the economic revitalization. That's the opposite of what I want.*
(B) restaurants near the Farmsley Center tend to be more expensive than restaurants in outlying areas	CA:S ~~A~~ ~~B~~ C D E 3ya: F built RS: F ppl spend $96 avg other stuff ⒸF NOT nec → M econ +	*Hmm. This would mean that people maybe spend more money if they're going to a show at F because the restaurants are more expensive. But I don't even know whether people are going to restaurants on the day they go to a show at F. I'd have to make a few assumptions here to make this work.*
(C) the Farmsley center generally earns more from films than from plays or other performance art projects	CA:S ~~A~~ ~~B~~ ~~C~~ D E 3ya: F built RS: F ppl spend $96 avg other stuff ⒸF NOT nec › M econ +	*I don't think this has anything to do with the conclusion at all. The conclusion is about F overall, not the different kinds of things people can watch at F. And what does it matter how F earns its money as long as it's earning money?*
(D) the Farmsley Center is the only downtown theatre large enough to afford to show newly-released major Hollywood films	CA:S ~~A~~ ~~B~~ ~~C~~ ~~D~~ E 3ya: F built RS: F ppl spend $96 avg other stuff ⒸF NOT nec → M econ +	*Here's a good reason why people might go to F vs. other places: this is the only place they can see big Hollywood films. Oh, but this answer is like answer A—I want something that will support the idea that F is NOT necessarily a major driver of M's revitalization. This one makes it sound like F IS an important factor.*
(E) most of the people who attend films or performances at the Farmsley Center do so because they are already in the area to shop	CA:S ~~A~~ ~~B~~ ~~C~~ ~~D~~ Ⓔ 3ya: F built RS: F ppl spend $96 avg other stuff ⒸF NOT nec → M econ +	*People go downtown to shop. While they're there, they think, "oh, hey, let's go see a show." I see. So people aren't coming downtown specifically because F is there; they're already downtown and just happen to see F and decide to stay. That would make it more likely that F isn't <u>necessarily</u> a driving factor in M's revitalization.*

Common Trap Answers

The common trap answers will mirror the trap answers we see on the regular question type. For example, if the "Complete the Argument" structure really reflects a Strengthen question, as our last problem did, then we should expect to see the same trap answers that we see on regular Strengthen questions: Reverse Logic (weakens rather than strengthens, as in answers A and D above) and No Tie to the Conclusion (as in answers B and C, above).

Takeaways for Complete the Argument Questions

Several question types can be written using a Complete the Argument structure, though most CA questions come in the Strengthen or Assumption formats. The CA format will always present an underlined blank in the argument, and there will not be a question stem following the argument.

Our first task is to figure out what kind of question we really have. The presence of the words "since" or "because" immediately before the blank indicate a Strengthen / Assumption-type question. On these, our task will be to find something that supports the argument in some way. Alternatively, if the language before the blank says something similar to "it should be expected that," then we are looking at an Inference-type CA. Finally, we might be asked to "illustrate" or "provide an example of" something that was discussed in the argument

Trap answer types will follow the normal patterns for questions of that type; for example, a Strengthen CA will have the usual Strengthen-type traps, and an Inference CA will have the usual Infer-type traps.

7

Problem Set

1. *Connecting Flight*

Which of the following most logically completes the argument?

John was flying from San Francisco to New York with a connecting flight in Chicago on the same airline. Chicago's airport consists of several small stand-alone terminals, and it often takes passengers thirty to forty minutes to move between terminals. John's plane into Chicago arrived on time. The flight attendant assured John that he would not miss his connecting flight thirty minutes later, because _____.

(A)   John's airline is known for always being on time

(B)   another passenger on John's first flight was also scheduled to take John's connecting flight

(C)   at the Chicago airport, airlines always fly in and out of the same terminal

(D)   John knew there was another flight to New York scheduled for one hour after the connecting flight he was scheduled to take

(E)   the airline generally closes the doors of a particular flight ten minutes before it is scheduled to take off

2. *Motor City*

Which of the following best completes the passage below?

A nonprofit organization in Motor City has proposed that local college students be given the option to buy half-price monthly passes for the city's public transportation system. The nonprofit claims that this plan will reduce air pollution in Motor City while increasing profits for the city's public transportation system. However, this plan is unlikely to meet its goals, as _____.

(A)   most college students in Motor City view public transportation as unsafe

(B)   most college students in Motor City view public transportation as prohibitively expensive

(C)   college students typically do not have the 9-to-5 schedules of most workers, and can thus be expected to ride public transportation at times when there are plenty of empty seats

(D)   a bus produces more air pollution per mile than does a car

(E)   a large proportion of the college students in Motor City live off campus

P

3. *Deep-brain Stimulation*

Which of the following most logically completes the argument given below?

Deep-brain stimulation is a new technique for combating severe depression. In a recent experiment, electrodes were implanted into the brains of six patients who had not responded to any currently approved treatment for depression. When an electrical current to the electrodes was switched on, four of the patients reported feeling a dramatic reduction in depressive symptoms. The long-term prospects of the new treatment are not promising, however, because _____.

(A)   other treatments for depression may also be effective

(B)   the other two patients reported only a slight reduction of depressive symptoms during the treatment

(C)   deep-brain stimulation relies on the expertise of highly skilled physicians

(D)   when the electrical current is interrupted, the effects of the treatment are reversed

(E)   in a subsequent experiment, a one-hour treatment with the electrodes resulted in a sustained remission from depression in the four patients for six months

4. *Mutual Funds*

Which of the following most logically completes the argument?

Many managers of mutual funds proclaim that they have been able to generate consistently higher rates of return on their investments than the general stock market by buying shares of undervalued companies. Classical economic theory, however, proposes the "efficient capital markets hypothesis," which indicates that stock prices accurately reflect the value of the underlying investments, incorporating all information available to the public. If the efficient capital markets hypothesis is correct, then it should be expected that _____.

(A)   mutual fund managers, in order to compete with each other, will bid up the prices of certain stocks beyond their true values

(B)   mutual fund managers use insider information, an illegal practice, to generate higher rates of return than the general stock market

(C)   stock prices will rise over time

(D)   based upon public information alone, companies cannot reliably be labeled undervalued or overvalued relative to the general stock market

(E)   some mutual fund managers are better than others at generating a higher rate of return on investments

5. *Law of Demand*

Which of the following best completes the passage below?

The law of demand states that, if all other factors remain equal, the higher the price of a good, the less people will consume that good. In other words, the higher the price, the lower the quantity demanded. This principle is illustrated when _____.

(A)   Company A has a monopoly over the widget market so an increase in widget prices has little effect on the quantity demanded

(B)   a manufacturer of luxury cars noticed that its customer base is relatively unresponsive to changes in price

(C)   a city experiences an increase in both gasoline prices and the number of people taking public transportation

(D)   an increase in the number of computer retailers led to a decrease in the average price of computers

(E)   a reduction in the price of oranges from $2 per pound to $1 per pound results in 75 pounds of oranges being sold as opposed to 50 pounds

Solutions

1. Connecting Flight: The correct answer is **C**.

Step 1: Identify the question.

Which of the following most logically completes the argument?	CA A B C D E	*The question appears before the argument, and the argument contains a blank at the end. Both of these things indicate that this is a Complete the Argument question.*

Step 2: Deconstruct the argument.

John was flying from San Francisco to New York with a connecting flight in Chicago on the same airline.	CA A B C D E J: SF → C → NY same line	*Straight fact describing his trip.*
Chicago's airport consists of several small stand-alone terminals, and it often takes passengers thirty to forty minutes to move between terminals.	CA A B C D E J: SF → C → NY same line C: mult terms, long time to move term	*Okay, it takes a long time to move between terminals in the Chicago airport.*
John's plane into Chicago arrived on time.	CA A B C D E J: SF → C → NY same line C: mult terms, long time to move term flt on time	*And another fact…*
The flight attendant assured John that he would not miss his connecting flight thirty minutes later, because _____.	CA A B C D E J: SF → C → NY same line C: mult terms, long time to move term flt on time ©FA: won't miss next flt	*Here we go: the FA claims that J won't miss his next flight. What's her evidence for that? That'll be the right answer.*

Step 3: State the Goal.

The FA claims that J will make his connecting flight in 30 minutes, so she must be assuming it's not going to take him more than 30 minutes to get to the gate for his next flight. I need to find an answer choice that somehow reflects that—something that makes it more likely that J will get to his next gate in less than 30 minutes.

Step 4: Work from wrong to right.

(A) John's airline is known for always being on time	CA A̶ B C D E J: SF → C → NY same line C: mult terms, long time to move term flt on time ⒸFA: won't miss next flt	*We already know that J's plane to Chicago is on time, so that doesn't change anything for this first flight. For the connecting flight, the only thing that would make the situation better is if that flight were late—because then John would have more time to get there. This one isn't it.*
(B) another passenger on John's first flight was also scheduled to take John's connecting flight	CA A̶ B̶ C̲ D̶ E̶ J: SF → C → NY same line C: mult terms, long time to move term flt on time ⒸFA: won't miss next flt	*Does that mean they can somehow get to the next gate faster because there are two of them? I don't think so. If they said they were going to hold the plane because there were two people coming, that would help… but they didn't say that.*
(C) at the Chicago airport, airlines always fly in and out of the same terminal	CA A̶ B C̲ D E J: SF → C → NY same line C: mult terms, long time to move term flt on time ⒸFA: won't miss next flt	*Ah—J isn't going to have to change terminals! We don't know how long it takes to move around the same terminal, but the argument does say that it typically takes 30 to 40 minutes to change terminals, so it likely takes less time when you're staying in the same terminal. This increases the likelihood that J will make his connecting flight. This might be it.*
(D) John knew there was another flight to New York scheduled for one hour after the connecting flight he was scheduled to take	CA A̶ B C̲ D̶ E J: SF → C → NY same linc C: mult terms, long time to move term flt on time ⒸFA: won't miss next flt	*This is only relevant if J misses his flight… but the FA claimed that J would make his flight.*

(E) the airline generally closes the doors of a particular flight ten minutes before it is scheduled to take off	CA A̶ B̶ Ⓒ D̶ E̶ J: SF → C → NY same line C: mult terms, long time to move term flt on time ⒸFA: won't miss next flt	*This hurts J's chances; now, he only has 20 minutes to make his next flight. Definitely not.*

2. Motor City: The correct answer is **A**.

Step 1: Identify the question.

Which of the following best completes the passage below ?	CA A B C D E	*The question appears before the argument, and the argument contains a blank at the end. Both of these things indicate that this is a Complete the Argument question.*

Step 2: Deconstruct the argument.

A nonprofit organization in Motor City has proposed that local college students be given the option to buy half-price monthly passes for the city's public transportation system.	CA A B C D E NPMC: give coll stud 1/2 off pub trans	*This is a fact—the organization has proposed this plan.*
The nonprofit claims that this plan will reduce air pollution in Motor City while increasing profits for the city's public transportation system.	CA A B C D E NP: give coll stud 1/2 off pub trans → ↓ air poll, ↑ prof	*Okay, the NP claims something, but I'm not labeling this the conclusion, because the conclusion is supposed to be in the final sentence of CA questions.*
However, this plan is unlikely to meet its goals, as _____.	CA A B C D E NP: give coll stud 1/2 off pub trans → ↓ air poll, ↑ prof ⒸBUT won't work	*This is the conclusion. The author thinks the plan won't work. Why?*

Step 3: State the Goal.

The author believes that the nonprofit's plan is not going to work, and I need to find a reason why. The plan is to let college students buy public transportation passes for half-price in order to reduce air pollution and increase profits.

Step 4: Work from wrong to right.

(A) most college students in Motor City view public transportation as unsafe	CA A̲ B C D E NP: give coll stud 1/2 off pub trans → ↓ air poll, ↑ prof ⒸBUT won't work	*If this is the case, then the students wouldn't want to use public transport at all, even if they were given a discount. That would make the plan unlikely to succeed. This might be it!*
(B) most college students in Motor City view public transportation as prohibitively expensive	CA A̲ B C D E NP: give coll stud 1/2 off pub trans → ↓ air poll, ↑ prof ⒸBUT won't work	*If they don't use public transport specifically because it's too expensive, then giving the students a discount is likely to make them use public transport more. This makes the plan more likely to succeed, not less likely.*
(C) college students typically do not have the 9-to-5 schedules of most workers, and can thus be expected to ride public transportation at times when there are plenty of empty seats	CA A̲ B C̶ D E NP: give coll stud 1/2 off pub trans → ↓ air poll, ↑ prof ⒸBUT won't work	*If this were true, it'd be good news for the public transport's profits—the students would be filling what are currently empty seats.*
(D) a bus produces more air pollution per mile than does a car	CA A̲ B C̶ D̶ E NP: give coll stud 1/2 off pub trans → ↓ air poll, ↑ prof ⒸBUT won't work	*At first, this sounds good—if a bus produces more air pollution than a car, then using more buses would create more air pollution, which would hurt the plan. But the plan isn't to use more buses; it's to put more people on the already-running buses. Plus, a car typically holds only 1 or 2 people; if 10 people stop using cars and take 1 bus instead, air pollution may indeed be decreased.*
(E) a large proportion of the college students in Motor City live off campus	CA Ⓐ B C̶ D̶ E NP: give coll stud 1/2 off pub trans → ↓ air poll, ↑ prof ⒸBUT won't work	*This makes it likely that the students need some method of transportation to get to school—if they're using cars now and switch to buses, then the plan just might work.*

MANHATTAN
GMAT

3. Deep-brain Stimulation: The correct answer is **D**.

Step 1: Identify the question.

Which of the following most logically completes the argument given below?	CA A B C D E	*The question appears before the argument, and the argument contains a blank at the end. Both of these things indicate that this is a Complete the Argument question.*

Step 2: Deconstruct the argument.

Deep-brain stimulation is a new technique for combating severe depression.	CA A B C D E DBS combat depr	*Straight fact.*
In a recent experiment, electrodes were implanted into the brains of six patients who had not responded to any currently approved treatment for depression.	CA A B C D E DBS combat depr Tested on 6 ppl	*This tells me how it works and that they tested it on 6 people.*
When an electrical current to the electrodes was switched on, four of the patients reported feeling a dramatic reduction in depressive symptoms.	CA A B C D E DBS combat depr Tested on 6 ppl, 4 better	*And four of the people got a lot better.*
The long-term prospects of the new treatment are not promising, however, because _____.	CA A B C D E DBS combat depr Tested on 6 ppl, 4 better ©BUT won't work	*Oh, but the author thinks the treatment's not really going to work long-term. Why?*

Step 3: State the Goal.

The author describes a new medical treatment but says it's probably not going to be good long-term; I need to find a reason why. So far, the only evidence they've given makes DBS sound promising, so I've got to find something that shows a flaw or weakness in the treatment.

P

Step 4: Work from wrong to right.

(A) other treatments for depression may also be effective	CA A̶ B C D E DBS combat depr Tested on 6 ppl, 4 better ⒸBUT won't work	*This is probably true in the real world, but talking about other treatments doesn't explain why DBS won't be a good treatment long-term.*
(B) the other two patients reported only a slight reduction of depressive symptoms during the treatment	CA A̶ B C D E DBS combat depr Tested on 6 ppl, 4 better ⒸBUT won't work	*When I saw the word "only," I was expecting them to say they had a bad result, but actually having even a slight reduction is better than nothing, especially for people who have tried other treatments that haven't worked. So, if anything, this is a plus for DBS. That's not what I want.*
(C) deep-brain stimulation relies on the expertise of highly skilled physicians	CA A̶ B C̶ D E DBS combat depr Tested on 6 ppl, 4 better ⒸBUT won't work	*I can believe this is true, but we would expect any major medical treatment to be performed by skilled physicians, so why would this make DBS not work long-term?*
(D) when the electrical current is interrupted, the effects of the treatment are reversed	CA A̶ B C̶ D̲ E DBS combat depr Tested on 6 ppl, 4 better ⒸBUT won't work	*That's interesting. So, when the current is on, the symptoms go away, but when the current is off, the depression comes back. That means they'd have to be connected to some machine all the time—they couldn't just get a treatment once a week or once a month. That definitely makes the treatment less practical and promising. Unless E is better, this might be it.*
(E) in a subsequent experiment, a one-hour treatment with the electrodes resulted in a sustained remission from depression in the four patients for six months	CA A̶ B C̶ Ⓓ E DBS combat depr Tested on 6 ppl, 4 better ⒸBUT won't work	*This is almost the opposite of D. If you get a one-hour treatment, then the symptoms go away for 6 months—that's great for DBS! This can't be the right answer.*

P

4. Mutual Funds: The correct answer is **D**.

Step 1: Identify the question.

Which of the following most logically completes the argument?	CA A B C D E	*The question appears before the argument, and the argument contains a blank at the end. Both of these things indicate that this is a Complete the Argument question.*

Step 2: Deconstruct the argument.

Many managers of mutual funds proclaim that they have been able to generate consistently higher rates of return on their investments than the general stock market by buying shares of undervalued companies.	CA A B C D E MF: buy ↓ val coms → > return than SM	*These managers claim something, but I'm betting the argument will disagree. Usually, when the author says someone else claims something, then the author disagrees. Let's see.*
Classical economic theory, however, proposes the "efficient capital markets hypothesis," which indicates that stock prices accurately reflect the value of the underlying investments, incorporating all information available to the public.	CA A B C D E MF: buy ↓ val coms → > return than SM BUT CET: stock $ is right based on public info	*Okay, the author is disagreeing. This sentence is a little hard to understand, but it sounds like it's saying that there aren't "undervalued" companies because the stock price should generally reflect the accurate value of the company.*
If the efficient capital markets hypothesis is correct, then it should be expected that _____.	CA A B C D E MF: buy ↓ val coms → > return than SM BUT CET: stock $ is right based on public info	*Hmm. I'm not sure how to write that down. It's just saying that if my second line is true, then something else should be true, too.*

Step 3: State the Goal.

This is one of the more rare variations of the complete the argument type. Rather than asking me to strengthen something or find an assumption, they're asking me to find something that follows, or must be true based on the given info. In other words, this is really an Inference question.

The CET says that stock prices generally accurately reflect the company's actual value. If that's true, then the MF managers must be wrong.

Step 4: Work from wrong to right.

(A) mutual fund managers, in order to compete with each other, will bid up the prices of certain stocks beyond their true values	CA A̶ B C D E MF: buy ↓ val coms → > return than SM BUT CET: stock $ is right based on public info	*They're supposed to be buying "undervalued" stocks, so bidding up the price doesn't make any sense. This doesn't follow from the argument.*
(B) mutual fund managers use insider information, an illegal practice, to generate higher rates of return than the general stock market	CA A̶ B̶ C D E MF: buy ↓ val coms → > return than SM BUT CET: stock $ is right based on public info	*I suppose this could be true of some people, but I don't think this is something that absolutely has to follow from the argument.*
(C) stock prices will rise over time	CA A̶ B̶ C̶ D E MF: buy ↓ val coms → > return than SM BUT CET: stock $ is right based on public info	*This might be true for many stocks, but there are also companies that go down and even go out of business.*
(D) based upon public information alone, companies cannot reliably be labeled undervalued or overvalued relative to the general stock market	CA A̶ B̶ C̶ D̲ E MF: buy ↓ val coms → > return than SM BUT CET: stock $ is right based on public info	*This one's a little difficult to understand. If we only know public info, then companies aren't under- or overvalued… so that would mean they're correctly valued… oh, wait, that's similar to what the theory said. It said that prices do accurately reflect the value of the companies. Okay, this might be it.*
(E) some mutual fund managers are better than others at generating a higher rate of return on investments	CA A̶ B̶ C̶ Ⓓ E̶ MF: buy ↓ val coms → > return than SM BUT CET: stock $ is right based on public info	*Again, I can believe this is true in general, but the argument, doesn't talk about whether some MF managers are better than others. Rather, it's talking about this CET thing and how it goes against what the MF managers say.*

5. Law of Demand: Correct answer is **E**.

Step 1: Identify the question.

Which of the following best completes the passage below?	CA A B C D E	*The question appears before the argument and the argument contains a blank at the end. Both of these things indicate that this is a Complete the Argument question.*

Step 2: Deconstruct the argument.

The law of demand states that, if all other factors remain equal, the higher the price of a good, the less people will consume that good.	CA A B C D E LD: = factors, ↑ $ → ↓ consume	*They're giving me a "general law," which is essentially a fact.*
In other words, the higher the price, the lower the quantity demanded.	CA A B C D E LD: = factors, ↑ $ → ↓ consume	*This basically says what I already wrote, so I'm not going to write anything else down.*
This principle is illustrated when _____.	CA A B C D E LD: = factors, ↑ $ → ↓ consume	*This is another one of those weird forms. They're not asking me to give a reason why or to find a conclusion. They're asking me to find an example that illustrates the "general law" they gave above.*

Step 3: State the Goal.

This is an interesting one. I need to find an example that illustrates this general principle: when something costs more, then people don't want to buy it as much. The opposite would be true, too: when something costs less, then people do buy it more.

Step 4: Work from wrong to right.

(A) Company A has a monopoly over the widget market so an increase in widget prices has little effect on the quantity demanded	CA A̶ B C D E LD: = factors, ↑ $ → ↓ consume	*This says that an increase in price does <u>not</u> change demand, but the LD said that an increase in price should lower demand, so this can't be an example of LD.*
(B) a manufacturer of luxury cars noticed that its customer base is relatively unresponsive to changes in price	CA A̶ B̶ C D E LD: = factors, ↑ $ → ↓ consume	*Again, this is saying that a change in price doesn't really affect demand, which is not what the LD theory said.*

(C) a city experiences an increase in both gasoline prices and the number of people taking public transportation	CA A̶ B ∈ D E LD: = factors, ↑ $ → ↓ consume	*Hmm. So maybe an increase in the gasoline price is causing people not to want to use as much gas? They didn't actually say that directly, though — they just said more people are taking public transport. Maybe the population is growing. It could be the case that people are still buying just as much gasoline even though the price went up. This one doesn't work.*
(D) an increase in the number of computer retailers led to a decrease in the average price of computers	CA A̶ B ∈ D̲ E LD: = factors, ↑ $ → ↓ consume	*Increase and decrease — that's good! Oh wait. It's not an increase in price vs. a decrease in number sold. It's an increase in number of stores selling computers to a decrease in price. That's not quite the same, but it's still closer than the first three answers. If E isn't better, I guess I'll choose this one.*
(E) a reduction in the price of oranges from $2 per pound to $1 per pound results in 75 pounds of oranges being sold as opposed to 50 pounds	CA A̶ B ∈ D̶ Ⓔ LD: = factors, ↑ $ → ↓ consume	*Tricky! Okay, they're giving me the other side of the rule. If it's true that higher price leads to lower consumption, then it's also true that higher consumption means there were lower prices. And that's what this one says — the price goes down and people buy more. This one's better than D!*

P

Chapter 8

of

Critical Reasoning

Wrong Answer Analysis

In This Chapter...

Chapter 8:
Wrong Answer Analysis

In previous chapters, we have examined a number of question types along with their common traps, or wrong answer types. This chapter is a summary of the "wrong answer" information scattered throughout the question-types chapters, and it also contains additional examples to illustrate the characteristics of these common traps.

We've talked about many different types, so we're going to group them into three big categories:

1. Out of Scope
2. Reverse Logic
3. The Mix Up

Out of Scope

Generally speaking, "out of scope" answers miss or go beyond the scope of the argument in some way. The "scope" refers to what the argument covers. If the author claims that women over five feet ten inches tall all make good basketball players, then the scope is limited to women (as opposed to men) with a certain physical characteristic (over five feet ten inches tall) and to the sport of basketball (as opposed to, say, hockey). If an answer focuses on men (the wrong group) and doesn't mention women at all, that answer is out of scope.

There are several different ways in which the test writers will try to take an answer out of the scope of the argument. On Assumption Family and Evaluate a Discrepancy questions, it's quite common to find answers that talk about the **wrong detail** (group, activity, action, characteristic, or other detail). For our mini-argument in the last paragraph, men would be the wrong group, hockey would be a wrong activity, less than five feet ten inches tall would be a wrong characteristic, and so on. The answer may sound as though it is related to the argument, but the details will take that answer out of scope.

A variation on the last trap is the **no tie to the conclusion** trap, which we see on Strengthen and Weaken questions, and the **no tie to the discrepancy** trap, which we see on Discrepancy questions. In all of these cases, we are asked to do something to the conclusion or discrepancy, and in all of these cases, the trap answer does not affect the conclusion or discrepancy at all.

Take a look at this example:

Question	"No Tie to the Conclusion" Wrong Answer
Which of the following, if true, best supports the claim that women who are under five feet ten inches tall cannot have successful careers as basketball players?	Women who are over five feet ten inches tall are more likely to excel at basketball.

In many ways, the wrong answer seems relevant: it's talking about women and basketball; it mentions the "five feet ten inch" height threshold. It does not, however, provide any information about women who are under five feet ten inches tall. The conclusion claimed something about this *specific* group of women. If the answer on a Strengthen the Conclusion question does not actually address the given conclusion, then it is out of scope. The same is true for Weaken questions.

Discrepancy questions provide us with some sort of discrepancy, and it is also possible for a wrong answer not to address the discrepancy. This is the same type of trap answer as a "no tie to the conclusion." For instance, an argument might tell us:

> Amy loves basketball, yet she's not attending tonight's game even though she has tickets.

It sounds like Amy would normally go to the game. Why isn't she? That's the discrepancy. A "no tie" wrong answer might say something like:

> Amy's friends also love basketball and plan to go to the game.

Why is this wrong answer not tied to our discrepancy at all? The argument mentions only Amy—what Amy thinks and what Amy plans to do. The answer choice talks about the wrong group—Amy's friends, rather than Amy. Unless the argument told us that Amy was influenced by her friends in some way (thereby making her friends part of the argument), we don't care what her friends think or do. That's out of the scope of the argument.

We also often see wrong answer choices that make an **irrelevant distinction or comparison**; these tend to appear primarily on Assumption Family questions. For instance, consider this argument:

> Students who earn A and B grades are more likely to participate in sports than are students who earn C grades. Therefore, participation in sports helps students to achieve higher grades.

Let's say that we're asked to find an assumption. An incorrect answer might say something like:

> Students who earn A grades participate in sports even more frequently than do those who earn B grades.

The argument grouped together the A and B students and treated them in the same way. The answer separates, or makes a distinction between, the A and B students. On Find the Assumption questions, our task is to find something that the author must believe to be true in order to draw his conclusion. Is it *absolutely necessary* to believe that the A-students participate in sports even more frequently than the B-students in order to believe the conclusion that sports participation in general helps students to achieve higher grades?

No, it's not absolutely necessary to believe that. *If* it were true, then that would help to strengthen the conclusion—but we weren't asked to strengthen the conclusion! The distinction between A and B students is irrelevant, since the argument puts them in the same category. In other words, the argument itself makes absolutely no distinction between A and B students, so why would it be necessary to make a distinction in order to accept the conclusion?

This example also illustrates another type of trap answer: the **real world distraction**. This type of answer sounds reasonable to assume in everyday, real-world conversations, but the information does not actually fulfill whatever we're supposed to be doing for that question type. For instance, on Find the Assumption (FA) questions, as we just discussed, we're trying to find something that must be true. It *could* be true that A students participate even more then B students, and we might even reasonably speculate that it is true in the real world, but it doesn't absolutely have to be true in order to draw the conclusion. We have to hold ourselves to the "must be true" standard on an FA question, so a "real-world" could-be-true answer is incorrect (though often very tempting!).

In sum, "out of scope" answers can take multiple forms.

8

Name	Why it's tempting	Why it's wrong	Most likely found in
Wrong detail	May use the same or similar words from the argument	It's not the right group, activity, action, characteristic, or other detail.	Find Assumption, Evaluate, Strengthen, Weaken, Inference, Discrepancy
No tie to the conclusion (or discrepancy)	Likely to use the same or similar words from the argument	The question asks us to address the conclusion or discrepancy; this answer does not affect the conclusion or discrepancy.	Strengthen, Weaken, Discrepancy

Irrelevant distinction or comparison	Does use specific groups, actions, or other details from the argument	Tries to separate two things that the argument places into the same category.	Find Assumption, Evaluate, Strengthen, Weaken
Real world distraction	Is the kind of thing that people might conclude or assume in the real world; could actually be true in the real world	The question asks us to find something that must be true and this answer doesn't have to be true.	Inference

Reverse Logic

One of the easier traps to fall into is the "reverse logic" trap, when we accidentally pick the opposite of what we really want, such as an answer that strengthens on a Weaken question. Reverse logic traps occur most frequently on Assumption Family and Structure Family questions.

One of the most common ways in which we fall into this trap is to misidentify the conclusion, particularly when the argument contains two "sides," or points of view. Consider this example.

> Some companies tie bonuses to company performance as well as personal performance, on the theory that individual performance is only valuable as far as it benefits the company as a whole in some way. This is counter-productive, however, because the highest-performing employees are essentially penalized by receiving a bonus commensurate only with the average performance of the overall company, thereby leading to a lack of motivation to continue to outperform their peers.

What are the claims here? Some companies think that "individual performance is only valuable if it benefits the company as a whole" and set up their bonus plans accordingly. Some unknown person, on the other hand, thinks that this viewpoint is "counter-productive" and will "[lead] to a lack of motivation" on the part of the best employees. Which is the main conclusion?

The author's point of view is always the main conclusion. In this case, the "unknown person" is the author. If a claim is attributed to a particular person or group, that claim is likely *not* the author's claim. A claim that is simply asserted, with no commentary as to who is doing the asserting, is likely to be the author's claim.

We can see how easy it would be to mix up the claims, though, and that in turn would make it easy to pick a "Reverse Logic" answer, since the two claims are on opposing sides of the fence.

Let's say that we have this question:

> Some companies tie bonuses to company performance as well as personal per-
> formance, on the theory that **individual performance is only valuable as far**
> **as it benefits the company as a whole in some way.** This is counter-productive,
> however, because the highest-performing employees are essentially penalized
> by receiving a bonus commensurate only with the average performance of the
> overall company, thereby leading to a lack of motivation to continue to outper-
> form their peers.
>
> In the argument given, the portion in boldface plays which of the following roles?

And here are our two answer choices:

> (A)   It is the main conclusion of the argument.
>
> (B)   It is a judgment that the argument opposes.

If we identify the boldface statement as the conclusion (of "some companies"), then we'd pick answer A.
But if we identify the "lack of motivation" comment as the true conclusion, then the boldface statement
goes against the conclusion and the answer is clearly B.

Alternatively, what if we were asked this question for the same argument?

Question	Reverse Logic trap answer	Correct Answer
Which of the following, if true, would most seriously under-mine the argument above?	The performance of employees who feel they aren't appropri-ately compensated for their efforts often drops.	High-performing employees typically state that their pri-mary motivation is the satisfac-tion of a job well done.
	Strengthens	*Weakens*

In this example, the Reverse Logic trap strengthens the conclusion instead of weakening it (and it is
even easier to fall into this trap if you misidentify the conclusion!). The trap answer, above, reinforces
(or strengthens) the author's conclusion: people whose pay is below their performance may lose motivation to work hard. The correct answer, on the other hand, does weaken the author's conclusion by offering a reason why employees might continue to work hard regardless of compensation levels.

In general, make sure to check the logical "direction" of the answers; if something fits one of the following categories, it's a trap!

Question Type	Reverse Trap answer will
Role	assign the opposite role of the correct role
Find Assumption	actually hurt the argument if it is true
Strengthen	weaken the conclusion
Weaken	strengthen the conclusion

The Mix Up

Our final major wrong answer category is "The Mix Up." These can appear in a few different varieties.

The **one word off** variety is simple, in the sense that only a single word can make the answer wrong, but also quite difficult and tempting… because only a single word makes the difference! (Note: it could also be two or three words.) These wrong answers most often show up in Describe the Role, Describe the Argument, and Inference questions.

For example, what's the difference between the below two answer choices?

> The first is a prediction that supports a position that the argument concludes.

> The first is a prediction that supports a position that the argument opposes.

Only one word is different—the very last word—and yet that one word changes everything. The first sample answer is describing a premise: something that supports the author's conclusion. The second, on the other hand, is describing a counter-premise: something that *goes against* the author's conclusion. If we're reading too quickly or skim over a word, that can be the difference between picking the right answer and falling for a tempting trap.

We also have to be on the alert for the **switching terms** trap, which occurs most often on Inference and Find the Assumption questions. The answer choice will use actual wording or terminology from the argument, but it will switch terms around or pair things that weren't actually paired in the argument. For instance, what if we were asked to infer something about the following argument excerpt?

Argument excerpt	Switching Terms Trap Answer
Studies have shown that holding a blood drive tends to stimulate the participation of members of an organization and increase the number of donations.	(B) Holding a blood drive helps an organization to increase the number of members.

See what answer choice B did there? It's certainly *possible* that answer choice B is true, but it doesn't accurately reflect what the argument actually said. Answer B contains many of the same words found in the argument, but in a mixed-up way. The argument said that the number of *donations* would increase, not the number of members. On an inference question, that is sufficient to eliminate this answer, because on inference questions, we are looking for an answer that must be true.

Problem Set

The problem set consists of problems that you have already seen in earlier chapters of this book. Note: if you have not yet done these problems, then do them normally under the 2-minute time constraint for the first time before doing the exercise described below.

For each of the following problems, identify the right answer, and try to articulate *why* each wrong answer is wrong. If you spot a particular category of wrong answer, write that down as well, but remember that the real test won't ask us to classify. Rather, our goal is to train ourselves to be able to identify wrong answers accurately and efficiently; the wrong answer categories are just a tool to help us practice this. Also note that some wrong answers may not fit into any of the common categories listed in this chapter.

1. *Gray Wolf Population*
From Chapter 3, Structure Family

> Government representative: Between 1996 and 2005, the gray wolf population in Minnesota grew nearly 50 percent; the gray wolf population in Montana increased by only 13 percent during the same period. Clearly, the Minnesota gray wolf population is more likely to survive and thrive long term.
>
> Environmentalist: But the gray wolf population in Montana is nearly 8 times the population in Minnesota; above a certain critical breeding number, the population is stable and does not require growth in order to survive.

The environmentalist challenges the government representative's argument by doing which of the following?

(A) introducing additional evidence that undermines an assumption made by the representative
(B) challenging the representative's definition of a critical breeding number
(C) demonstrating that the critical breeding number of the two wolf populations differs significantly
(D) implying that the two populations of wolves could be combined in order to preserve the species
(E) suggesting that the Montana wolf population grew at a faster rate than stated in the representative's argument

P

2. *Malaria*
From Chapter 3, Structure Family

In an attempt to explain the cause of malaria, a deadly infectious disease, early European settlers in Hong Kong attributed the malady to poisonous gases supposedly emanating from low-lying swampland. In the 1880s, however, doctors determined that Anopheles mosquitoes were responsible for transmitting the disease to humans after observing that **the female of the species can carry a parasitic protozoan that is passed on to unsuspecting humans when a mosquito feasts on a person's blood.**

What function does the statement in boldface fulfill with respect to the argument presented above?

(A) It provides support for the explanation of a particular phenomenon.
(B) It presents evidence that contradicts an established fact.
(C) It offers confirmation of a contested assumption.
(D) It identifies the cause of an erroneous conclusion.
(E) It proposes a new conclusion in place of an earlier conjecture.

3. *Oil and Ethanol*
From Chapter 4, Assumption Family

Country N's oil production is not sufficient to meet its domestic demand. In order to sharply reduce its dependence on foreign sources of oil, Country N recently embarked on a program requiring all of its automobiles to run on ethanol in addition to gasoline. Combined with its oil production, Country N produces enough ethanol from agricultural by-products to meet its current demand for energy.

Which of the following must be assumed in order to conclude that Country N will succeed in its plan to reduce its dependence on foreign oil?

(A) Electric power is not a superior alternative to ethanol in supplementing automobile gasoline consumption.
(B) In Country N, domestic production of ethanol is increasing more quickly than domestic oil production.
(C) Ethanol is suitable for the heating of homes and other applications aside from automobiles.
(D) In Country N, gasoline consumption is not increasing at a substantially higher rate than domestic oil and ethanol production.
(E) Ethanol is as efficient as gasoline in terms of mileage per gallon when used as fuel for automobiles.

4. *Charity*
From Chapter 4, Assumption Family

Studies show that impoverished families give away a larger percentage of their income in charitable donations than do wealthy families. As a result, fundraising consultants recommend that charities direct their marketing efforts toward individuals and families from lower socioeconomic classes in order to maximize the dollar value of incoming donations.

Which of the following best explains why the consultants' reasoning is flawed?

(A)   Marketing efforts are only one way to solicit charitable donations.
(B)   Not all impoverished families donate to charity.
(C)   Some charitable marketing efforts are so expensive that the resulting donations fail to cover the costs of the marketing campaign.
(D)   Percentage of income is not necessarily indicative of absolute dollar value.
(E)   People are more likely to donate to the same causes to which their friends donate.

5. *Food Allergies*
From Chapter 4, Assumption Family

Food allergies account for more than thirty thousand emergency department visits each year. Often, victims of these episodes are completely unaware of their allergies until they experience a major reaction. Studies show that 90 percent of food allergy reactions are caused by only eight distinct foods. For this reason, individuals should sample a minuscule portion of each of these foods to determine whether a particular food allergy is present.

Which of the following must be studied in order to evaluate the recommendation made in the argument?

(A)   The percentage of allergy victims who were not aware of the allergy before a major episode
(B)   The percentage of the population that is at risk for allergic reactions
(C)   Whether some of the eight foods are common ingredients used in cooking
(D)   Whether an allergy to one type of food makes someone more likely to be allergic to other types of food
(E)   Whether ingesting a very small amount of an allergen is sufficient to provoke an allergic reaction in a susceptible individual

P

6. *Smithtown Theatre*
From Chapter 5, Assumption Family

The Smithtown Theatre, which stages old plays, has announced an expansion that will double its capacity along with its operating costs. The theatre is only slightly profitable at present. In addition, all of the current customers live in Smithtown, and the population of the town is not expected to increase in the next several years. Thus, the expansion of the Smithtown Theatre will prove unprofitable.

Which of the following, if true, would most seriously weaken the argument?

(A)   A large movie chain plans to open a new multiplex location in Smithtown later this year.
(B)   Concession sales in the Smithtown Theatre comprise a substantial proportion of the theatre's revenues.
(C)   Many recent arrivals to Smithtown are students that are less likely to attend the Smithtown Theatre than are older residents.
(D)   The expansion would allow the Smithtown Theatre to stage larger, more popular shows that will attract customers from neighboring towns.
(E)   The Board of the Smithtown Theatre often solicits input from residents of the town when choosing which shows to stage.

7. *Digital Coupons*
From Chapter 5, Assumption Family

The redemption rate for e-mailed coupons is far lower than that for traditionally distributed paper coupons. One factor is the "digital divide"—those who might benefit the most from using coupons, such as homemakers, the elderly, and those in low-income households, often do not have the knowledge or equipment necessary to go online and receive coupons.

Which of the following, if true, does the most to support the claim that the digital divide is responsible for lower electronic coupon redemption rates?

(A)   Computers are available for free in libraries, schools, and community centers.
(B)   The redemption rate of ordinary coupons is particularly high among elderly and low income people that do not know how to use computers.
(C)   Many homes, including those of elderly and low income people, do not have high-speed internet connections.
(D)   More homemakers than elderly people would use computers if they had access to them.
(E)   The redemption rate for coupons found on the internet has risen in the last five years.

8. *World Bank*
From Chapter 5, Evidence Family

In 2010, China comprised about 10 percent of the world's gross domestic product (GDP), and its voting share in the World Bank was increased from under 3 percent to 4.4 percent. During the same timeframe, France comprised about 4 percent of the world's GDP and saw its voting share in the World bank drop from 4.3 percent to 3.8 percent.

Which of the following can be logically concluded from the passage above?

(A)   World Bank voting shares are allocated based upon each country's share of the world's GDP.

(B)   The new ratio of voting share to percentage of world GDP is lower for China than it is for France.

(C)   Gross domestic product is the most important factor in determining voting share at the World Bank.

(D)   China should be upset that its voting share does not match its proportion of the world's GDP.

(E)   France lost some of its voting share to China because China comprised a larger portion of the world's GDP.

9. *Bar Codes*

Two-dimensional bar codes are omni-directional; that is, unlike one-dimensional bar codes, they can be scanned from any direction. Additionally, two-dimensional bar codes are smaller and can store more data than their one-dimensional counterparts. Despite such advantages, two-dimensional bar codes account for a much smaller portion of total bar code usage than one-dimensional bar codes.

Which of the following, if true, most helps to resolve the apparent paradox?

(A)   Many smaller stores do not use bar codes at all because of the expense.

(B)   For some products, the amount of data necessary to be coded is small enough to fit fully on a one-dimensional bar code.

(C)   Two-dimensional bar codes are, on average, less expensive than one-dimensional bar codes.

(D)   Two-dimensional bar codes can also be scanned by consumer devices, such as cell phones.

(E)   One-dimensional bar codes last longer and are less prone to error than two-dimensional bar codes.

Solutions

1. Gray Wolf Population

(A) introducing additional evidence that undermines an assumption made by the representative

This is the correct answer.

(B) challenging the representative's definition of a critical breeding number

This is a Mix-Up answer. The environmentalist discusses critical breeding number, not the representative.

(C) demonstrating that the critical breeding number of the two wolf populations differs significantly

This doesn't fit into one of the standard trap categories. The environmentalist does mention the term "critical breeding number" but does not say that this number differs significantly. Rather, the environmentalist says that the population size differs.

(D) implying that the two populations of wolves could be combined in order to preserve the species

This is a Real World Distraction answer. It might be an interesting strategy in the real world, but the argument doesn't mention it.

(E) suggesting that the Montana wolf population grew at a faster rate than stated in the representative's argument

This is a Mix-Up answer. The environmentalist does mention a number, but that number does not represent a rate of growth.

2. Malaria

(A) It provides support for the explanation of a particular phenomenon.

This is the correct answer.

(B) It presents evidence which contradicts an established fact.

This doesn't fit into one of the standard trap categories. The boldface text does contradict what people once thought about malaria, but what they once thought was not an established fact.

(C) It offers confirmation of a contested assumption.

This is a "one word off" trap—nothing was contested in the argument.

P

(D) It identifies the cause of an erroneous conclusion.

> *This could be a Reverse Logic trap; we're looking for something that supports the conclusion.*

(E) It proposes a new conclusion in place of an earlier conjecture.

> *This is a general Mix-Up answer; the argument does do this in general, but not the statement in boldface.*

3. Oil and Ethanol

(A) Electric power is not a superior alternative to ethanol in supplementing automobile gasoline consumption.

> *This Out Of Scope answer is the Wrong Detail. The argument is about oil and ethanol, not electric power.*

(B) In Country N, domestic production of ethanol is increasing more quickly than domestic oil production.

> *This doesn't fit into one of the standard trap categories. It sounds pretty good at first glance, but isn't actually necessary (which is a requirement for a correct answer on an assumption question).*

(C) Ethanol is suitable for the heating of homes and other applications aside from automobiles.

> *This seems somewhat Out Of Scope. What does the heating of homes have to do with the argument?*

(D) In Country N, gasoline consumption is not increasing at a substantially higher rate than domestic oil and ethanol production.

> *This is the correct answer.*

(E) Ethanol is as efficient as gasoline in terms of mileage per gallon when used as fuel for automobiles.

> *This Out of Scope answer is too specific on the detail, so we can call this a Wrong Detail. Knowing how efficient the two are generally might help, but they don't necessarily have to be equally efficient.*

4. Charity

(A) Marketing efforts are only one way to solicit charitable donations.

This Out Of Scope answer discusses an Irrelevant Distinction. It may be true that there are other ways to solicit donations besides marketing efforts, but the argument itself is about marketing efforts.

(B) Not all impoverished families donate to charity.

This answer is One Word Off. It makes a statement about "all" impoverished families, but the argument never says that all of these families act in the same way. (Note: many people will eliminate this answer because the word "all" is extreme. It's true that this argument does not provide support for the extreme word "all," but extreme words can appear in correct CR answers—if the argument provides support for the extreme word.)

(C) Some charitable marketing efforts are so expensive that the resulting donations fail to cover the costs of the marketing campaign.

This is an especially tricky Wrong Detail answer. The argument never talks about whether the marketing campaign will be "profitable" (that is, make more money than was spent on the marketing campaign). It might seem like this should be the goal of any charitable marketing campaign… but the argument doesn't address this.

(D) Percentage of income is not necessarily indicative of absolute dollar value.

This is the correct answer.

(E) People are more likely to donate to the same causes to which their friends donate.

This sounds plausible in the Real World, but it's just a distraction here—the argument doesn't address this issue.

5. Food Allergies

(A) The percentage of allergy victims who were not aware of the allergy before a major episode

This answer makes an Irrelevant Distinction. Knowing the exact percentage doesn't actually tell us anything.

(B) The percentage of the population that is at risk for allergic reactions

This answer is Out Of Scope because it talks about all allergies in general, not just food allergies.

(C) Whether some of the eight foods are common ingredients used in cooking

This doesn't fit into one of the standard trap categories. The argument does not hinge on how commonly used the foods must be in order to warrant testing. Further, the argument does not limit itself to foods that must be cooked.

P

(D) Whether an allergy to one type of food makes someone more likely to be allergic to other types of food

This answer makes an Irrelevant Distinction; the argument doesn't address whether some-one is allergic to multiple types of food.

(E) Whether ingesting a very small amount of an allergen is sufficient to provoke an allergic reaction in a susceptible individual

This is the correct answer.

6. Smithtown Theatre

(A) A large movie chain plans to open a new multiplex location in Smithtown later this year.

This one can be considered either Out of Scope (a different movie chain doesn't matter to this conclusion) or Reverse Logic (if anything, the new movie theatre might take some busi-ness from Smithtown Theatre, strengthening the author's claim).

(B) Concession sales in the Smithtown Theatre comprise a substantial proportion of the theatre's rev-enues.

This one is Out of Scope because it has No Tie to the Conclusion. Knowing this information about concession sales tells us nothing new about the Theatre's plans to expand.

(C) Many recent arrivals to Smithtown are students that are less likely to attend the Smithtown Theatre than are older residents.

This is a Reverse Logic trap because it strengthens the author's claim (and this is a weaken question).

(D) The expansion would allow the Smithtown Theatre to stage larger, more popular shows that will attract customers from neighboring towns.

This is the correct answer.

(E) The Board of the Smithtown Theatre often solicits input from residents of the town when choosing which shows to stage.

This sounds good in the Real World, but it really has No Tie to the Conclusion. Two traps for the price of one!

7. Digital Coupons

(A) Computers are available for free in libraries, schools, and community centers.

P

If anything, this answer choice weakens the author's claim, and this is a strengthen question. This is a Reverse Logic trap.

(B) The redemption rate of ordinary coupons is particularly high among elderly and low income people that do not know how to use computers.

This is the correct answer.

(C) Many homes, including those of elderly and low income people, do not have high-speed internet connections.

This argument focuses on the Wrong Detail. The argument says nothing about having to have high-speed internet connections.

(D) More homemakers than elderly people would use computers if they had access to them.

This answer is making an Irrelevant Distinction between two groups that are treated the same in the argument.

(E) The redemption rate for coupons found on the internet has risen in the last five years.

This answer focuses on the Wrong Detail. The argument claims that paper coupons are in wider use because some people have difficulty accessing electronic coupons.

8. World Bank

(A) World Bank voting shares are allocated based upon each country's share of the world's GDP.

This sounds as though it could be reasonable in the Real World, but they didn't provide enough data points to say that this is definitely true.

(B) The new ratio of voting share to percentage of world GDP is lower for China than it is for France.

This is the correct answer.

(C) Gross domestic product is the most important factor in determining voting share at the World Bank.

We can think of this as an Irrelevant Comparison because it says that something is the "most important factor" when the argument doesn't actually say that at all.

(D) China should be upset that its voting share does not match its proportion of the world's GDP.

This might be reasonable to believe in the Real World, but the argument mentions nothing about how China "should" feel about anything.

P

(E) France lost some of its voting share to China because China comprised a larger portion of the world's GDP.

> *We can consider this a Mix-Up answer because it includes many words and terms from the argument... but this answer imposes a cause-effect relationship that wasn't given in the argument.*

9. Bar Codes

(A) Many smaller stores do not use bar codes at all because of the expense.

> *This choice makes an Irrelevant Distinction. The argument talks about stores that do use bar codes, not stores that don't.*

(B) For some products, the amount of data necessary to be coded is small enough to fit fully on a one-dimensional bar code.

> *This one is very tempting, but it's also a One Word Off trap. The choice addresses only "some" products—not enough to affect the conclusion.*

(C) Two-dimensional bar codes are, on average, less expensive than one-dimensional bar codes.

> *This is a Reverse Logic trap. If this choice were true, it would make the discrepancy even more strange, because it offers another reason why people would want to use 2D bar codes.*

(D) Two-dimensional bar codes can also be scanned by consumer devices, such as cell phones.

> *This can be considered a Reverse Logic trap (because it makes 2D bar codes more attractive) or a No Tie to the conclusion trap (because scanning with consumer devices isn't part of the scope of the argument).*

(E) One-dimensional bar codes last longer and are less prone to error than two-dimensional bar codes.

> *This is the correct answer.*

Appendix A

of

Critical Reasoning

Official Guide Problem Sets

In This Chapter...

Official Guide Problem Sets

Official Guide Problem Sets

Now that you have completed *Critical Reasoning*, it is time to test your skills on problems that have actually appeared on real GMAT exams over the past several years.

The problem set that follows is composed of questions from two books published by the Graduate Management Admission Council® (the organization that develops the official GMAT exam):

>*The Official Guide for GMAT Review, 13th Edition* (pages 33–39 & 500–538)
>*The Official Guide for GMAT Verbal Review, 2nd Edition* (pages 116–152).

These books contain Verbal questions that have appeared on past official GMAT exams. (The questions contained therein are the property of The Graduate Management Admission Council, which is not affiliated in any way with Manhattan GMAT.)

Although the questions in *The Official Guides* have been "retired" (they will not appear on future official GMAT exams), they are great practice questions.

Solve each of the following problems in a notebook, making sure to demonstrate how you arrived at each answer by showing all of your work. If you get stuck on a problem, look back at the Critical Reasoning strategies and content contained in this guide to assist you.

Note: Problem numbers preceded by "D" refer to questions in the Diagnostic Test chapter of *The Official Guide for GMAT Review, 13th Edition* (pages 33–39).

Describe the Argument:

>*13th Edition:* 34, 84, 85, 123
>*Verbal Review:* 79

Describe the Role:

>*13th Edition:* 18, 28, 63, 76, 78, 89, 98, 116
>*Verbal Review:* 48, 74

Find the Assumption:

>*13th Edition:* 21, 41, 46, 48, 75, 77, 83, 93, 96, 106, 109, 113, D28
>*Verbal Review:* 7, 34, 44, 52, 56, 63, 67, 76

Evaluate the Argument:

>*13th Edition:* 7, 10, 15, 27, 36, 42, 47, 53, 68, 70, 72, 110, 114, 124, D21, D22, D29
>*Verbal Review:* 3, 28, 40, 42, 54, 66, 70

Flaw:

13th Edition: 8, 100

Strengthen the Argument:

13th Edition: 1, 5, 11, 14, 16, 19, 23, 29, 30, 31, 35, 40, 45, 50, 52, 56, 64, 67, 95, 101,
102, 108, 111, 118, 120, 121, D25, D27, D32
Verbal Review: 1, 2, 6, 9, 13, 17, 21, 23, 25, 29, 30, 32, 33, 35, 37, 45, 51, 55, 58, 62,
65, 68, 69, 77, 78, 82

Weaken the Argument:

13th Edition: 2, 4, 20, 25, 32, 37, 43, 51, 58, 62, 71, 73, 79, 80, 82, 87, 88, 90, 97, 107,
112, 115, 117, 119, 122, D18, D20, D23, D26, D30, D34
Verbal Review: 4, 5, 11, 15, 16, 18, 20, 22, 24, 26, 27, 31, 36, 39, 41, 46, 47, 49, 50, 71,
80, 81, 83

Explain the Discrepancy:

13th Edition: 3, 6, 9, 13, 17, 22, 24, 44, 49, 57, 61, 86, 92, 94, 99, D19, D33
Verbal Review: 8, 59, 60, 61, 72, 73

Inference:

13th Edition: 26, 38, 54, 55, 60, 66, 91, 103, 104, 105, D24, D31
Verbal Review: 12, 14, 19, 43, 53, 57, 64, 75

Complete the Argument:

13th Edition: 12, 33, 39, 59, 65, 69, 74, 81
Verbal Review: 10, 38

mbaMission